ENGLAND AS IT IS

The Development of Industrial Society Series

William Johnston

ENGLAND AS IT IS

Political, Social and Industrial in the Middle of the Nineteenth Century

Volume 1

IRISH UNIVERSITY PRESS
Shannon   Ireland

First edition London 1851

This I U P reprint is a photolithographic facsimile of the first edition and is unabridged, retaining the original printer's imprint.

© *1971 Irish University Press Shannon Ireland*

All forms of micropublishing
© *Irish University Microforms Shannon Ireland*

ISBN 0 7165 1774 4 Two volumes
ISBN 0 7165 1775 2 Volume 1
ISBN 0 7165 1776 0 Volume 2

T M MacGlinchey Publisher
Irish University Press Shannon Ireland

PRINTED IN THE REPUBLIC OF IRELAND BY
ROBERT HOGG PRINTER TO IRISH UNIVERSITY PRESS

The Development of Industrial Society Series

This series comprises reprints of contemporary documents and commentaries on the social, political and economic upheavals in nineteenth-century England.

England, as the first industrial nation, was also the first country to experience the tremendous social and cultural impact consequent on the alienation of people in industrialized countries from their rural ancestry. The Industrial Revolution which had begun to intensify in the mid-eighteenth century, spread swiftly from England to Europe and America. Its effects have been far-reaching: the growth of cities with their urgent social and physical problems; greater social mobility; mass education; increasingly complex administration requirements in both local and central government; the growth of democracy and the development of new theories in economics; agricultural reform and the transformation of a way of life.

While it would be pretentious to claim for a series such as this an in-depth coverage of all these aspects of the new society, the works selected range in content from *The Hungry Forties* (1904), a collection of letters by ordinary working people describing their living conditions and the effects of mechanization on their day-to-day lives, to such analytical studies as Leone Levi's *History of British Commerce* (1880) and *Wages and Earnings of the Working Classes* (1885); M. T. Sadler's *The Law of Population* (1830); John Wade's radical documentation of government corruption, *The Extraordinary Black Book* (1831); C. Edward Lester's trenchant social investigation, *The Glory and Shame of England* (1866); and many other influential books and pamphlets.

The editor's intention has been to make available important contemporary accounts, studies and records, written or compiled by men and women of integrity and scholarship whose reactions to the growth of a new kind of society are valid touchstones for today's reader. Each title (and the particular edition used) has been chosen on a twofold basis (1) its intrinsic worth as a record or commentary, and (2) its contribution to the development of an industrial society. It is hoped that this collection will help to increase our understanding of a people and an epoch.

The Editor
Irish University Press

ENGLAND AS IT IS,

POLITICAL, SOCIAL, AND INDUSTRIAL,

IN THE

MIDDLE OF THE NINETEENTH CENTURY.

By WILLIAM JOHNSTON, Esq.,

BARRISTER AT LAW.

IN TWO VOLUMES.—Vol. I.

LONDON:

JOHN MURRAY, ALBEMARLE STREET.

1851.

" It behoves us ever to bear in mind that, while actions are always to be judged by the immutable standard of right and wrong, the judgment which we pass upon men must be qualified by considerations of age, country, situation, and other incidental circumstances, and it will then be found that he who is most charitable in his judgment is generally the least unjust."

SOUTHEY, *Book of the Church.*

PREFACE.

THE Essays contained in these volumes had their origin in a design of writing letters to a friend on the Continent, in order to make him acquainted with the present state of England. It is hoped that a considerable amount of authentic information on subjects of public interest will be found collected in these pages. An Index is supplied in order to facilitate reference to the statistical facts, which have been gleaned from a great mass of public documents. These documents are not difficult of access, but they are so unwieldy as to be troublesome to consult, and often repulsive from the painful elaboration of their details. It is hoped that, by selecting some parts, and abridging others, of the ponderous books in which public information is officially registered, some service may have been done in the promoting of useful knowledge. The writer is aware that, as essays upon the important subjects of which he has treated, some of his papers must appear meagre, and all of them incomplete. It was not his object, however, to discuss these subjects fully. If he had done so, he must have written a library instead of two volumes. His object was to supply materials for present reflection and future history. For this purpose he has sought the most authentic information he could obtain ; and where he has thought it necessary to state his own views, he has refrained from stating them at length.

For the political tone of the book the writer does not think it necessary to make any apology. Though he does not take what is called the popular side, he yields to no one in ardent desire to elevate the minds, and to better the condition, of the people. His dislike of *liberalism* is founded on his earnest conviction—be that conviction right or wrong—that the doctrines of *liberalism* are directly adverse to the happiness of the great bulk of the population. He is very little disposed to flatter the rich and great of any political party, but he would seek a remedy for existing evils, rather by inducing an earnest and generous sense of duty in every rank of life, than by promoting democratic progress, which throws power and advantage into the hands of the wealthy, the busy, the bold, and the unscrupulous; but leaves the humble, the conscientious, and the sincere, without help, without justice, and without hope.

It may perhaps be proper to add that a part of the papers on Revenue, and on Trade, has already appeared in the ' Quarterly Review.'

CONTENTS OF VOLUME I.

ENGLAND:

POLITICAL, SOCIAL, AND INDUSTRIAL.

CHAPTER I.

THE RURAL ASPECT OF ENGLAND.

LOOKING to the rural parts of England, it may be said that there are few countries for which Nature has done more, and none for which Art has done so much. In the grandeur and beauty of city architecture England cannot compare with continental kingdoms; but nowhere else in the world can the country parts boast of so much ornamental cultivation. In some of the less picturesque districts, careful culture and judicious planting have produced a beauty and home-felt charm of their own; while in the romantic regions, though instances of bad taste struggling to improve upon nature may now and then be seen, yet upon the whole the delightfulness of natural beauty has been enhanced by the association of shelter, comfort, and not inappropriate skill. So it is, then, that, whether we gaze upon the mountains of Westmoreland, "from base to summit," making it our occupation and delight—

> " To note in shrub and tree, in stone and flower,
>   That intermixture of delicious hues
>   Along so vast a surface, all at once
>   In one impression, by connecting force
>   Of their own beauty imaged in the heart,"—

or take our journey to the south—

> " To some low cottage in a sunny bay,
>   Where the salt sea innocuously breaks,
>   And the sea breeze as innocently breathes
>   On Devon's leafy shore,"—

we find such beauty as Switzerland and Italy only can surpass ; and such variety within our own land as neither Switzerland nor Italy could by itself supply.

They who remember travelling in England before the mode of transit by railways was invented, can bear witness to the wondrous beauty of scenery, or the touching rural charm of villages and hamlets, which, in favourable weather, made an easy seat on the outside of a mail or stage-coach so enviable a position. They can call to mind " the groves, the gardens, the farm-houses, the showy equipages flitting along from one fine mansion to another —the country houses, the village steeples peeping up from their embosoming oaks, the noble cathedrals rising up from the bosom of the towns like a mighty mother with her children clustering in circles around her," all of which they passed in their cheerful journey. And they who have sojourned at a country inn of the olden time (how unlike the real pomp and affected precision of modern railway hotels !), and have taken advantage of a leisure day, in spring or autumn, to ramble over hill and dale in the neighbourhood, have they not been ready to exclaim with Dyer,

> " Ever charming, ever new,
>   When will the landscape tire the view ?

> The fountain's fall, the river's flow,
> The woody valleys, warm and low;
> The windy summit, wild and high,
> Roughly rushing on the sky!
> The pleasant seat, the ruin'd tower,
> The naked rock, the shady bower,
> The town and village, dome and farm,
> Each gives each a double charm,
> As pearls upon an Ethiop's arm."

It is pleasant to reflect that there is scarcely an aspect of our country which has not been depicted in delightful verse; which will live as long as men live in England who have hearts capable of appreciating the true and the beautiful in nature and in language. Nor do I allude now to the more noble and striking forms of majestic nature which have been depicted in some of the most memorable passages of Shakspeare, Scott, Byron, and Wordsworth; but even the more homely forms of beauty, which no great vigour of imagination or elevation of feeling is required to appreciate. Perhaps when the old feelings of England *proper* have passed away under the influence of modern "improvements" and mercantile calculation, they who still speak the tongue in which Cowper wrote may, in far off lands of Western Canada or of Southern Australia, have their hearts softened and their minds turned back to the land of " their forefather's grave," by the simple yet most natural and accurate descriptions of our rural scenery which Cowper has so admirably given :—

> " I have loved the rural walk through lanes
> Of grassy swarth, close cropp'd by nibbling sheep,
> And skirted thick with intertexture firm
> Of thorny boughs; have loved the rural walk
> O'er hills, through valleys, and by river's brink,
> E'er since, a truant boy, I pass'd my bounds
> To enjoy a ramble on the banks of Thames."
>
> *The Task*, book i.

Or take the following, of an English common, such as may even yet be found without travelling very far from London :—

> " The common overgrown with fern, and rough
> With prickly gorse, that, shapeless and deform'd,
> And dangerous to the touch, has yet its bloom,
> And decks itself with ornaments of gold,
> Yields no unpleasing ramble; there the turf
> Smells fresh, and, rich in odoriferous herbs
> And fungous fruits of earth, regales the sense
> With luxury of unexpected sweets."
>
> *The Task*, book i.

One great charm in the general tone of the English landscape arises from the abundance of timber all over the face of the cultivated land. From one end of the civilized world to the other, the hedge-rows and hedge-row timber of England have been, and are, the admiration of the traveller. A great destruction of this timber is, however, now in progress, and it appears likely to increase. In order successfully to compete with foreign farmers, who are now as free to bring their produce into English markets as English farmers are, scientific agriculturists declare that it is expedient to make our fields larger and more open to sun and air, by removing hedges and fences ; that the shade of trees is injurious to the ripening of grain, and therefore that they should be removed ; that " timber-smothered " land is a reproach to scientific and economical farming ; that to keep pace with the advancement of agricultural knowledge, and to meet the activity and competition of the age, the hedge-rows, which have heretofore been considered the beauty of England, must, from considerations of utility, be abandoned ; that land must be looked upon as nothing else than a manufactory of agricultural produce ; and that farmers who think of anything else than profit, are little

better than fools. Such are the theories of those who
bring the wisdom of city counting-houses, or scientific
lecture-rooms, to bear upon rural affairs. The love of
rural life, however, and the taste for its charms, seem to
be deeply seated in the character and affections of the
common people of England; and it may be hoped that,
notwithstanding the advance of the mercantile spirit, and
the devotedness to profit among the middle class, there
will long continue among the great body of the people a
feeling for what is fresh, and sweet, and beautiful, in
country life.

The late Dr. Arnold, who appears to have had a pas-
sionate admiration for the grand and picturesque in
English scenery, could not find delight in the plainer
aspect of the agricultural and pastoral country. This
seems to me to indicate some defect in his sympathies,
which, in such a man, is rather surprising. He found the
country about Rugby "positively dull;" and says he
regarded it as a mere working place. His supreme
delight was in the wildness of Westmoreland; yet that he
had a relish for less exciting scenes appears in his fond-
ness for his other residences. "As for my coming down
into Westmoreland," he writes, "I may almost say that
it is to satisfy a physical want in my nature, which craves
after the enjoyment of nature, and for nine months in the
year can find nothing to satisfy it. I agree with old
Keble that one does not need mountains and lakes for
this: the Thames at Laleham, Bagley Wood, and Shot-
over at Oxford, were quite enough for it. I only know
of five counties in England which cannot supply it, and I
am unluckily perched down in one of them. These five
are Warwick, Northampton, Huntingdon, Cambridge,
and Bedford; I should add, perhaps, Rutland, and you
cannot add a seventh; for Suffolk, which is otherwise just

as bad, has its bits of sea-coast.   But Halesworth, so far as
I remember it, would be just as bad as Rugby.   We have
no hills, no plains—not a single wood, and but one single
copse—no heath, no down—no rock, no river—no clear
stream—scarcely any flowers, for the lias is particularly
poor in them—nothing but one endless monotony of enclosed fields and hedge-row trees."   Notwithstanding this
testimony, I think I have seen and enjoyed extremely
picturesque forest scenery in Northamptonshire ; and in
the rich undulating grounds of Warwickshire I have
found much delight.   But let us take a working silk-
weaver's description of that sort of country which probably
Dr. Arnold would have found unpicturesque and dull.*
It is John Bamford, the " radical," who is trudging through
Leicestershire on a fine morning in August.   "We were
now," he says, " in a right farming country, where large
stacks, barns, and cattle-sheds were quite common on the

---

* I cannot refrain from quoting here Cowper's admirable picture of
the ordinary, and, as it were, tamer sort of English scenery :—

> " Thence with what pleasure have we just discern'd
> The distant plough slow moving, and beside
> His labouring team, that swerved not from the track,
> The sturdy swain diminish'd to a boy !
> Here Ouse, slow winding through a level plain
> Of spacious meads with cattle sprinkled o'er,
> Conducts the eye along his sinuous course
> Delighted.   There, fast rooted in their bank,
> Stand, never overlook'd, our favourite elms,
> That screen the herdsman's solitary hut;
> While far beyond, and overthwart the stream,
> That, as with molten glass, inlays the vale,
> The sloping land recedes into the clouds ;
> Displaying on its varied side the grace
> Of hedge-row beauties numberless, square tower,
> Tall spire, from which the sound of cheerful bells
> Just undulates upon the listening ear,
> Groves, heaths, and smoking villages, remote."

road sides. The roads were broad and in good condition; and there were very often wide slips of good land on each side, apparently much trodden by cattle. Occasionally we came to a neat homely-looking cottage, with perhaps a large garden and a potato-ground attached, and with rose-shrubs and honey-bines clustering around the door. These were specimens of our real English homes; there was no mistaking them; in no other country do such exist; and he or she who leaves this land expecting to meet with like homes in foreign ones will be miserably disappointed. In England alone is the term home, with all its domestic comforts and associations, properly understood. May it long continue the home of the brave, and eventually become the home of the really free! There had been some rain a few days before; the Trent had been flooded, and, of all the verdant pastures I have ever beheld, none have surpassed the rich vivid green of the meadows betwixt Shardlow and Kegworth. As the sweet air came across them, cooling one's dewy brows, one almost felt tempted to stop and seek an abiding-place in that delicious valley." Bravo, honest silk weaver! there was no sulky, self-sufficient Radicalism in your heart on that delightful summer morning! Long may such rural homes as you describe be found in our land, and long may we have men in the humbler classes of society who feel an affection for their rural homes, which no love of change can dissipate, and no rage for hasty improvement destroy!

The earlier letters of Southey give us some delightful descriptions of scenery, which one quotes in preference to descriptions taken from works of fiction, because there is no reason to believe that the pictures in these letters were at all "got up" for the sake of effect. Writing from the beautiful county of Brecon, he says—" What have I seen?

—woods, mountains, and mountain-glens, and streams! In these words are comprehended all imaginable beauty. Sometimes we have been winding up the dingle side, and every minute catching the stream below, through the wood that half hid it, always hearing its roar; then over mountains where nothing was to be seen but hill and sky, their sides rent by the winter streams; sometimes a little tract of cultivation appeared up some coomb-place, so lovely, so beautiful: they looked as if no tax-gatherer ever visited them. I have longed to dwell in these solitary houses in a mountain vale, sheltered by the hills and the trees that grow finely round the houses; the vale rich by the soil swept down the hills, a stream before the door, rolling over large stones—pure water, so musical too!"

Take another picture—a *De Wint* after a *Salvator;* not by way of companion, but by way of contrast—the scene six miles from Norfolk—Yarmouth. "This part of England looks as if Nature had wearied herself with adorning the rest with hill and dale, and squatted down here to rest herself. You must suppose a very Dutch-looking Nature to have made it of such pancake flatness. An unpromising country—and yet, Edith, I could be very happy with such a home as this. I am looking through a window over green fields, as far as I can see—no great distance. The hedges are all grubbed up in sight of the house, which produces a very good effect. A few fine acacias, white thorns, and other trees are scattered about; a walk goes all round, with a beautiful hedge of lilacs, laburnams, the Gueldres rose, barberry shrubs, &c. &c. Edith, you could not wish a sweeter scene; and being here, I wish for nothing but you. Half-an-hour's walk would reach the sea-shore."

How charming all this is, and with what pleasing unconscious art the figure is brought into the second picture

to give it life and feeling. With "Edith" in the foreground, who indeed could wish a sweeter scene?

The lofty mountain and the romantic glen, the over-
hanging wood, the picturesquely scattered rocks, and the
bounding river attract all eyes and all hearts among those
to whom Nature has given a conception of the grand and
a sense of the beautiful; but to the full enjoyment of the
merely rural scenery of fields and country lanes, it seems
that some knowledge is necessary of the wild flowers and
picturesque weeds, which actually escape the observation
of the uninformed or the negligent. A correspondent of
Constable, the eminent painter of English rural scenes,
points out to him the minor details which should appear
in one of his summer pictures. "I think," he says, "it
is July in your green lane. At this season all the tall
grasses are in flower—bogrush, bulrush, teazle. The
white bind-weed now hangs its flowers over the branches
of the hedge; the wild hemlock and carrot, flower in banks
of hedges, cow-parsley, water-plantain, &c. The heath-
hills are purple at this season; the rose-coloured persi-
caria in wet ditches is now very pretty; the catchfly
graces the hedgerow, as also the ragged robin; bramble
is now in flower, poppy, mallow, thistle, hop, &c." This
very enumeration seems to carry us into the country, and
to place us among the watchers of Nature's less prominent
beauties.

In fine, notwithstanding the occasional harshness and
dampness of our climate, there are perhaps few countries
in the world where more enjoyment may be had in habitual
intercourse with Nature in the open air. Once we get
out of our smoky, toilsome towns, and beyond the prim-
ness and overdone snugness of the region immediately
around them, Nature is in this country generally found
most bountiful of her various beauty.

CHAPTER II.

STATISTICS OF THE LAND—FARMERS AND GENTRY.

WE learn from Mr. Porter's 'Progress of the Nation,' and sundry other books, that the land of the *United Kingdom*, including the Channel and the Northern Islands, amounts to 77,394,433 acres, of which 46,522,970 are under some sort of cultivation. Here is his table:—

	Acres Cultivated.	Acres Uncultivated.	Acres Unprofitable.	Total.
England . . .	25,632,000	3,454,000	3,256,000	32,342,400
Wales	3,117,000	530,000	1,105,000	4,752,000
Scotland . . .	5,265,000	5,950,000	8,523,930	19,738,930
Ireland . . .	12,125,280	4,900,000	2,416,664	19,441,944
British Islands	383,690	166,000	569,469	1,119,159
	46,522,970	15,000,000	15,871,463	77,394,433

These, again, are divided into 19,135,990 acres of arable land and gardens; 27,386,980 acres of meadows, pastures, and marshes; 15,000,000 acres of waste land capable of improvement, but in its present state estimated at the value of 5,000,000*l.* sterling a year; and 15,871,463 acres incapable of improvement.

Mr. Spackman estimates the rental of the land of the United Kingdom at 58,753,615*l.*, and adds that the direct and local taxation applicable to it amounts to 18,314,908*l.*, of which 13,881,911*l.* is paid by the landed interest, and 4,432,997*l.* by the manufacturing interest. The capital embarked in the cultivation of the soil he estimates at

250,000,000*l.* There is, however, no accurate statistical information of the state of agriculture in England and Scotland. In Ireland it is better known, the rural constabulary having been employed to furnish it.* Pebrer, quoted by Alison, gives the following as his estimate of the agricultural produce of the United Kingdom :—

Grain of all sorts	£86,700,000
Hay, grass, field turnips, vetches, &c. .	113,000,000
Potatoes	19,000,000
Gardens, orchards, and nurseries . .	3,800,000
Timber cut down, hops, seeds, &c. . .	2,600,000
Cheese, butter, eggs, &c.	6,000,000
Manure and labour in rearing cattle . .	3,500,000
Hemp and wool, labour included . .	12,000,000
	£246,000,000

Mr. Porter makes the produce more valuable :—

19,135,000 acres at 7*l.* per acre . . .	£133,945,000
27,000,000 acres at 6*l.* per acre . . .	162,000,000
15,000,000 acres wastes	5,000,000
	£300,945,000

Mr. Spackman's estimate is only 250,000,000*l.* for the annual produce of the land of the United Kingdom, though

---

* It should be borne in mind that all the calculations of the money value of produce which were made before the repeal of the corn laws came into action, were based upon prices 30 per cent. higher than they have been during the last two years. The amount of the crops in Ireland has been *officially* ascertained of late years, but doubts have been thrown upon the accuracy of the official returns. Mr. James Macqueen estimates the annual agricultural produce of the United Kingdom to have been 686,524,132*l.* under protection prices, and 470,580,485*l.* according to the prices of 1850 ! The annual value of the land of Great Britain, as assessed to the income-tax in 1848, was 41,179,713*l.* It appears to me that, if the value of the produce be taken at five or six times the rent-returning value of the land, it is as high an estimate as may be safely made.

he takes wheat at 60*s.* the quarter, and all other grain
at 30*s*   His calculation is—

22,000,000 qrs. of wheat . . .	£66,000,000
34,000,000 qrs. of all other grain . .	51,000,000
Hay, seeds, garden, and green crops .	30,000,000
2,000,000 head of cattle . . .	30,000,000
10,000,000 sheep and lambs . . .	15,000,000
Potatoes	25,000,000
Wool	8,000,000
Butter	5,000,000
Cheese	5,000,000
Poultry, milk, eggs, fruit, and vegetables	3,000,000
200,000 horses	3,000,000
Pigs	2,000,000
All other animals	1,000,000
Hops	1,500,000
Timber	2,500,000
Value of uncultivated wastes and woods .	2,000,000
	£250,000,000

Mr. Spackman estimates the yield of wheat in England
at 18,000,000 quarters; of barley, 6,000,000 quarters;
of oats, rye, beans, and peas, 12,000,000 quarters: at the
value of 54,000,000*l.* for wheat, 9,000,000*l.* for barley,
and 18,000,000*l.* for the other sorts of grain and pulse.
Mr. M'Culloch (*On Taxation*, p. 389) gives his estimate
of the corn grown *in England* as follows:—

Wheat, 14,000,000 qrs. at 50*s.* . . .	£35,000,000
Barley, 5,000,000 qrs. at 30*s.* . . .	7,500,000
Oats, peas, and beans, 12,000,000 qrs. at 25*s.*	16,000,000
	£58,500,000*

---

* The 'Edinburgh Review' (April, 1850) states that Mr. M'Culloch's
calculation in 1844 gave the following results for the " three kingdoms :"—

Produce from arable land . . .	£132,021,548
Pasture and uncultivated land . . .	89,750,000
	£227,771,548

And

—being 22,500,000*l.* under the estimate of Mr. Spackman.
Mr. M'Culloch estimates the entire landed rental of
England and Wales at about 34,000,000*l.* (*On Taxation,*
p. 119); but soon afterwards, on discussing the income-
tax, he estimates the landed rental of England and
Wales at 40,000,000*l.* to 41,000,000*l.* (p. 147). When
he arrives at p. 389 of the same book, he says the rental
of the whole landed property of Great Britain is certainly
under 40,000,000*l.* As no one has studied such matters
more than Mr. M'Culloch, I mention these inconsistencies
as illustrating the difficulty there must be in arriving at
any *positive* conclusion. Mr. Spackman, in his Appendix,
gives the gross rental of England and Wales as amounting
to 40,167,088*l.*; that of Scotland to 5,586,628*l.*; and that
of Ireland to 13,562,946*l.*; making a total of 59,316,662*l.*,
from which deductions of 563,047*l.* are made, leaving a
net total rental of 58,753,615*l.* for the United Kingdom.
It is to be feared that, from what has taken place in
Ireland during the last three years, the rental there has
fallen off in a very serious degree. In the House of
Commons, on the 19th of February, 1850, Mr. Disraeli,
in his very elaborate speech on the burdens which affected
the landed interest, based some calculations on the assumption that the rental of England was 60,000,000*l.*,
a-year.* I know not where he found this statistical fact;
but no doubt he had an authority. It appears that the
average of rent per acre in England and Wales in 1842-3
was 1*l.* 1*s.* 8½*d.*, having risen to that sum from 18*s.* 6¾*d.*,
which was the rate in 1814-15.† In all the English

And this the reviewer *fancifully* divides into the following proportions:—

Cattle, cattle-food, and roots, not subject (as he says) to foreign competition	£137,295,009
Cereal crops (exposed to competition)	90,476,539

* Times report, Feb. 20, 1850.   † Spackman, Appendix, 185.

counties but five, there appears to have been some increase. These counties are Durham, Middlesex, Northumberland, Oxford, and Surrey. It is curious that in
Middlesex the decrease of rental is very considerable,
being 14s. 5½d per acre. The next in degree is Northumberland, 2s. 9d. per acre. The other three have declined only a few pence per acre each.

Very different views are taken of the amount of capital
required for the cultivation of land : 5l. to 6l. an acre is
a common estimate; but the high farming of modern
times is calculated to require almost double that sum.*

---

* In Mr. Doubleday's Financial History the following table of the
expense of cultivating 100 acres at different periods is given:—

	1790.			1803.			1813.			1835.		
	£.	s.	d.	£.	s.	d.	£.	s.	d.	£.	s.	d.
Rent . . .	88	6	3¼	121	2	7¼	161	12	7¼	150	0	0
Tithe . . .	20	14	1¾	26	8	0¼	38	17	3¼	30	0	0
Rates . . .	17	13	10	31	7	7¾	38	19	2¾	30	0	0
Wear and tear	15	13	3¼	22	11	10¼	31	2	10¾	20	0	0
Labour . .	85	5	4	118	0	4	161	12	11¼	180	0	0
Seed . . .	46	4	10¼	49	2	7	98	17	10	53	0	0
Manure . .	48	0	3	68	6	2	37	7	0¼	20	0	0
Team . . .	67	4	10	80	8	0¼	134	19	8½	120	0	0
Interest . .	22	11	11½	30	3	8½	50	5	6	16	0	0
Taxes . . .		..			..		18	1	4	5	0	0
Total . . .	411	15	11¾	547	10	11½	771	16	4½	624	0	0
Deduct rent .	88	6	3¼	121	2	7¼	161	12	7¼	150	0	0
Net expenses .	323	9	8½	426	8	4½	610	3	9¼	474	0	0
Price of wheat	s. 46 per qr.			s. d. 56 9 per qr.			s. d. 108 9 per qr.			s. d. 44 2 per qr.		

The first three columns are taken from the information furnished to a
Parliamentary Committee. The last is furnished by a Durham farmer,
and I suspect not an economical one. The expense of seed is set down
as considerably more in 1835 than in 1790, though the price of wheat
was less in 1835. Certainly it has been the practice of *good* farming to
use less seed of late years than was formerly thought necessary.

Although it appears to be now adopted as a legislative theory that we should not attempt to trust to our own supplies of corn, but should encourage the import of all kinds of food from foreign countries, it is not to be inferred from thence that we have by any means reached the limit of our powers of production in this country. Writing nearly forty years ago, an author of great reputation said that the British empire might unquestionably be able not only to support from its own agricultural resources its then existing population, but double, and in time perhaps even treble the number.* Doubtless the population has increased greatly since he wrote, but not at a more rapid rate than agricultural energy and skill. If all the cultivable ground of the United Kingdom were actually cultivated, so as to produce as much food as in the existing state of agricultural knowledge it could be made to produce, it is calculated by those who have given their attention to such subjects that it might support without difficulty three times our present population. In fact, notwithstanding the rapid advance of our population since 1815, our agriculture—under a system of graduated restriction upon foreign import—kept pace with that advance, and the additional supply brought in was very small. It appears from a Parliamentary return of last year, that in each of the years between 1814 and 1846 the import of foreign wheat and wheat-flour was under a million quarters.† The table below will show that

---

* Malthus 'On Population,' book iii., chap. xii.

† Quarters Imported.

							Price.
							s. d.
1815	.	.	.	116,382	.	.	. 74 4
1816	.	.	.	225,263	.	.	. 78 6
1819	.	.	.	124,858	.	.	. 74 6
1820	.	.	.	34,725	.	.	. 67 10
1821	.	.	.	9	.	.	. 56 1

production kept pace tolerably well with consumption ; and though some will argue that consumption was kept down by high price, I think that view of the case is answered by reference to the three years 1834, 35, and 36, when the average price was 44s. 8d. per quarter. It is worthy of notice that the smallest importation of all took place in 1822, a year when, owing to the failure of the potato crop of 1821, the Irish peasantry were in a state of starvation, and large sums were raised by public subscription for their support. Yet it was the apprehension of a similar misfortune in 1846 which was made the pretext for repealing all restriction upon the import of foreign corn into the United Kingdom.

From statements made in Parliament in 1845, supported by Parliamentary returns, it appeared that the rental of land in Great Britain had advanced from 39,405,705l., which it was in 1814, to 45,753,615l.* in 1843, while that of houses had increased from 16,259,399l. in 1814 to 38,475,738l. It appears, says Mr. Alison,

	Quarters Imported.	Price.
		s. d.
1822	2	44 7
1823	12,188	53 4
1824	16,692	63 11
1825	527,007	68 6
1826	316,638	58 8
1827	576,707	56 8
1828	841,947	60 5
1832	375,789	58 8
1833	83,714	52 11
1834	64,552	46 2
1835	27,527	39 4
1836	30,096	48 6
1837	244,086	55 10
1843	982,287	50 1
1845	313,245	50 10

* Ireland not included.

that while the rent of land has increased in Great Britain in the last thirty years by about 12 per cent., the rent of houses has advanced 140 per cent., or nearly twelve times as much; and although the *produce* of the soil has increased about 46 per cent. in the same period, the rent has only increased 12 per cent.*

In the House of Commons it appears that the phrase " real property " signifies something different from what it does in the adjacent neighbourhood of Westminster Hall. In the former place it appears to mean the rental of lands and tenements assessed to the property-tax. In the debate of the 19th of February, 1850, the Secretary of State for the Home Department (Sir George Grey) said that the total value of real property assessed in 1843 was 85,802,735*l.* Of this the land represented 40,167,088*l.*; houses, 35,556,400*l.*; railways, 2,417,610*l.*; and all other property, 7,661,637*l.*† In 1848 the rated value

---

* England in 1815 and 1845, p. 98.

† To the Lords Committee on Parochial Assessments (May, 1850) Mr. Cornwall Lewis stated that in 1843 the " real property " assessed to the income-tax was as follows:—

Lands	£40,167,088
Houses	35,556,399
Tithes	1,960,330
Manors	152,216
Fines (supposed to be on copyhold renewals)	319,140
Quarries	207,009
Mines	1,903,794
Iron-works	412,022
Fisheries	11,104
Canals	1,229,202
Railways	2,417,609
Other Property	1,466,815
	£85,802,728

In 1848—

Lands had increased to	£41,179,713
Houses had increased to	37,282,140
Railways had increased to	5,465,584

But

of land was 41,179,713*l.*; houses, 37,282,140*l.*; railways, 5,465,584*l.*; and all other property, 7,245,034*l.*; making a total of 91,172,471*l.*

From these facts we may in some degree estimate the advance which has taken place in the general income of the upper and middle classes who possess property in land and in houses. With 1849, however, commenced a free importation of foreign corn and a general fall in prices, and it remains to be seen whether income can be maintained under such an altered state of circumstances.

Mr. M'Culloch observes * that the greatest possible misconception prevails among the mercantile and moneyed classes with regard to the situation and circumstances of the owners of land. He affirms that the land belonging to opulent proprietors " bears no sort of proportion " to that which belongs to persons of middling and very small fortune. In the majority of English counties, he adds, property is subdivided to a far greater extent than is commonly supposed, and there are few that lead a more laborious life, or are more under the necessity of abstaining from luxurious indulgences, than the owners and occupiers of small landed properties. Instead of the landlords being " generally as rich and luxurious as is imagined, or at least represented by the demagogues in manufacturing towns," he estimates that the average income of landowners in England is 170*l.* a-year, and as a few have much more, it follows that many must have a great deal less. Mr. Disraeli held a similar argument during the session of 1849 in the House of Commons. My own belief, however, is that, in the last forty years, thousands of small estates have been absorbed into the larger pro-

But upon the aggregate of all other property there was a decrease from 7,661,637*l.* in 1843 to 7,245,034*l.* in 1848.

* 'Treatise on Taxation,' pp. 119,120.

perties. The rich have been adding field to field, and house to house, while the poorer proprietors have in numerous instances sold their possessions under the pressure of distress, or in the prospect of more profitable investment. The smaller proprietors now are not, as they once were, owners of fields, but of houses and gardens—the proprietors, in short, of residences, but not deriving their support from the land. It is to be regretted that such facts in England cannot be stated with exactness. Calculation may approximate to the truth, but there is no such thing as a precise statistical return of the ownership, occupation, and average produce of land in the different counties of England.

It occurs to me that there is no more apparent want in the rural districts of England than that of an intelligent middle class of landowners, cultivating their own property, and residing upon it throughout the year. Farmers of the ordinary class generally divide their time between the labours of their calling, and amusements with which neither mental cultivation nor refinement of taste have much to do. On the other hand, the gentry, or "county people," are for the most part possessed with rather lofty ideas of their own local importance, and their habits of life are such as to repel intimacy save with the opulent. If the farming men now and then mix with the landowners in their field sports, it is upon a footing of understood inferiority, and the association exists only out of doors, or in the public room of an inn after a cattle-show or an election. The difference in manners of the two classes does not admit of anything like social and family intercourse. The chief link between different orders of society in the country is formed by the clergy, but they constitute a middle class rather between the rich and the poor than between the gentry and the farmers. The clergy have, indeed, the rank of gentry, though not generally the riches, and their families find no congenial society in the families of farmers. The labourer's cottage, which they visit in the performance of the offices of religion and of charity, knows much more of the clergyman and his family, than does the better provided house of the farmer, who frequently desires to manifest a surly independence of the parson.

Farming has of late years in England been by no means so thriving a business as the industry devoted to it might be supposed to deserve. "We see," says Alison, "cultivation everywhere extended, and the most strenuous efforts made frequently to drain and improve the soil; but we perceive scarcely any traces of these exertions leading to the accumulation of fortunes among their authors. It is painfully evident that these efforts are made, not to accumulate money, but to avert ruin. The farmers are contented if they can live; to make fortunes has become so rare among them that it is scarce ever thought of. We often hear of shopkeepers and merchants buying villas in the country to enjoy themselves in summer, but we never hear of farmers buying houses in town for recreation in winter. They do not even acquire small properties in the country." Upon the whole it does not seem to me that the rural advantages of England are productive of as much practical good to the people as they might be under such social arrangements as it is easy to conceive, however difficult it might be to carry them into execution.

CHAPTER III.

POPULATION—OCCUPATIONS OF THE PEOPLE.

An official numbering of the people in Great Britain and Ireland takes place every tenth year. The last account was taken in 1841. It is a very laborious matter to make up and classify the returns. The returns themselves are probably far from accurate. They depend on the good faith or attentiveness of the master of each inhabited house, who fills up the blanks in the paper left at his door, and I am not aware that any check exists upon these returns, or that there could be an efficient check. For some years past there has been an official registration of births and deaths, but we have no enrolment of the inhabitants of any district, except when the decennial census is taken. I have now before me seven or eight different accounts, all of them purporting to be abstracts of the official enumeration of 1841, but no two of them agree to within a few thousands. Mr. Spackman's synoptical table does not precisely agree with the elaborate enumerations abstracted from the official returns in the body of his book. According to these abstracts, the numbers in 1841 were

England {(including 5016 travelling on the night of the census)	15,000,154*
Wales	911,603
Scotland	2,620,184
Ireland	8,175,124
British Isles	124,040
	26,831,105

* The official abstract returned to Parliament in 1844 gives—
England

We may take the population of the United Kingdom in round numbers at 27,000,000 in 1841, or 19,000,000 excluding Ireland. Since the commencement of the century the increase of the population of Great Britain each ten years has been between 16 and 17 per cent., so that we may estimate the present population of Great Britain at about 22,000,000. In Ireland, it is probable, the population in the last three years has rather diminished, owing to the pressure of extreme distress.

The abstract of the population returns of 1841, presented to Parliament by the Population Commissioners in 1844, contains the following :—

" The agricultural class forms not quite 8 per cent. of the whole population, while trade and manufactures employ $16\frac{1}{2}$ per cent. The altered proportion which the agricultural bears to the commercial classes for Great Britain generally will at first perhaps excite surprise. The proportions which the agricultural, the commercial, and the miscellaneous classes bore to each other were in—

	Agricultural.	Commercial.	Miscellaneous.
1811	35	44	21
1821	33	46	21
1831	28	42	30
1841	22	46	32

These comparative statements refer in the first three decennial periods to families, but upon the present occasion to individuals.

" The total number of agricultural labourers in Great

England	.	.	14,995,508, of whom 7,321,875 are males, and
			7,673,633 are females.
Wales	.	.	911,321
Scotland	.	.	2,620,610

—according to the census taken in 1841.

Britain of both sexes amounts to 1,138,563, being the largest number returned under any one head except domestic servants, who amount to 1,165,233. The total number of both sexes included under these two heads is, in localities varying much as to other circumstances, pretty nearly the same."

The Commissioners say they have reason to believe that in some instances servants kept in farm-houses, and employed generally about the premises, have been returned as domestic servants, whereas in 1831 such persons were included as agricultural labourers. Mr. Spackman accuses the returns of being, not only in this respect, but in all other respects, framed so as to give an erroneous impression of the comparative numbers connected with agriculture and with manufactures. In the returns of 1831, out of 5,812,276 males of the age of 20 years and upwards in Great Britain and Ireland, only 430,063 were returned as manufacturers, while the agriculturists were enumerated as 1,243,057 in Great Britain, and 1,227,054 in Ireland, making together 2,470,111. Those engaged in trade, commerce, domestic service, and in labour not strictly either agricultural or manufacturing, were 2,297,137. In 1841 the form of statement was changed; trades and manufactures were joined together in the summaries, and but two great classes were recognised—those who were actually engaged in agriculture, and those who were not. Mr. Spackman contends that a very large proportion of those engaged in commerce and trade should be classed with the agricultural interest as being employed by those who derive their income from the land, or, as he puts it, " dependent on agriculture." He also includes Ireland in his calculation, which adds largely to the proportion of agriculturists. His summary is as follows :—

Number of persons, male and female, engaged in
  agriculture in Great Britain and Ireland   . 3,344,207
In trade and commerce 2,413,951
In manufactures $\begin{Bmatrix} \text{Great Britain} & . & 1,140,906 \\ \text{Ireland} & . & . & 300,000 \end{Bmatrix}$ 1,440,906

The agriculturists he thus distributes :—

England   1,157,816
Wales   103,632
Scotland   229,337
Islands in the British Seas   8,493
Ireland   1,844,929
                                                    _____
                                                   3,344,207

According to his assortment of the population, the
agriculturists and those depending on agriculture pre-
dominate in all the counties of England save seven, and
one division of a county. The exceptions, in which the
manufacturing interest occupies the larger portion of the
population, are—Chester, Derby, Lancaster, Leicester,
Nottingham, Stafford, Warwick, and the West Riding of
Yorkshire. In Lancashire, containing 1,667,054 inhabitants, he sets down 292,129 as engaged in manufactures,
and 1,133,091 as dependent on these manufacturers. In
the West Riding of Yorkshire, containing 1,154,101 inhabitants, he gives the number of 168,084 as actually
engaged in manufactures, and an additional 724,294 dependent on them. To the metropolitan county of Middlesex, containing 1,576,636 inhabitants, he allots 18,164
engaged in agriculture, and 1,006,692 dependent on
agriculture !*

---

* The following are the ten English counties which contain the
largest agricultural population :—

Lincoln   57,561
Devon   54,522
Essex   51,116
Norfolk   50,365
                                            Lancashire

Let us now return to the Commissioners' abstracts presented to Parliament in 1844, which give to agriculture only those actually engaged upon the soil, and claim for "manufactures and commerce" all the rest. They inform us that

"Of tradesmen and handicraftsmen by far the largest number are included under the head of *boot and shoe makers*, amounting in the whole to 214,780, or nearly one-third more than the butchers, bakers, buttermen, milkmen, grocers, and greengrocers put together.

"It was important to ascertain correctly the numbers employed upon the staple article of manufacture of this kingdom, inasmuch as, in the absence of any official returns upon this point (except those of the Factory Commissioners), the estimates of persons qualified to judge and to arrive at correct conclusions have varied very greatly. The numbers employed in and about the manufacture of COTTON have been estimated much beyond and as far below the truth. The actual number, including men, women, and children, amounts to 302,376.

"To the numbers included strictly under the head of cotton manufacture, might be added, as employed upon this fabric in its more advanced stages, most of those returned under the head of *lace* and *hose;* if to these be

Lancashire	.	.	.	.	49,569
York (West Riding)		.	.	.	49,297
Kent	.	.	.	.	47,585
Somerset	.	.	.	.	44,467
Suffolk	.	.	.	.	43,858
Wiltshire	.	.	.	.	36,390

This table includes only the number of persons actually at work. In Lincoln, for example, the 57,561 persons consist of 56,151 males and 1410 females employed in agriculture, and 286,704 are set down as dependent on them; the whole population of the county when the enumeration was made being 362,002.

added the fair proportion of those who appear under the general heads of weavers, spinners, and factory-workers, we may fairly assume the numbers to whom the cotton manufacture furnished employment in Great Britain as near upon half a million in June, 1841."

It appears from the Commissioners' statement that, comparing the state of circumstances in 1844 with that of the preceding seven years, the proportion of women and of persons under 20 years of age employed in factories was gradually diminishing. In the cotton manufacture the official return of 1841 is as follows:—Males, above 20 years of age, 105,810; females, 83,830; males, under 20 years of age, 48,968; females, 63,768. This statement does not include those engaged in the manufacture of *lace* or *hose*, or other fabrics of which the material is not specified.

Notwithstanding the immense extent of our iron-works, the whole number of persons employed in iron mines in 1841 was only 10,949, and in the manufactories 29,497. These numbers comprised 497 females employed in the mines, and 451 in the manufactories. Since that period restrictions have been imposed by statute upon the practice of employing females in mines. The coal-mines of Great Britain occupied, in 1841, 118,233 persons. The Population Commissioners remark that the number of persons employed under ground in mines of all kinds amounts to 193,825, being nearly equal to an eighth of the total numbers employed in the cultivation of the surface.

The potteries and large glass manufactories support a population of 32,200, in the proportion of 24,600 males, and 7600 females.

The manufacture of gloves in Great Britain employed, in 1841, 9225 persons: of these 3135 were males.

The total male population of Great Britain, of 20 years of age and upwards, not including the army, the navy, or merchant seamen, was, in 1841, 4,707,600. Of the occupations of all those who have occupations, accounts of almost painful minuteness are given by the Population Commissioners. It is as well to know that they exist, and may be found in the 'Commons Sessional Papers' of 1844. From spinners of cotton down to makers of coffins —from shoemakers down to shovel and shroud makers, the enumeration is carefully carried on. It would not be easy to carry the enumeration further.

The proportions of persons employed in agriculture and in "manufactures and commerce" of course differ exceedingly, say the Commissioners, in different localities. The greatest difference occurs in Lancashire and Middlesex : in the first 28, and in the second 20 per cent. of the whole population is engaged in trade and manufactures, while agriculture claims only 3 per cent. in the first and 1 per cent. in the second. The difference between the two classes is least in the counties of Bedford, Dorset, Hertford, Norfolk, Northampton, Salop, and Southampton, in all of which the division is very nearly equal. The counties in which the percentage engaged in agriculture greatly exceeds that employed in trade and commerce are Essex, Hereford, Huntingdon, Lincoln, and Rutland ; and in none of these does the difference amount to $6\frac{1}{2}$ per cent., while the excess in the returns of "trade and manufactures" ranges from 10 per cent. up to 25 per cent. in the counties of Chester, Derby, Lancaster, Leicester, Middlesex, Nottingham, Stafford, Warwick, and the West Riding of York.

In Middlesex one-fifth of the "occupations" consists of domestic servants, and they form 9 per cent. of the whole population. In all England the number set down as domestic servants—many of them however being assistants in farm-houses, and really engaged in agricultural labour, or in labour directly connected with agriculture—amounts to 1,165,233, of whom 908,825 are females.

The population of London, including a circle round St. Paul's Cathedral of 8 miles radius, was

In 1801	.	.	.	.	.	864,845
In 1811	.	.	.	.	.	1,009,546
In 1821	.	.	.	.	.	1,225,694
In 1831	.	.	.	.	.	1,474,069
In 1841	.	.	.	.	.	1,873,676

And the number now (1850) is probably 2,200,000, for London, far from exhibiting any sign of diminishing populousness, is week by week extending on every side, and covering with streets the ground that in the boyhood of middle-aged persons was pasture and meadow, divided by hedge and ditch, over which the schoolboy scrambled in his holiday excursions. In 1841 the enumerators gave the male population of the metropolis as 876,956, and the female 996,720. This excess of female population, so much beyond the ordinary excess, is doubtless attributable to the number of female servants brought from all parts of the country to attend upon the opulent classes of the metropolis.

To show the rapidity with which the population of towns increases compared with the population of rural districts Mr. Alison gives the following table :*—

Cities and Towns.				1821.		1841.
London	.	.	.	1,225,694	..	1,873,676
Manchester	.	.	.	154,807	..	296,183
Liverpool	.	.	.	131,801	..	286,487
Glasgow	.	.	.	147,043	..	274,533
Dublin	.	.	.	185,881	..	238,531
Birmingham	.	.	.	106,722	..	182,190

* England in 1815 and 1845, p. 26.

Cities and Towns.				1821.		1841.
Edinburgh	.	.	.	138,235	. .	138,182
Bristol	.	.	.	87,779	. .	122,296
Leeds	.	.	.	83,796	. .	152,054
Dundee	.	.	.	30,575	. .	62,794

Counties.						
Argyle	.	.	.	97,316	. .	97,371
Dumfries	.	.	.	70,878	. .	72,830
Perthshire	.	.	.	139,050	. .	137,390
Devon	.	.	.	439,040	. .	533,460
Westmoreland	.	.	.	51,359	. .	56,454
Northumberland	.	.	.	198,965	. .	250,278
Salop	.	.	.	206,153	. .	239,048
Buckingham	.	.	.	134,068	. .	155,983
Hereford	.	.	.	103,243	. .	113,878
Wilts	.	.	.	222,157	. .	258,733

The grave question, whether or no the population of this country is "redundant" with reference to the existing means for its support, is one which must be determined according to the views which are taken of the degree in which the whole property of the country should be made subservient to the use of the whole population. According to the present distribution of property, the numbers of the people appear to be redundant. There are far more seeking to be employed than employers have any need of; and notwithstanding the great numbers supported either as paupers chargeable upon the property of the district to which they belong, or as recipients of private bounty, still there are many who suffer severe distress—many who have no fixed income to live upon, and who find the greatest difficulty in selling their labour to any employer. In this sense the population is redundant, but, on the other hand, if all the land in the British dominions were made to produce as much as all the labour that could be applied to it could cause it to produce, there can be no question that our present population is but a fraction of what might—under such circumstances—be supported.

The Right Honourable Sydney Herbert, a former minister of the Crown, announces as an important truth that " our wealth and our population have *both* outgrown the narrow area of our country. We want more room. We have too much capital and too many people—more capital than we can employ with profit—more people than we can maintain in comfort." Many persons contend that this statement is upon the face of it fallacious; for if we have capital, and if we have people, it is certain that, between the two, any additional amount of subsistence or comfort that may be required may also be obtained; and the difficulty under which we labour is not want of room, but want of some means by which the capital in the country may be devoted to the employment, in productive industry, of those who are now without work. The statement of Mr. Herbert points to the remedy of emigration, and other facts, intended to direct the public mind to the same conclusion, were strongly stated in the *Times* journal of the 15th of February, 1850, from which I make the following extract :—

" It has been asked a thousand times, and certainly is a very natural question, ' Why do not our parishes send to our colonies that surplus population the existence of which is evidenced by the crowded state of our workhouses, and the increased burden of our rates?' On every consideration, philanthropical, political, economical, it strikes every tyro in public affairs as a marvel and a mystery that we do not send our redundant myriads almost anywhere, and anyhow, instead of keeping them at home. It is only the first blush of the matter we are speaking of; but at the first blush never was there a case so plain. In the year ending Lady-day, 1849,—so the Poor-Law Board tells, — England and Wales spent 5,792,963*l.* in the relief of the poor. It is estimated—

for it cannot yet be ascertained with perfect exactness—
that on the 1st of July last 997,796 paupers were receiving relief, in or out of the workhouse, in this part of
the empire.   This is near a million persons, at an average
cost of about 5*l.* 16*s.* a head.   Only think of that in this
wealthy, enterprising, and well-governed empire!   The
year in question is a considerable improvement on the
previous year; yet, it must be admitted, bad is the best.
The computation is that every sixteenth person, or one
person in every three households, is a pauper, hanging
like a dead weight on the industry of the other fifteen.
This, too, in only one form of charity, besides untold
millions spent in endowed almshouses, hospitals, asylums
for every imaginable infirmity, coal funds, clothing funds,
charity schools, voluntary labour rates, church collections,
alms done in secret, and several hundred other species of
benevolence.   Such is the case at home ;—a million
paupers costing the country at the rate of 5*l.* 16*s.* a year.
From this prospect look across the Atlantic, and sail
round the Cape to the Antipodes.   Everywhere we possess
lands flowing with milk and honey, and either with no
Canaanites at all or very harmless ones.   We possess
without dispute, without let or hindrance, as fully and as
freely as our own paddocks and lawns, land enough not
only for one million, but for a hundred millions.   The
inhabitants of these regions clamour for our labourers ;
the cattle ask to be milked, the sheep to be eaten, the
harvest to be reaped, and all nature to be occupied and
enjoyed.   The woods and dales are vocal with invitation.
Then, as for the means of conveyance, it is not a barren
wilderness that separates our land of promise from our
house of bondage, but the ocean—an ocean in which we
are ever at home—an ocean which we call our own, and
justly, for no nation can traverse it more freely and safely

than we do—an ocean filled with our merchantmen, and
protected by our fleets—an ocean the greatest perils of
which are those which a vessel escapes from when it loses
sight of our own shores—an ocean which, so far from
being any real obstacle, is, in fact, the readiest, easiest,
safest, and cheapest means of communication between the
extremes of poverty and abundance we have just described.
Only one other link in the chain is wanting, and that is
the expense. It is supplied by the simple fact that one
million paupers cost us annually about 5l. 16s. a head.
One year's maintenance of one million paupers would
place them with a sovereign apiece in their pockets in
Upper Canada. Two years' maintenance would land
them at Cape Town or Port Natal. Three years' maintenance would distribute them over Australia, Van Die-
men's Land, and New Zealand. Such are the broad
features of a case, such the simple conditions of a problem,
without a parallel for interest and importance."

This is very effective declamation, but I think, if the
author of it had ever travelled in an emigrant ship, he
would have wished to be " at home " in some other sense
than that of being on the waves which Britannia rules.*
I admire the adventurous spirit which leads men to seek
in far off lands the comfort and independence which are
so difficult of attainment at home ; but when a family has

---

* Long after this was written I found in the *Times* of August 1, 1850,
some remarks upon an entertainment given on board an emigrant ship,
before starting for New Zealand. " Doubtless," says the writer, " there
was some oddity in the comparison suggested between the present holiday
look of the vessel and its possible state three or four months hence, when
it may be driving before a north-wester off the Cape—its cabins and cribs
all peopled with sickness and sorrow, its hatches battened down, its windows
closed, and the sounds above associated with the idea of actual danger."
Afterwards the same writer observes, " There is no disguising the bitter
truth—emigration is a very great leap, and a leap almost in the dark."

to cross several thousand miles of ocean in a crowded
ship, it is impossible to deny that the adventure is one of
hideous discomfort, and of some peril. I confess, however, that I know no better remedy for popular distress
than emigration, until the time shall come when men of
wealth will not place their happiness in the possession of
that which they cannot use, but which they at the same
time prevent others from using. I never expect to see
that time. I think emigration necessary, not because
more room is wanted for our population to employ their
capital, and to raise food for themselves and their little
ones, but because they who possess the wealth of the
country, and its land, do not find that they can make a
profit for themselves by employing the people upon it to
produce more food. On this account the food is not produced, and the people are not employed. Why would
our population be better off in the distant colonies ? Because they would either find unappropriated land, or land
for which the owner requires more labour in order to
make it profitable. If in this country to raise more food
were merely the object, without reference to the profit to
be obtained by the sale of it, there would be plenty of
work for all, and more than plenty of food. At the end
of Mr. Alison's first volume on the ' Principles of Population,' he goes into calculations to show that, after setting aside one-half of the arable land of the United Kingdom for the production of luxuries, the remaining half
might be made to produce, in grain and potatoes, enough
of food for 123,000,000 persons ! Nor is his agriculture
very sanguine, according to modern notions, for he estimates only 3 quarters of wheat per acre, or food for three
persons for a year, from the portion of land devoted to grain,
and food for nine persons for a year from each acre devoted
to potatoes. " It is needless, however," he adds, in a pero-

ration composed in his elaborately ornate manner, "it is
needless to say that these numbers are never likely to be
realized.   It seems the law of nature that, ages before a
nation has arrived at the limit of its subsistence, its decay
is prepared by a great variety of causes which, by destroy-
ing national virtue, pave the way for natural decline.
A survey of the fate of all the great empires of antiquity,
and a consideration of the close resemblance which the
vices and the passions by which they were distinguished
at the period of the commencement of their decline bear
to those by which we are agitated, leads to the melancholy
conclusion that we are fast approaching, if we have not
already attained, the utmost limit of our greatness; and
that a long decay is destined to precede the fall of the
British empire.   During that period our population will
remain stationary or recede, our courage will perhaps
abate, our wealth will certainly diminish, our ascendancy
will disappear, and at length the Queen of the Waves
will sink into an eternal, though not forgotten, slumber.
It is more likely than that these islands will ever contain
human beings for whom sustenance cannot be obtained,
that its fields will return in the revolutions of society to
their pristine desolation, and the forest resume its wonted
domain, and savage animals regain their long-lost habita-
tions; that a few fishermen will spread their nets on the
ruins of Plymouth, and the beaver construct his little
dwelling under the arches of Waterloo Bridge; the towers
of York arise in dark magnificence amid an aged forest,
and the red deer sport in savage independence round the
Athenian pillars of the Scottish metropolis."

CHAPTER IV.

TAXATION—REVENUE—EXPENDITURE.

AMONG the many wondrous things accomplished by the British nation between 1795 and 1815, certainly the payment of enormous taxation was not the least extraordinary. Alluding to our financial condition at the close of the war, Mr. Alison says, " the revenue raised by taxation within the year 1815 had risen to 72,000,000 from 21,000,000 in 1796." Besides this contribution in the form of tax, the capitalists were enabled to lend so much money to government that the expenditure for public purposes (including war) reached in each of the years 1814 and 1815 the enormous amount of 117,000,000. Either the will or the way to pay taxes has been much enfeebled since that time, for now, with a population increased probably by two-fifths since 1815, it is with no slight difficulty that a much smaller revenue is raised. All matters of public finance in this country are rendered somewhat perplexing to the investigator by the different ways in which the public accounts are stated, the very same terms being sometimes used to signify different things. Thus we find in public returns for the year 1849 the *net* revenue of Customs set down as 22,194,600*l*., and the *net* revenue of Excise as 14,985,865*l*. ; but in such returns " net revenue " appears to relate to what has been received after deducting drawbacks, allowances, &c., but *not* deducting the expenses of collection. Other returns of " net revenue " show what the Exchequer of the United

Kingdom has actually received in the years 1848 and 1849, after deducting the charges of collection. The figures are as follow :—

	1848.	1849.
Customs	£20,999,132	•• £20,636,921
Excise	14,154,054	•• 13,985,363
Stamps (including legacy-duty) .	6,643,772	•• 6,867,548
Taxes (not on articles of consumption)	4,314,704	•• 4,303,849
Property and Income-tax . .	5,347,364	•• 5,408,159
Post-Office	815,000	•• 832,000
Poundage on Pensions, &c. . .	4,559	•• 4,561
Crown Lands	81,000	•• 160,000
Small branches of hereditary revenue	9,202	•• 42,342
Surplus fees of regulated public offices	53,548	•• 70,022
Total of ordinary revenue .	£52,422,338	£52,310,768
Total ordinary and extraordinary	£53,388,717	£52,951,748

The public accounts of 1848 and 1849 exhibit a further receipt, beyond both the ordinary and extra-ordinary revenue, arising from the sale of 3 per cent. stock, authorized by 11 and 12 Vict. c. 125, to raise 2,000,000*l.* for the public service. Out of the sum so raised by sale of stock, 1,604,312*l.* 10*s.* was added to the receipt of 1848, and 395,687*l.* 10*s.* to the receipt of 1849.

The following were the sums expended under various heads in 1848, or in the year ending the 5th of January, 1849 :—

Expenses of Collection . . .	£4,154,499
Other Payments	651,099
Interest and Management of the *permanent* National Debt	23,978,113
Terminable Annuities . . .	3,795,076
Interest on Exchequer Bills . .	790,327
Civil List	395,245
Annuities and Pensions charged on the Consolidated Fund	509,762
Salaries and Allowances . . .	271,381

Diplomatic Salaries and Pensions . .	£166,492
Courts of Justice	1,098,403
Miscellaneous Charges on the Consolidated Fund	342,549
Army	6,647,284
Navy	7,922,286
Ordnance	3,076,124
Kaffir War	1,100,000
Miscellaneous Charges on the Annual Grants of Parliament, including 276,377*l.* for relief of Distress in Ireland and Scotland . .	4,092,090

The following was the expenditure of 1849 :—

Charges of Collection	£4,020,726
Other payments	606,309
	4,627,035
Interest and Management of the *permanent* Debt	23,991,942
Terminable Annuities . . .	3,725,993
Interest on Funded Debt . . .	27,717,935
Interest on Exchequer Bills . . .	606,025
	28,323,961
Civil List	396,600
Annuities and Pensions	464,687
Salaries and Allowances	268,629
Diplomatic Salaries and Pensions . .	160,833
Courts of Justice	1,105,282
Miscellaneous Charges on Consolidated Fund	398,859
Army	6,549,108
Navy	6,942,397
Ordnance	2,332,031
Miscellaneous by Annual Grants of Parliament, including 113,542*l.* for relief of destitute Emigrants from Ireland . .	3,911,231
	£50,853,623*
Besides 4,627,036*l.*, paid out of the Revenue, as above, before it reached the Exchequer. The excess of Income over Expenditure on the 5th Jan. 1850, was	£2,098,126

* The error of 5*l.* in this summation is caused by the odd shillings and pence which are not set down.

It is worthy of observation that, owing to the bias of the legislative classes of late years towards the encouragement of foreign commerce, almost all the efforts in favour of freedom of trade have had reference to Customs duties or other restrictions upon importation. Customs duties or prohibitions are the restrictions which most directly interfere with the operations of merchants. It is, however, I believe, not denied that the greatest public obstruction to the productive industry of the country is the Excise. This arises not so much from the enhancement of the price of the articles produced and sold, as from the vexatious restrictions and interferences which are made necessary in order to secure the collection of the Excise duty, and to prevent production going on surreptitiously, and independently of the impost which the law imposes. It is in vain that fines are imposed, and in many cases rigorously levied. The temptation to evade the Excise duties is so great that no mere prohibition or penalty is found sufficient to prevent the exercise of the smuggler's ingenuity. Neither the enactments of Parliament, nor the most solemn regulations of Her Majesty's Commissioners of Inland Revenue, have that effect upon the general conscience which is the best safeguard against the commission of offences. It is found difficult to persuade mankind in general, and impossible to convince manufacturers of spirits, malt, paper, and soap, in particular, that to send these articles into the world without the payment of duty, is a violation of the moral law.

The following is called an account of the net receipt of Excise for the years 1848 and 1849, but the expenses of collection are not deducted.

	1848.	1849.
Bricks	£455,845	£456,452
Game Certificates	11,167	9,062
Hops	392,381	205,936
Licences	1,103,435	1,107,890
Malt	5,225,071	4,964,066
Paper	745,795	810,554
Post-horse duty	146,012	144,194
Post-horse licences	6,593	6,801
Soap	990,512	1,026,080
Spirits	5,455,475	5,757,336
Railways	232,270	235,475
Stage-carriages	196,874	188,785
Hackney-carriages	70,409	73,234

£14,985,865

Unfortunately we never can have actual freedom of industry until the greater part, if not the whole, of this heavy taxation is repealed.

It is curious to see how very largely the revenue of Great Britain depends on what goes into the mouth.   In the above list we have malt, hops, spirits, licences to sell beer and spirits and wine, producing upwards of 12 millions.   Then take a selection from the Customs duties :—

	1849. Gross Receipt.
Butter	£138,406
Cheese	97,686
Cocoa	16,644
Coffee	643,210
Corn and Meal	617,814
Eggs	35,694
Fruits	582,906
Hams	3,284
Rice	15,207
Spices	112,825
Spirits	1,803,527
Sugar	3,855,928
Refined sugar	68,328
Molasses	214,695
Tea	5,471,641

—which make not far short of 14 millions more. If to these we add another substance, which Sir James Graham, late a secretary of state, classes with beer and spirits,* as the " stimulants " of the people, we have about four millions and a half from tobacco. The gross receipt in 1849 was—

Unmanufactured tobacco	£4,328,217
Manufactured tobacco and snuff . . .	96,814

We have now a total of between 30 and 31 millions of money derived from taxation of the various articles which the mass of the people eat, drink, or smoke. If I were to include the duties levied upon the import of wine, the sum would be increased by 1,835,071*l.*; but foreign wines are consumed only by the comparatively rich. The duty of between 30 and 31 millions is levied upon articles of universal consumption in England. All but a mere fraction of this may be regarded as voluntary taxation. The " stimulants " might be done without. I have, however, no wish that they should be. I should be glad to see the moderate and prudent consumption of them more general; but, at the same time, I believe the Government will never have fully discharged its duties to society till the most stringent measures are resorted to for checking the vice of drunkenness, which is the parent of almost every other vice among the lower classes of society.

The operation of indirect taxation upon the interests of the working classes appears to me less obvious and more complicated than many persons consider it to be. If every measure which tended to increase the price of the necessaries and comforts of life was therefore a burthen to all classes, so far as it went; and if every measure which tended to diminish the price was therefore

---

* House of Commons debate, Feb. 21, 1850.

a relief, the philosophy of taxation would be a much simpler matter than it really is.   It is assumed by many political debaters, both in and out of parliament, that such simplicity really exists.   Whoever reflects upon the subject, however, will see that the matter is in reality and truth much more complex than these debaters admit. They will see that a measure which in its operation increases the price even of the necessaries of life, may increase also the remuneration of those who produce such necessaries, and render them better able to pay a higher price, than in the absence of such a measure they would be to pay a lower price.   Taxation may operate, not as a burthen upon all alike, in proportion to their consumption of the commodity taxed, but as a transfer of wealth from the non-workers to the workers, causing the non-workers to pay and the workers to receive a larger price than otherwise would be paid and received, respectively, for what the one wants and the other supplies.

P.S. August, 1850.—An account of income and expenditure has just been laid before parliament, including half of the last year and half of the present.   It is called " An Account of the Net Public Income of the United Kingdom of Great Britain and Ireland, in the year ended 5th July, 1850 (after abating the expenditure thereout defrayed by the several revenue departments)."   The following is the statement of income :—

	£.	s.	d.
Customs	20,615,636	3	9
Excise	14,383,829	5	2
Stamps	6,802,954	1	9
Taxes (Land and Assessed)	4,351,531	1	2
Property-Tax	5,459,844	0	0
Post-Office	834,000	0	0
Crown Lands	160,000	0	0
Carried forward	£52,607,794	11	10

Brought forward	£52,607,794	11	10
1s. 6d. and 4s. in £ on pensions and salaries	4,561	12	7
Small branches of hereditary revenues of the Crown	46,390	1	6
Surplus fees of regulated public offices	119,889	7	7
Total of ordinary Revenue	52,778,635	13	6
Produce of the sale of old Stores and other extra receipts	460,769	17	0
Impost and other moneys	102,382	12	1
Money received from the East India Company	60,000	0	0
Unclaimed Dividends (more than paid)	27,884	7	5
	53,429,672	10	0
Expenditure one year to July 5, 1850	49,991,313	12	8
Balance in favour of Revenue	£3,438,358	17	4

—which exceeds by 3,396,961l. the balance in hand on the 5th July last year. The alteration is effected partly by an increase of revenue, and in a yet more considerable degree by a diminution of expenditure :—

The increase of Income amounts to	£1,013,426
The decrease in the public Expenditure amounts to	2,383,535
	£3,396,961

The surplus on 5th July, 1850, appears to be thus disposed of :—

Issued to Commissioners for reducing the National Debt	£837,842
Interest on donations and bequests	11,138
Reduction of Unfunded Debt (Exchequer Bills)	5,300
Excess of advances over repayments, on account of local Works, &c.	700,996
Increase of balances in the Exchequer	1,883,082
	£3,438,358

The following is an account of the public expenditure

of the United Kingdom for one year, to the 5th July, 1850, exclusive of the sums applied to the redemption of funded or paying off unfunded debt, and of the advances and repayments for local works, &c. :—

FUNDED DEBT.

Interest and management of the permanent Debt . . .£23,981,852	1	1	
Terminable Annuities . . 3,726,757	2	0	
Total Charge of the Funded Debt, exclusive of 11,138*l.* 11*s.*, the interest on donations and bequests . . . 27,708,609	3	1	

UNFUNDED DEBT.

Interest on Exchequer Bills . 403,896	16	6	
			28,112,505 19 7
Civil List 396,681	2	2	
Annuities and Pensions for Civil, Naval, Military, and Judicial services, &c., charged by various Acts of Parliament on the Consolidated Fund . . . 409,824	16	8	
Salaries and Allowances . . 278,862	19	8	
Diplomatic Salaries and Pensions 158,963	5	7	
Courts of Justice . . . 1,086,136	1	2	
Miscellaneous charges on the Consolidated Fund . . 341,690	14	7	
			2,672,158 19 10
Army 6,577,358	0	2	
Navy 6,381,724	0	0	
Ordnance 2,375,464	13	8	
Miscellaneous, chargeable on the Annual Grants of Parliament . 3,872,101	19	5	
			19,206,648 13 3
			£49,991,313 12 8

Much has been said in a very triumphant tone by the advocates of the free importation of foreign products, as if the improved balance in the Exchequer were clearly traceable to the complete establishment of free importation of corn, from February, 1849. Now, without dis-

puting that, so far as the experiment has yet been tried,
the amount of mischief to the public revenue which many
anticipated from it, has not occurred, it seems a very
hasty and unfounded assumption that free trade has been
the cause of the favourable financial change.   For, in the
first place, more than two-thirds of the improved balance
arises from diminution of expenditure.   Some zealous
friends of free trade are of opinion that to it we are indebted even for the more economical spirit which has of
late prevailed in Government departments, and which has
caused the reduction of expense; but let us remember
that in the days of political darkness, while all the leading
Whigs, including Lord John Russell, were supporters of
the laws giving large protection to native agriculture—in
the days when the Whig Prime Minister, Lord Melbourne, declared that in his opinion it would be madness
to repeal the Corn Laws—the Government was far more
economical than it is now.   Take a few items of the
expenditure of 1835, and compare them with the expenditure of 1849-50 :—

	Year ending 5th Jan. 1836.	Year ending 5th July, 1850.
Army . . .	. £6,493,925	£6,577,358
Navy . . .	. 4,503,908	6,381,724
Ordnance .	. 1,068,223	2,375,464
Courts of Justice .	. 465,004	1,086,136
Miscellaneous . .	. 2,061,395	3,872,101

From these figures it is perfectly clear that, while as yet
the brightness of free trade philosophy had not penetrated
the minds of Whig politicians, at least to anything like
the extent in which it now pervades and illuminates their
policy, they were far more economical than they are at
present.

In the second place, it is to be remembered that various
causes affect so miscellaneous a revenue as that of Great

Britain, and we have not to go back many years for changes of much greater importance than that which has taken place since the establishment of free trade in corn. In the year 1841, while the Corn Law of 1848 was still in force, the gross revenue of the customs yielded 23,515,374*l*. Since then many duties have been reduced, and some have been repealed. But let us take some important articles upon which the duties remain the same :—

In 1841 the Duties received on Tea, Tobacco, and
            Foreign Wine amounted to   .   . £ 9,244,692
1846 the same Duties amounted to   .   . 11,323,295
1849 the same Duties amounted to   .   . 11,731,743

It was no application of the principles of free trade which caused the remarkable increase between 1841 and 1846. The customs duties had, indeed, been largely tampered with in 1842 and 1845, for the purpose of promoting commerce ; but, excluding the above articles, which had not been touched, the customs revenue was *less* in 1846 than in 1841 by 3,315,661*l*. When we can show an increase within a few years, *before* the establishment of free trade, of more than 2,000,000*l*. in the year upon three articles of consumption, it is certainly unreasonable to assume that an increase of little more than 1,000,000*l*. upon all the items of revenue in Great Britain, *since* the adoption of free trade, must be the result of that new system.

The following is a statement of the net amount of *ordinary* revenue paid into the Exchequer in different years, and of the sums paid out, from which conclusions may be drawn as to the *triumphant* character of the financial statement of 1849-50 :—

Years.   Receipt.

1835, the economical Year	.	£46,425,263
1841, Year of Financial Distress	.	47,917,521
1845, Grand Prosperity Year .	.	51,719,118*
1846, Fall of the Peel Administration		52,950,202

Exclusive of Cost of Collection.

Years.

1835.	Expenditure	. £44,901,701
	Expense of collecting the Revenue	. . 3,582,635
1841.	Expenditure	. 50,185,729
	Expense of collecting the deficient Revenue	. 3,582,639
1845.	Expenditure	. 49,242,713
	Expense of collecting the Revenue	. . 3,919,368
1846.	Expenditure	. 50,943,831
	Expense of collecting the Revenue	. . 3,877,446

In the year 1841 the *net* revenue of the Customs was 21,898,844*l*., and in the year 1849 it was 20,636,921*l*. The Excise in 1841 gave to the Exchequer 13,678,835*l*., and in 1849, 13,985,363*l*. The stamps, under which head are included legacy and probate duty, duty on plate, and several other matters, yielded, in 1841, 7,135,217*l*., and in 1849 6,867,548*l*. Yet the year 1841 was one of large deficiency, and so would every year since have been, but for the large sum derived from property and income tax, laid on in 1842. The apparent charges of collection are very considerably swelled of late years by the great expense of the Post-Office. Under the old system, nearly three-fourths of the whole sum received by the Post-Office from the public, went into the Exchequer; under the new system, not much more than one-third appears as revenue. In 1848 the gross receipt of the Post-Office was 2,192,478*l*., and the sum paid into the Exchequer was 815,000*l*. In 1849 the gross receipt was 2,213,149*l*., and the Exchequer received only 832,000*l*. The large amount of difference in both cases goes to swell

* This included 5,026,570*l*. of Property and Income tax which did not exist in 1841.

the "charges of collection." If the cost of the Post-Office packets, now defrayed by a separate estimate, were also deducted from the Post-Office revenue, it would reduce it to between 100,000*l*. and 200,000*l*. a-year.* Besides the "charges of collection," which generally amount to nearly 4,000,000*l*. a-year, and in the years 1848 and 1849 exceeded that sum, there are " other charges " deducted from the various branches of the revenue in its progress to the Exchequer. These are of a very miscellaneous character, and commonly amount to from 600,000*l*. to 700,000*l*. a-year. Independently of these sums, the charges of the collection of the Customs revenue amounts to about five per cent. on the sum received, and on the revenue of the Excise the charge is rather more.

In the last two Sessions of Parliament considerable attention has been given to the growth of the expenses of the army and navy, and under both these heads reductions have been made. It is, however, in the expenses of internal government that the steadiest increase has taken place. Much of this expense is defrayed by local taxation ; but the charges upon the public income have also greatly increased. The miscellaneous expenses provided for by annual grants of Parliament amounted, in 1835,

---

* The revenue from the Post-Office, paid into the Exchequer under the old system, was about 1,600,000*l*. a-year. The change is now approved of on considerations wholly apart from those of revenue; but it is worthy of remark that the gentleman whose name is associated with the new system proposed it chiefly on financial grounds ; his proposition being that a cheap and uniform postage was the surest to return a maximum postage revenue. Upon this ground the experiment was assented to by the House of Commons in 1839 ; the sagacious Chancellor of the Exchequer of that period taking a pledge from the House that, *if* the result were a decrease of revenue, it would, in some way or another, make good the loss ! In the first year the Post-Office revenue fell to one-fourth of what it had been.

to 2,061,395*l.* ; in the year ended 5 July, 1850, they amounted to 3,872,101*l.* A separate charge, under the head " Courts of Justice," amounted, in 1835, to 465,004*l.* ; for the year 1849 this charge is 1,105,282*l.* ; but in the year ending 5 July, 1850, it appears to be reduced to 1,086,136*l.*

The charge for interest on the national debt [*] is generally stated, in round numbers, at 28,000,000*l.* a year. According to the public accounts for the year 1841 (up to 5 January, 1842), the charge for the funded debt was 28,553,680*l.*, and for interest on Exchequer bills 896,464*l.* ; total, 29,450,144*l.* In 1845 the charge for funded debt was 27,827,265*l.*, and for Exchequer bills 426,606*l.* In 1849, for funded debt 27,717,935*l.*, and for interest on Exchequer bills 606,025*l.* The charge on the funded debt, in 1849, is divided into interest and management of " permanent debt," 23,991,942*l.*, and terminable annuities, 3,725,993*l.* An analysis, however, of the funded debt, and the annual charge which it occasions, will be given from the official documents in a subsequent notice of public and private indebtedness in the United Kingdom.

The following is a statement of expenses provided for by Parliament in the miscellaneous estimates, over and above the great branches of public expenditure, army, navy, ordnance, and the revenue departments :—

---

[*] In the public accounts the sums due for interest are charged as paid, whether they are called for or not, and then at certain periods the arrears of unpaid dividends are carried to the credit of the public, or handed over to the Commissioners for the reduction of the National Debt. By a Parliamentary Return of 1850 it appeared that the amount of back dividends due and not demanded was 1,101,342*l.*, of which there had been advanced to Government 936,690*l.* ; leaving in the Bank 164,652*l.*

Sums granted in 1849 *for Salaries and Expenses of Public Departments :—*

Salaries and Expenses of the

Two Houses of Parliament	£93,200
Department of Her Majesty's Treasury . .	57,200
Secretary of State for the Home Department .	25,400
Secretary for Foreign Affairs	76,000
Secretary for the Colonies . . .	36,900
Board of Trade	43,000
Lord Privy Seal	2,000
Paymaster-General's establishment . .	23,900
Comptroller of the Exchequer . . .	6,626
State Paper Office	2,700
Ecclesiastical Commissioners	3,540
Expenses connected with the Poor Law . .	240,000
Mint	45,694
Commissioners of Railways . . .	7,996
Record Office	12,822
Inspectors of Factories, Mines, &c. . .	11,879
Foreign and Secret Service . . .	39,000
Stationery, printing, and binding, for the several public departments	277,762
Law expenses, Treasury . . .	26,000
Mint Prosecutions	9,000
Sheriffs' expenses and Queen's Prison . .	17,700
Insolvent Debtors' Court	10,370
Charges formerly paid out of County Rates .	258,000
Prisons, and expenses of convicted criminals .	702,523

Sums granted in support of Education, Science, and Art :—

Public education in the year 1849 (this is exclusive of 120,000*l.* for Ireland)	£125,000
School of Design	10,000
Universities of Oxford and Cambridge (Professorships)	2,006
University of London	4,000
British Museum (new buildings) . . .	36,288
,, ,, for purchase of Antiquities . .	1,500
Geological survey	18,000
Magnetic observatories, &c. (beyond sea) . .	5,000
Monument of Nelson in London . . .	2,800
Charges of British Museum for year ending March 25, 1850	42,915

There are considerable charges, besides the above, for educational establishments in Scotland and Ireland. The last grant enumerated in the official list is 12,000*l.* for the purchase of books, apparatus, instruments, &c., for the colleges established in Ireland.

———•———

CHAPTER V.

FOREIGN TRADE.

IMMENSE as the foreign trade of Great Britain undoubtedly is, the ideas which generally prevail on the Continent with respect to its *comparative* importance are much exaggerated. In France it appears to be taken for granted by public writers that the principal part of the industry of Great Britain is devoted to the production of goods for foreign markets; and that the principal dependence of this country is upon the sale of domestic or colonial productions to foreigners. This is a most erroneous supposition. Let us take the last year (1849), when the exports of Great Britain exceeded, by 20 per cent., the exports of the preceding year. According to the official return of the Board of Trade, the total value of the exports of the principal articles of British and Irish produce and manufactures for the year 1849 was 58,848,042*l.*; and this includes the value of the raw material, which, in respect to some of the most important articles of British export, is of foreign production. Now, this sum, large though it be, is probably not more than an eighth part of the annual production of wealth in the United Kingdom. Mr. W. F. Spackman, in his work on ' The Occupations of the People,' gives the following estimate, as an approximation to a correct statement :—

Agriculture, annual creation of wealth in Great Britain £250,000,000
Manufactures (deducting the value of the raw material)   127,000,000
Mining interest   37,000,000
                                                         _____
                        Carried forward . . £414,000,000

Brought forward	.	.	£414,000,000
Colonial interest .	.	.	.	.	18,000,000
Foreign commerce (including the shipping interest)	15,000,000
Fisheries .	.	.	.	.	.	.	3,000,000

£450,000,000

Mr. Porter estimates the annual value of the produce of the land of the United Kingdom at upwards of three hundred millions. As to the gross value of manufactured productions, Mr. Spackman estimates it at 187,184,292*l*., of which 118,600,000*l*. are for the home trade, and 58,584,292*l*. for the foreign trade. His general conclusion is, that of the products of manufacturing industry the foreign trade absorbs *one* third, and the home trade *two* thirds. It is probable that foreign writers may have been misled by looking too exclusively at our cotton manufacture. Of the products of that particular branch of industry the larger portion is exported. It is calculated that the home consumption is to the export consumption as 20 to 25.

The official return of exports for 1849 gives—

Of cotton cloth, 1,335,654,751 yards, value	.	£18,834,601
Lace and net, 105,918,378 yards	,, .	.	487,300
Thread, 4,950,451 lbs. .	.	,, .	.	427,422
Stockings .	.	.	.	,, .	.	439,551
Cotton yarn, 149,502,495 lbs. .	,, .	.	6,701,920

£26,890,794

The import of raw cotton in the year 1849 is officially returned as 6,745,259 cwt. Taking this at the value of 50*s*. the cwt., the sum paid out of the kingdom for the raw material would be 16,863,147*l*. ; so the gain upon this branch of trade is not so very great as might at first be supposed, from looking merely at its vast extent.

The following is a list, taken from the official return for 1849, of the export of all articles of home production, the total value of which exceeded half a million of money :—

Coal and culm	£1,088,148
Cotton manufactures	26,890,794
Earthenware	807,466
Haberdashery and millinery . . .	1,183,229
Hardware and cutlery	2,198,597
Linen cloth, thread and yarn . . .	4,103,463
Machinery and mill-work	709,074
Iron and steel	4,967,643
Copper and brass	1,863,287
Lead and tin	1,140,563
Silk manufactures of all kinds . . .	1,000,357
Wool, sheep or lambs'	535,801
Woollen manufactures of all kinds . .	8,420,342

The most remarkable feature in the progress of our export trade is, that the increase of the quantity of goods exported is prodigiously greater than the increase of the money value of our exports. In our Customhouse returns, what is called the " official value," according to rates fixed in 1694, remains unchanged, and its fluctuations mark only fluctuations of quantity. The "declared value," which is also entered, fluctuates according to the value of the article in the market. In the first year of the present century the " official value " of the exports was 24,927,684*l.* and the real or declared value 39,730,659*l.* In 1846 the official value was 134,385,829*l.*, showing the quantity of goods exported to be about five and a half times as much as in 1801 ; but the real or declared value of the exports in 1846 was 59,837,660*l.* ; so that, while the business done had increased more than 400 per cent., the price or remuneration obtained had increased only 50 per cent. This change appears more in the cotton manufacture than in any other, because more than any other it has been affected by the progress of mechanical invention as well as by a decrease in the money value of the raw material. The change, however, may be seen, more or less, in almost every product of our industry. If we compare the export of bar and rod iron in 1848 and 1849, we find the quantity in 1848 was 338,688 tons, and in 1849 it was 398,007 tons; but the declared value in 1849 was only 2,567,783*l.*, while in 1848 it was 2,615,554*l.*

The official return of imports states only the quantities and the duties paid. Looking at the Board of Trade returns for 1849, the most remarkable feature is the increase in the quantity of food imported. Two important causes have led to this effect; first, the failure or partial failure of late years in the potato crop, upon which hundreds of thousands of the people in Great Britain, and millions in Ireland, entirely depended; secondly, the removal of the duties which formerly existed upon the import of corn: for though by the self-guiding operation of the late Corn Law these duties vanished as corn became dear, they certainly restrained importation when corn was cheap. The average annual import of foreign bread-corn into Great Britain, from the commencement of the century to the year 1844, was about three-fourths of a million of *quarters*, or 360,000,000 lbs. In 1849, though the potato had in a great measure recovered from the disease of 1847 and 1848, the import of bread-corn has been enormous. The quantities taken into home consumption in 1849 have been—of wheat, 4,509,626 quarters; of Indian corn, 2,249,571 quarters; of wheat flour, 3,937,219 cwt.; of Indian corn meal, 102,181 cwt.; besides 1,554,860 quarters of barley, 1,368,673 quarters of oats, and 1,417,863 cwt. of potatoes. Even at the comparatively cheap rate at which this immense supply of foreign food has been purchased, the value is so considerable that the equivalent payment must constitute a very serious drain upon the wealth of the country.

The foreign animals imported in 1849 were below the number imported in 1848. They were—

Oxen and bulls	.	.	.	.	.	.	.	21,751
Cows	.	.	.	.	.	.	.	17,921
Calves	.	.	.	.	.	.	.	13,645
Sheep	.	.	.	.	.	.	.	126,247
Lambs	.	.	.	.	.	.	.	3,018
Swine	.	.	.	.	.	.	.	2,653

Of meat the import was—

	Cwt.
Bacon	.	.	.	.	.	.	.	384,325
Pork	.	.	.	.	.	.	.	348,276
Beef	.	.	.	.	.	.	.	149,917

Of foreign butter, the amount taken for home consumption was 279,462 cwt., and of cheese 390,978 cwt.*

Other imports of 1849, for home consumption, which may be classed with food, were cocoa, 3,233,372 lbs.; coffee, 34,431,074 lbs., of which 29,769,730 lbs. were from our own colonies; lard, 185,838 cwt; oil-cake, 59,144 tons; rice, 537,326 cwt.; sugar (unrefined), 5,922,154 cwt.; molasses, 812,330 cwt.; and tea, 50,024,688 lbs. The import of foreign eggs reached the extraordinary number of 97,884,557, which paid a duty of 35,694*l.* There were 433,450 cwt. of foreign currants taken for home consumption, 31,165 cwt. of foreign figs, 193,811 cwt. of raisins, and upwards of 340,000 boxes or chests of oranges and lemons. Of pepper there were 3,257,746 lbs., and of pimento 3419 cwt. Of rum (independently of the quantity re-exported) we received 3,044,758 gallons, and of brandy 2,187,500 gallons. Of French wine, 355,504 gallons; of Cape wine,

---

* The reader must bear in mind the distinction between quantities imported and quantities taken for home consumption, the amount re-exported being excluded.

241,890 gallons; and all other sorts of foreign wines, 5,890,295 gallons. The supply of eatables and drinkables is quite astounding; and when it is considered that all this importation from abroad comes in addition to our own produce (greater in proportion to our extent of territory than that of any other kingdom in the world), it might perhaps be hastily concluded that every one in Great Britain was well fed. Unfortunately, however, the business of distribution is not so well managed as that of supply, and surrounded by all this abundance there are thousands of the people who scarcely obtain the necessaries of life.

Great as our progress in mercantile intercourse may have been since the close of the war in 1815, it has not equalled (according to the information published by Mr. Spackman) the progress of our great rivals in activity, the French and the Americans. He gives the following facts :—

ENGLAND. Average of 5 years' *Imports*,	1816 to 1820	31,273,309
,, ,,	1840 to 1844	70,510,112
Increase		120 per cent.
FRANCE. Average of 5 years' *Imports*,	1816 to 1820	13,045,168
,, ,,	1840 to 1844	45,564,747
Increase		250 per cent.
AMERICA. Average of 5 years' *Imports*,	1816 to 1820	22,391,982
,, ,,	1840 to 1844	22,206,071
Increase		Nil.
ENGLAND. Average of 5 years' *Exports*,	1816 to 1820	40,211,045
,, ,,	1840 to 1844	52,256,963
Increase		30 per cent.

FRANCE. Average of 5 years' *Exports*, 1816 to 1820   17,420,900
  „   „   1840 to 1844   41,242,251

              Increase .   .   .   .   143 per cent.

AMERICA. Average of 5 years' *Exports*, 1816 to 1820   12,900,429
  „   „   1840 to 1844   20,448,221

              Increase .   .   .   .   62½ per cent.

Supposing this statement to be correct, it will be seen that our rate of progress—at all events as regards the *value* of imports and exports—is much inferior to that of France ; and, as regards exports, to that of America. It is very remarkable that a country making such progress in population and wealth as the United States should appear to be stationary as regards imports. This can only be accounted for by supposing a gradually increasing and more earnest direction of the industry of the people to the supply of their own wants. The political economist may see in this no reason for congratulation ; but the American patriot may well rejoice to find his country growing more and more sufficient to itself, and more able to maintain a noble existence independently of the favour of foreign powers and the fluctuations of foreign commerce.*

---

* The accounts of trade and navigation for the six months ending 5th July, 1850, show a very great increase in the commercial dealings of Great Britain with foreign countries. I shall select from the account of the " Export of British and Irish Produce from the United Kingdom " the articles of which the aggregate declared value exceeded 100,000*l.* in the half-year.

Exported in Six Months, to July 5, 1850.		Same period 1849.
Beer and ale	£311,535	£232,365
Coals	592,807	520,875
Cotton manufactures of all descriptions	13,606,389	12,508,822
Earthenware	477,742	369,937
Haberdashery and millinery . .	735,475	532,607
Hardware	1,256,929	924,643
Leather unwrought and wrought .	291,126	227,681

                                                    Linen

The total exports for the six months ending July 5th, 1850, are returned as having been entered at a declared value of 31,778,504*l.* ; while, in the corresponding period of 1849 (which was largely in excess of the preceding year), the amount was only 26,515,439*l.* The partisans of the Free Trade policy, naturally enough, refer to these returns with great exultation, claiming them as unquestionable evidence of the beneficial effect of that policy.* This was to have been expected ; and if the returns had been the other way, doubtless the opponents of Free Trade would have used them as evidence of the failure of the system. It should be recollected, however, that the injurious effect anticipated from the new system was on British agriculture and on the home trade ; and that, when it was contended that a large amount of the increased imports to be expected from the new policy would have to be paid for in gold, it was not, and could not be, known that California would give the United States that supply of the precious metal which otherwise would most probably have been taken from the accumu-

Exported in Six Months, to July 5, 1850.		Same period 1849.
Linen manufactures of all descriptions	£2,331,504	£1,889,967
Machinery and mill-work	470,747	250,335
Iron and steel	2,826,577	2,315,522
Copper and brass	884,792	807,474
Lead and tin	706,197	503,590
Rape and linseed oil	207,269	128,495
Painters' colours	133,169	107,928
Salt	113,480	137,582
Silk manufactures	484,775	307,572
Soap	102,361	81,151
Stationery	189,629	124,440
Refined sugar	168,316	192,036
Wool (sheep or lambs')	242,012	224,784
Woollen manufactures of all descriptions	4,916,274	3,523,449

* In August and September the exports, as compared with 1849, have decreased.

lated stock of England.   It should also be borne in mind
that rapid increases of export are no novelties in this
country—that they have occurred before, without the
stimulus of Free Trade ; and, therefore, there is no just
ground for absolutely assuming that Free Trade is, and
must be, the cause of the increase in 1849 and 1850.
In the year 1815 the value of British and Irish produce
and manufactures exported was 51,603,028*l.* ;* then came
peace with all Europe, which certainly made commerce
more free than it was before, but in 1819 the exports fell
to 35,208,321*l.*   All who have studied the history of
that period must be aware that restriction of money has
as much to do with diminution of trade as any laws
restrictive of the importation of foreign produce.   In 1822
the exports rose to nearly 37 millions ; but in 1823, notwithstanding Mr. Huskisson's " liberal" commercial
policy, they were down again to 35,458,048*l.*   The prodigious prosperity of 1824-5 was attained with an export
of 38,877,388*l.* ; but the financial crash at the close of
that year brought exports down to 31,536,723*l.* in 1826.
Between 1832 and 1836, without any Free Trade measures to run them up, they rose from 36,450,594*l.* to
53,368,571*l.* ; and then in 1837 fell again to 42,069,245*l.*
After reaching 53,233,580*l.* in 1839, they fell in the year
of Sir Robert Peel's tariff reforms (1842) to 47,381,023*l.*
In 1845, with the sliding scale of 1842 in full operation
to restrict the import of foreign grain, they rose to the
unprecedented amount of 60,111,081*l.* ;† and in 1848,
after that restriction was abolished, they amounted only
to 48,946,325*l.*‡   In 1849 the financial crash and panic

---

* See Spackman's Tables, p. 117.

† Spackman's Tables, p. 117.   The Financial Blue Book gives the
export of 1845 as 58,316,315*l.*, and that of 1846 as 59,837,660*l.*

‡ Board of Trade Returns.

of 1847 had been recovered from, and they rose to 58,848,942*l.* The increase goes on with no less progress in 1850 than it did in 1849; but so also does the abundance of money, and the confidence of bankers and merchants in the general credit. If that were again to receive a serious shock (as under the present state of the banking and currency laws it probably may), it is reasonably to be doubted that Free Trade would keep up the commerce of the country. Nevertheless, whatever be the cause, it is gratifying that the improvement in the export trade should be so considerable in the year 1850, and should spread itself over so large a variety of objects. The only increase to be regarded with a doubtful feeling is that of machinery and mill-work, which has almost doubled since last year. It may be that in these articles of export we supply to foreign countries the means of doing without the products of our industry in future years. But this is the debateable ground of political economy.

With respect to the imports of the first six months of 1850, the one point that awakens attention is the diminution of the import of articles of food. The following is a list of articles of diminished import:—

Imports of	Six Months to July 5, 1850.	Same period 1849.
Living animals	12,948	14,296
Cocoa	2,691,132 lbs.	3,617,396 lbs.
Coffee	19,975,965 ,,	22,992,510 ,,
Wheat	1,562,516 qrs.	2,246,576 qrs.
Indian corn	815,445 ,,	1,192,394 ,,
Flour	1,160,777 cwt.	1,802,627 cwt.
Bacon	245,730 ,,	302,383 ,,
Beef	83,537 ,,	117,440 ,,
Pork	160,114 ,,	253,408 ,,
Cheese	147,698 ,,	150,459 ,,
Rice	332,798 ,,	472,837 ,,
Tea	33,724,609 lbs.	33,772,341 lbs.

Imports of	Six Months, to July 5, 1850.	Same period 1849.
Timber (Colonial) . .	44,021 loads . .	51,056 loads
Cotton wool . . .	3,138,867 cwt. . .	4,600,016 cwt.
Brimstone . . .	314,034 ,, . .	402,506 ,,
Flax and tow . . .	482,293 ,, . .	538,419 ,,
Currants . .	137,791 ,, . .	175,284 ,,
Hides (untanned) .	247,002 ,, . .	283,248 ,,
Mahogany . . .	13,044 tons . .	16,407 tons
Palm oil . . .	152,815 cwt. . .	177,667 cwt.
Opium	63,536 lbs. . .	67,248 lbs.
Clover-seed . . .	66,593 cwt. . .	97,243 cwt.
Flax-seed and linseed .	93,967 qrs. . .	122,881 qrs.
Rum	1,801,779 galls. . .	2,232,299 galls.
Brandy	1,783,565 ,, . .	1,854,945 ,,
Tallow	168,939 cwt. . .	259,304 cwt.
Sawn timber (Colonial) .	57,193 loads . .	72,174 loads
Quicksilver . . .	176,819 lbs. . .	969,338 lbs.

In all the articles enumerated there is a diminution of import as compared with last year, though the amount of wheat and wheat-flour imported would seem enormous when compared with six months' foreign supply in any other year than 1849. It is to be observed that not an ounce either of the wheat or wheat-flour has gone into the bonded warehouses for future use. While the wheat imported is 1,562,516 quarters, the quantity taken out for home consumption is 1,581,299 quarters. The wheat-flour imported is 1,160,777 quarters; the quantity taken for home consumption is 1,161,656 quarters. The import of potatoes is nearly double of that of last year.

The following are the more important articles in which an increase of importation has taken place in the first six months of 1850, as compared with the first six months of 1849 : —

	Six Months to July 5, 1850.	Same period 1849.
Oats	568,859 qrs. . .	493,171 qrs.
Butter . . .	150,371 cwt. . .	135,069 cwt.
Eggs . . number	62,025,283 . .	56,454,745
Lard	208,247 cwt. . .	110,246 cwt.

	Six Months to July 5, 1850.		Same period 1849.
Lemons and Oranges .	276,286 chests	··	221,343 chests.
Bark, for Tanners and			
Dyers . . .	149,625 cwt.	··	147,650 cwt.
Caoutchouc . . .	3,416 ,,	··	3,373 ,,
Clocks . . .	£39,834 value	··	£31,855 value.
Cochineal . . .	8,967 cwt.	··	6,279 cwt.
Indigo . . .	41,076 ,,	··	30,249 ,,
Logwood . . .	19,006 ,,	··	9,874 ,,
Madder . . .	57,756 ,,	··	49,285 ,,
Embroidery and Needle-			
work . . .	£104,391 value	··	£63,196 value
Hemp, undressed . .	255,744 cwt.	··	209,063 cwt.
Tanned Hides . .	809,306 lbs.	··	740,889 lbs.
Thread lace (made by			
hand) . . .	£53,282 value	··	£52,279 value
Women's Boots . .	13,105 pairs	··	8,329 pairs
,, Shoes . .	59,714 ,,	··	50,860 ,,
Men's Boots and Shoes .	21,298 ,,	··	13,728 ,,
Boot fronts . . .	304,357 ,,	··	283,068 ,,
Gloves . . .	1,921,984 ,,	··	1,764,209 ,,
Cambrics and French			
Lawns . . .	20,086 pieces	··	15,339 pieces
Damask and Diaper .	10,640 sq. yds.	··	3,103 sq. yds.
Copper, wrought and un-			
wrought . . .	56,748 cwt.	··	15,334 cwt.
Lead and Spelter . .	11,637 tons.	··	7,211 tons
Tin	9,690 cwt.	··	6,690 cwt.
Train-oil and Blubber .	6,216 tuns	··	5,949 tuns
Cocoa-nut Oil . .	37,105 cwt.	··	16,542 cwt.
Olive ,, . .	13,070 tuns	··	8,283 tuns
Potatoes . . .	1,113,738 cwt.	··	708,440 cwt.
Saltpetre . . .	315,369 ,,	··	290,204 ,,
Rapeseed . . .	34,564 qrs.	··	6,791 qrs.
Raw Silk . . .	2,688,800 lbs.	··	2,519,264 lbs.
Silk and Satin Broadstuffs	233,238 ,,	··	167,733 ,,
,, Ribbons . .	196,606 ,,	··	143,170 ,,
,, Handkerchiefs .	409,398 pieces	··	259,095 pieces
Cassia Lignea . .	931,707 lbs.	··	196,183 lbs.
Cinnamon . . .	375,881 ,,	··	354,293 ,,
Cloves . . .	256,761 ,,	··	108,119 ,,
Pepper . . .	1,480,102 ,,	··	772,739 ,,
Sugar . . .	3,263,661 cwt.	··	3,014,944 cwt.

	Six Months to July 5, 1850.		Same period 1849.
Foreign Timber (sawn and unsawn) . .	136,110 loads	. .	96,461 loads
Tobacco . . .	5,956,419 lbs.	. .	5,483,417 lbs.
Wine	4,112,396 galls.	. .	2,986,106 galls.
Wool (sheep and lambs')	33,584,730 lbs.	. .	23,325,171 lbs.
Woollen manufactures	£310,582 value.	. .	£296,637 value.

Here we find an increase of many foreign articles which (were as much attention given to the stimulating of home industry as to the encouragement of foreign trade) might be procured of native manufacture, thus putting wages into the pockets of thousands who are now unemployed. Needlework, lace made by hand, women's boots and shoes, boot-fronts, gloves, cambrics, damasks, silk manufactures, have all been imported in larger quantity than in 1849, while large subscriptions are made to send out of England the persons who could manufacture these articles, because, it is said, there is no profitable occupation for them at home! The increase of the import of sheep's wool is a gratifying fact, especially as nearly two-thirds of the very large quantity imported come from British possessions abroad. This fact, together with the remarkable increase of the export of manufactured woollens and of linen manufactures, are features of change in which even the most conservative will rejoice. The import of foreign timber, it will be seen, increases, while that of British colonial timber diminishes—a circumstance which, probably, the politico-economic directors of British Colonial policy regard with much equanimity. The great increase in the import of spices is merely a mercantile supply—the quantity taken for consumption is nearly the same as last year.

CHAPTER VI.

THEORY OF " PROGRESS."

Every one is ready to admit that the present century, and especially the last thirty years of it, has been an era of great " progress ;" but much difference of opinion exists as to the nature of that progress. The activity of all classes appears to have been accelerated in a prodigious degree, and many writers take it for granted that this activity has been, upon the whole, turned to good account. They contend that the progress of *improvement* has been commensurate with the quickened movement of society. Others there are who take a far less favourable view of the remarkable changes in the state of society during the present century. They represent the improvements and advantages as having been confined to the upper and middle classes—to those who are above the condition of the labouring poor. They doubt that " the masses " have shared in the advantages of progress ; or they go even further than that, and assert that the great bulk of the people are in a worse and more dependent condition than they were before the " improvements " (which are considered to be the glory of the present age) had been heard of. Let us calmly and impartially examine some of the authorities on both sides of this great question.

Mr. Macaulay, if not the most accurate, unquestionably the most eloquent of the champions of the " improvement " theory, tells us, in the first volume of his History, that,

" the more carefully we examine the history of the past, the more reason shall we find to dissent from those who imagine that our age has been fruitful of new social evils. The truth is, that the evils are, with scarcely an exception, old. That which is new is the intelligence which discerns, and the humanity which remedies them." This is a strong assertion, but not a considerate one. It is true that evils in the state of society are more observed, and brought more under public consideration, than they were wont to be ; but it is also true that the new circumstances which have grown up—more especially that of the concentrating larger masses of people in towns — form prolific sources of evils, which, if they existed at all in the olden time, existed in a much mitigated degree. It is impossible but that there must be new social evils of immense magnitude ; and the real question is, whether they have been counterbalanced by the opposite tendencies of the age, so as to produce upon the whole an improvement.

M. Guizot says, in one of his lectures on history (I quote from the English translation), that " no reasonable person will deny the immensity of the social reform which has been accomplished in our times. Never have human relations been regulated with more justice, nor produced a more general well-being as the result. Not only this, but I am convinced a corresponding moral reform has also been accomplished. At no epoch, perhaps, has there been, all things considered, so much honesty in human life, so many human beings living in an orderly manner : never has so small an amount of public force been necessary to repress individual wrongdoing." This was written before M. Guizot's experience of 1848, and I think it indicates that he had taken a view rather of the external and temporary attitude of the people in their relation to politics and police, than of their domestic condition and the state of their lives at home.

Mr. Mackay, the author of a book on ' The Western World,' to which I refer because it has been mentioned, I think, on more than one occasion in the House of Commons, is good enough to assure the public, without any kind of hesitation upon the point, that " it is true that more has been done for mankind during the last seventy years than perhaps during the previous seven hundred ;" but, he adds, " the development of a nation in Europe is a slow process at the best, as compared with the course of things in this respect in America." It is not necessary to criticise this gentleman ; but we shall see presently something of the nature of the " development" with which he is so satisfied.

We now, however, come to a high scientific authority on the side of the " improvement" theory. Mrs. Somerville, at the close of her volumes on ' Physical Geography,' says that " no retrograde movement *can* now take place in civilization ; the diffusion of Christian virtues and of knowledge ensured the progressive advancement of man in those high intellectual and moral qualities that constituted his true dignity. But much yet remains to be done at home, especially in religious instruction and the prevention of crime ; and millions of our fellow-creatures in both hemispheres are still in the lowest grade of barbarism. Ages and ages must pass away before they can be civilized ; but if there be any analogy between the period of man's duration on earth and that of the frailest plant or shell-fish of the geological periods, he must still be in his infancy ; and let those who doubt of his indefinite improvement compare the first revolution in France with the last, or the state of Europe in the middle ages with what it is at present. For, notwithstanding the disturbed condition of the Continent, and the mistaken means the people employ to improve their position, crime is less frequent and less atrocious than it was in former times, and the universal indignation it now raises is a strong indication of improvement. In our own country, men who seem to have lived before their time were formerly prosecuted and punished for opinions which are now sanctioned by the legislature and acknowledged by all. The moral disposition of the age appears in the refinement of conversation. Selfishness and evil passions may possibly ever be found in the human breast, but the progress of the race will consist in the increasing power of public opinion—the collective voice of mankind, regulated by the Christian principles of morality and justice. The individuality of man modifies his opinions and belief; it is a part of that variety which is a universal law of nature, so that there will probably always be a difference of views as to religious doctrine, which, however, will become more spiritual and freer from the taint of human infirmity ; but the power of the Christian religion will appear in purer conduct and in the more general practice of mutual forbearance, charity, and love." *

---

* Contrast with this the following passage from Wilberforce's ' Practical View :'—

" Let the community in general be supposed to have been for some time in a rapidly improving state of commercial prosperity ; let it also be supposed to have been making no unequal progress in all those arts and sciences and literary productions which have ever been the growth of a polished age, and are the sure marks of a highly-finished condition of society. It is not difficult to anticipate the effects likely to be produced on vital religion, both in the clergy and laity, by such a state of external prosperity as has been assigned to them respectively. And these effects would be infallibly furthered where the country in question should enjoy a free constitution of government. We formerly had occasion to quote the remark of an accurate observer of the stage of human life, that a much looser system of morals commonly prevails in the higher than in the middling and lower orders of society. Now, in every country of which the middling classes are daily growing in wealth and consequence, by the success of their commercial speculations, and most

This is the very poetry of science, soaring into prophecy.
No doubt, if human life were indeed what is drawn by
scientific speculation, and coloured by the pure glow of a
female imagination, little more were to be desired.   Mrs.
Somerville, surrounded by all the emblems of scientific
research, and in an afflatus of cosmogony and benevolence,
predicting universal good, would be more attractive

> " than Naiad by the side
> Of Grecian brook, or lady of the Mere,
> Sole sitting by the shores of old Romance."

But stern reality, alas ! disturbs these pleasing visions.
We regard with admiring wonder the inventions of science,
and our respect for human ingenuity is vastly increased ;
but when we inquire how far the use of them has benefited the great mass of the people, we are compelled to
dismiss all sense of triumph in their achievements.   Mr.
M'Culloch, the political economist, who is not likely to be
betrayed into any excess by the vivacity of his feelings, or

---

of all in a country having such a constitution as our own, where the
acquisition of riches is the possession also of rank and power, with the
comforts and refinements, the vices also of the higher orders are continually descending, and a mischievous uniformity of sentiments, and
manners, and morals, gradually diffuses itself throughout the whole
community.   The multiplication of great cities also, and, above all, the
habit, ever increasing with the increasing wealth of the country, of fre-
quenting a splendid and luxurious metropolis, would powerfully tend to
accelerate the discontinuance of the religious habits of a purer age, and
to accomplish the substitution of a more relaxed morality.   And it must
even be confessed that the commercial spirit, much as we are indebted
to it, is not naturally favourable to the maintenance of the religious
principle in a vigorous and lively state.

" In times like these, therefore, the strict precepts and self-denying
habits of Christianity naturally slide into disuse, and even among the
better sort of Christians are likely to be softened, so far at least as to be
rendered less abhorrent from the general disposition to relaxation and
indulgence.   In such prosperous circumstances, men, in truth, are apt to
think very little about religion."

to be carried away by the warmth of his imagination, says,
" It is doubtful whether the condition of the labouring
part of the population has not been deteriorated during
the last five-and-twenty years; and, at all events, it is but
too certain that their comforts and enjoyments have not
been increased in anything like the same proportion as
those of the classes above them.   Inasmuch, however, as
the labouring poor constitute the majority of the population, their condition is of the utmost importance, not only
in regard to their own well-being, but also in regard to
that of the other classes.   The poverty and depressed
condition of any very large class, especially if it be
strongly contrasted with vast wealth, extravagance, and
luxury on the part of others, is a most undesirable state
of things, and one which can hardly fail to produce discontent, sedition, and disturbance of all kinds." *   This
was written, or at least published, just before the era of
Free Trade.   If, then, any one should be disposed to say
that the new legislation has altered all this, he must refer,
for additional instruction upon the point, to the most conspicuous and strenuous of all the advocates of the new
system.   The *Times* newspaper says, " In the midst of
the splendour and abundance of this country, there is so
appalling an amount of squalor and destitution that the
imagination almost recoils from conjuring up before it the
alternate pictures that would convey a faithful idea of the
social condition of one of our great cities.   It would be
easy to dwell upon the contrasts between the extremes of
human fortune presented to the eye of the observer as he
passes along the London streets, and yet how faint are its
outward signs in comparison with the inward agony of
extreme destitution in the midst of civilization." †   But

---

* M'Culloch on Taxation, p. 394.   † *Times*, January 19, 1850.

are there not houses of refuge for the destitute poor—
workhouses where the wretched can, at all events, have
food and shelter in their extremity? No doubt; but
these are not the abodes of comfort but of misery. Much
of this is perhaps inevitable, but that alleviation which
might be attained by a more careful classification of the
inmates is not obtained. All varieties are huddled
together, and they who suffer least are the lowest and
coarsest, who scarcely have a conception of anything
beyond the gratification of their animal wants. Not to
refer to the poet Crabbe, lest it should be said he described a bygone state of things, let the same newspaper
be again called on to bear witness. " But there is hardly
in all the earth a sadder sight than the multitudes of
from 300 to 1000 shut up in the workhouses. Broken
hearts and fortunes, high spirits still untamed, minds in
ruin and decay, good natures corrupted into evil, cheerful
souls turned to bitterness, youth just beginning to struggle
with the world, and vast masses of childhood are there
subjected, not to the educated, the gentle, and the good,
but the rude, the rough, the coarse, the ignorant, and
narrow-minded. The qualifications for the governor of a
workhouse are those we expect in a gaoler, or a policeman,
or the keeper of wild beasts. Human nature, if it be
ever so fallen, is yet too fine a thing to be bullied into
goodness. None can reclaim it but the good and noble.
We want a race of heroes and apostles for the reformation
of our paupers, and their conversion into men. With
our workhouse staff such as it is, low, vulgar, and brutal,
and with the evil association of the unfortunate with the
wicked, and the weak with the audacious, it is impossible
but that the miserable inmates should be more and more
depraved, embittered, and exasperated—witness the un-
intermitted current of misery to the county gaol, which is

fast sinking into the punishments ward of the union workhouse." *

I must confess that, in my own opinion, this striking picture is somewhat over-coloured, and I am disposed to believe that, as regards the treatment applicable to a large class of the inmates of workhouses, they are not such places of discipline and frugality as it is desirable they should be. The shameless, habitual pauper deserves, I think, a severer treatment than he receives ; but whenever persons whose better feelings still remain to them are forced by crushing misfortune to become inmates of such houses, their misery must indeed be extreme. Can it be said, however, with correctness, as Mr. Macaulay says, that there are no new social evils, when we find such severity of pressure, such extremity of distress, concurrently with an unparalleled progress of wealth and luxury ? Is it not true that the pain of poverty is enhanced by contrast, and that, to do justice to the poor, we should make their circumstances better in proportion as the general circumstances of the country are better ; and is it not a monstrous evil that the poor grow poorer while the rich grow more rich ? In a country where the general lot is a hard one, the privations of poverty may be borne without the bitter sense of degradation.—

> " Though poor the peasant's hut, his feasts though small,
> He sees his little lot the lot of all ;
> Sees no contiguous palace rear its head,
> To shame the meanness of his humble shed ;
> No costly lord the sumptuous banquet deal,
> To make him loathe his vegetable meal."

No doubt the living even of the humblest classes is in some measure refined, in comparison with the living of times past. It may be true that " bread is now given to

---

* *Times*, November 30, 1849.

the inmates of a workhouse," such as formerly was
" seldom seen even on the trencher of a yeoman or of a
shopkeeper," and that the time was when " the great
majority of the nation lived on rye, barley, and oats."
This is what Mr. Macaulay tells us, but another very
picturesque writer, namely, the Lord Chief Justice Fortescue, who wrote in the reign of Henry VI., says that
" the inhabitants of England are rich in gold and silver,
and in all the necessaries and conveniences of life.   They
drink no water unless at certain times upon a religious
score, and by way of doing penance.   They are fed in
great abundance with all sorts of flesh and fish, of which
they have plenty everywhere ; they are clothed throughout
in good woollens ; their bedding and other furniture in
their houses are of wool, and that in great store ; they
are also well provided with all other sorts of household
goods and necessary implements for husbandry ; every
one according to his rank hath all things which conduce
to make life easy and happy."   This Fortescue wrote
when suffering exile under similar circumstances to those
of Clarendon two hundred years afterwards, who also in
his turn wrote, concerning England, that for " twelve years
before the meeting of the Long Parliament the kingdom
enjoyed the greatest calm, and the fullest measure of
felicity, that any people in any age for so long time together have been blessed with, to the wonder and envy of
all the other parts of Christendom."   I am afraid that
" modern improvement " cannot justly claim the credit
of having produced such results as these old writers
describe.

CHAPTER VII.

PRESENT CONDITION OF THE PEOPLE—PHYSICAL.

NOTWITHSTANDING Mr. Macaulay's abstract optimism in respect to the present condition of the people, he is now and then led by his genius into a picturesque truth which cannot be said to corroborate his theory. Before the revolution, he says, " many thousands of square miles, now enclosed and cultivated, were marsh, forest, and heath. Of this wild land much was by law common, and much of what was not common by law was worth so little, that the proprietors suffered it to be common in fact. In such a tract squatters and trespassers were tolerated to an extent now unknown. The peasant who dwelt there could at little or no charge procure occasionally some palatable addition to his hard fare, and provide himself with fuel for the winter. He kept a flock of geese on what is now an orchard rich with apple blossoms. He snared wild fowl on the fen which has long since been drained and divided into corn-fields and turnip-fields. He cut turf among the furze-bushes on the moor which is now a meadow bright with clover, and renowned for butter and cheese. The progress of agriculture, and the increase of population, deprived him of these privileges. But against this disadvantage a long list of advantages is to be set off." The last sentence, intended as a saving clause for Mr. Macaulay's theory, is not, I think, very well sustained by the context. He enumerates better roads, paved and lighted streets, which afford at night a

VOL. I.

brilliantly lighted walk, and which are better watched than they used to be. He mentions also the improved surgery which gives a man a better chance of being cured of his wounds after an accident, and the improved state of the general health by sanitary measures. It is to be feared that these improvements minister much more to the comfort and safety of those who have acquired the property, so pleasingly described by Mr. Macaulay, than to the advantage of those who have lost it. Few are the labourers who, after a day's toil, find enjoyment in the " brilliantly-lighted walk " which modern pavements and gas-lamps afford. Infinitely more delightful to them is a bench to rest on, with the solace of a pipe and a pot of beer, though the room in which they partake of these comforts be ever so dimly lighted. Their taste is not for brilliancy. The improved watching, though of high importance to their richer neighbours, is a matter of indifference to them. What cares the "vacuus viator" for the thief? Mr. Macaulay must for the moment have forgotten his Juvenal. As to the improved surgery, it certainly operates much more decidedly in favour of those who can pay fees, than in favour of those who cannot. With regard to sanitary measures, they have as yet been applied only to towns, and even in them their progress, for so far, has rather been in making known the horrors that exist, than in relieving them.*

---

* "How pitiful is the condition of many thousands of children born in this world ! Here, in the most advanced nation of Europe—in one of the largest towns in England—in the midst of a population unmatched for its energy, industry, manufacturing skill—in Manchester, the centre of a victorious agitation for commercial freedom—aspiring to literary culture—where Percival wrote and Dalton lived—13,362 children perished in seven years over and above the mortality natural to mankind. These little children, brought up in unclean dwellings and impure streets, were left alone long days by their mothers to breathe the subtle sickly vapours

Let us consider the state of the working population in some of those towns, that we may form an adequate conception of the compensation which their condition affords for the loss of rural rights and privileges. A gentleman whose merit must have been very great, since it has raised him to I know not what of influence and distinction, gave the world some years ago a very graphic account of the state of the Manchester workpeople. He wrote under the name of Dr. James Phillips Kay, and that he was very learned may be inferred from the following passage in the first page of his treatise :—" The sensorium of the animal structure, to which converge the sensibilities of each organ, is endowed with a consciousness of every change in the sensations to which each member is liable, and few diseases are so subtle as to escape its delicate perceptive power." The Doctor, however, soon emerges from these profundities to deal with matters which require no very delicate perceptive power for their appreciation. " The population employed in the cotton factories rises," he informs us, " at five o'clock in the morning, works in the mills from six till eight o'clock, and returns home for half an hour or forty minutes to breakfast. This meal generally consists of tea or coffee, with a little bread. Oatmeal porridge is sometimes, but of late rarely used, and chiefly by the men ; but the stimulus of tea is preferred, and especially by the women. The tea is almost always of a bad, and sometimes of a deleterious quality ;

—soothed by opium, a more " cursed" distillation than " hebenon "— and when assailed by mortal diseases, their stomachs torn, their bodies convulsed, their brains bewildered, left to die without medical aid— which, like hope, should 'come to all'—the skilled medical man never being called in at all, or only summoned to witness the death and sanction the funeral."—*Blue Book of the Registrar-General, presented to Parliament* 1848.

the infusion is weak, and little or no milk is added. The operatives return to the mills and workshops until twelve o'clock, when an hour is allowed for dinner. Amongst those who obtain the lower rate of wages this meal generally consists of boiled potatoes. The mess of potatoes is put into one large dish, melted lard and butter are poured upon them, and a few pieces of fried bacon are sometimes mingled with them, and but seldom a little meat. Those who obtain better wages, or families whose aggregate income is larger, add a greater proportion of animal food to this meal, at least three times in the week, but the quantity consumed by the labouring population is not great. The family sits round the table, and each rapidly appropriates his portion on a plate, or they all plunge their spoons into the dish, and with an animal eagerness satisfy the cravings of their appetite. At the expiration of the hour they are all again employed in the workshops or mills, where they continue until seven o'clock, or a later hour, when they generally again indulge in the use of tea, often mingled with spirits, accompanied by a little bread. Oatmeal or potatoes are, however, taken by some a second time, in the evening." There is nothing very fascinating in this fare, yet it is one of the least unfavourable features of the condition of these working people. " The population nourished on this aliment," continues our Doctor, " is crowded into one dense mass, in cottages separated by *narrow, unpaved, and almost pestilential streets*, in an atmosphere loaded with the smoke and exhalations of a large manufacturing city. The operatives are congregated in rooms and workshops during twelve hours in the day, in an enervating, heated atmosphere, which is frequently loaded with dust or filaments of cotton, or impure from constant respiration, or from other causes. They are engaged in an employment which absorbs their attention and unremittingly employs their physical energies. They are drudges who watch the movements and assist the operations of a mighty material force, which toils with an energy ever unconscious of fatigue. The persevering labour of the operative must rival the mathematical precision, the incessant motion, and the exhaustless power of the machine." So much for the fate of the Manchester labourer while at his labour: let us now see what compensation he has in his hours of relaxation. Dr. Kay proceeds to say that, "having been subjected to the prolonged labour of an animal—his physical energy wasted, his mind in supine inaction — the artisan has neither moral dignity, nor intellectual nor organic strength, to resist the seductions of appetite. His wife and children, too frequently subjected to the same process, are unable to cheer his remaining moments of leisure. Domestic economy is neglected—domestic comforts are unknown. A meal of the coarsest food is prepared with heedless haste and devoured with equal precipitation. Home has no other relation to him than that of shelter—few pleasures are there—it chiefly presents to him a scene of physical exhaustion from which he is glad to escape. Himself impotent of all the distinguishing aims of his species, he sinks into sensual sloth, or revels in more degrading licentiousness. His house is ill furnished, uncleanly, often ill-ventilated, perhaps damp ; his food, from want of forethought and domestic economy, is meagre and innutritious ; he is debilitated and hypochondriacal, and falls the victim of dissipation." Such is the testimony to the condition of the humbler classes in Manchester, of a gentleman of the most " liberal " commercial views, who, as a physician in the town, had the best opportunities of observation. Describing the quarters of the town inhabited exclusively by the working classes, he

says, "the houses in such situations are uncleanly, ill
provided with furniture ; an air of discomfort if not of
squalid and loathsome wretchedness pervades them : they
are often dilapidated, badly drained, damp, and the
habits of their tenants are gross ; they are ill-fed, ill-
clothed, and uneconomical ; at once spendthrifts and
destitute, denying themselves the comforts of life in order
that they may wallow in the unrestrained licence of
animal appetite." Yet it must be admitted that luxury
has made great, and refinement has made some, progress
in Manchester. The houses of the opulent are numerous,
and, if deficient in that which a taste for simple elegance
would have provided, abound, even to overflowing, with
every expensive convenience. I have selected by no
means the most apalling passages of Dr. Kay's book, and
they who wish to familiarise themselves with far more
revolting pictures than I have ventured to transcribe, of
the foul degradation to which the lowest classes of a large
manufacturing town habitually submit, must refer to the
painful pages in which I have read them. Nor is it to
be supposed that in these respects Manchester holds a
bad pre-eminence. Dr. Kay says that, were similar investigations made in other large towns, it would be discovered that not a few exist with which Manchester might
be *very favourably* compared ! Such investigations were
made by the Sanitary Commission, and the details of filth
and misery, of grossness and degradation, which the
Reports of that Commission present, are absolutely too
horrible for general perusal. Let us take one slight
glance at Stockport, prolific in patriots and poisonous
gases. In the Heaton Norris district " there are forty-
four houses in the two rows, and twenty-two cellars, all
of the same size ; the cellars are let off as separate dwellings ; these are dark, damp, and very low, not more than

six feet between the ceiling and the floor. The street
between the two rows is seven yards wide, in the centre
of which is the common gutter, or more properly sink,
into which all sorts of refuse is thrown; it is a foot in
depth. Thus there is always a quantity of putrifying
matter contaminating the air. At the end of the rows is
a pool of water, very shallow and stagnant, and a few
yards farther a part of the town's gas-works. In many
of these dwellings there are four persons in one bed."
In the noble seaport of Liverpool, renowned over all the
world for its commercial greatness and wealth, there are
from 35,000 to 40,000 of the population living beneath
the general surface of the ground in cellars, from many
of which there is no drainage at all. The consequences
must be left to the imagination.* It is to be remarked
that here, as in Manchester also, the lowest of the low in
the scale of human existence are Irish. There is no conceivable depth of debasement to which this people does
not sink with a most fatal facility. Easily excited into a
temporary and frantic exertion for any imaginary good,
they seem incapable of, or fatally indisposed to, any sober
continuous struggle for that just and reasonable position
in society to which the honest and diligent labourer is
entitled.

The metropolis itself, with all its glories and its gor-
geousness, is comfortable and splendid only for the middle
and upper classes and their servants. Nowhere is there
more intense misery of the poor than in London; and if
we have not anything quite so bad in the way of habita-
tions as the Manchester "cottages" and the Liverpool

---

* An able digest of the most striking points in the Reports of the
Health of Towns Commission may be found in an eighteenpenny
pamphlet by the Rev. C. Girdlestone, Longmans, 1845. See also
'Quarterly Review,' No. 142, art. vii.

cellars, we have our localities of old, mouldy, decaying houses, let off in rooms to as wretched a population as any in the United Kingdom. True it is that if this population choose to make a pilgrimage to Piccadilly, Regent-street, or the West-end squares, after the lamps are lighted, it may indulge in the most brilliant night-walks in the world. But this is little consolation to the wearied silk-weaver of Bethnal Green, or the labourer who rents a room in the courts off Drury-lane, or in the back slums of Whitechapel or of Westminster. I see not what they have gained by our great improvements ; since, wherever improvement gains a footing, *they* are driven away. Something of late has been done in the erecting of model lodging-houses ; but I venture to suggest that the habits of the working people must be re-modelled before these cheap hotels for their accommodation can come into very general use. One is glad, however, to see any attempt, however artificial it may seem, to give the labouring classes an opportunity of sharing the advantages which modern " progress " has given to those above them.*

Among the great cities of the United Kingdom, Glasgow ranks next in population after London. In no city

---

* " I hear from day to day of the inadequate means of the people to support themselves. If we take a general view of the subject it is impossible not to see that the labouring classes have not advanced in proportion to the other classes. The higher and the middle classes have increased in wealth and the power of obtaining comforts and luxuries ; but the labouring classes have not done so. If we compare the condition of the working classes with what it was a century ago (say 1740), it is impossible not to see that, while the higher and middle classes have improved, and increased their means of obtaining comforts—of obtaining foreign articles of luxury, and facilities of travelling from place to place—the labouring classes—the men who either till the soil or work in factories—have retrograded, and cannot now get for their wages the quantity of the necessaries of life they could a century ago."—*Lord John Russell*, 1844.

has the progress of opulence been more conspicuous, or the increase of poverty, wretchedness, and crime more lamentable. Mr. Alison, the historian, who is officially connected with Glasgow, bears testimony to these facts. In the second volume of his treatise on ' The Principles of Population' he mentions it as " a fact extremely well worthy of observation that, even in Glasgow, where the progress of opulence for the last half-century has been unprecedented in European annals, and equalled only in the far-famed rapidity of trans-Atlantic increase, and where the vast wealth of the richer classes has been poured forth with noble, it may be added unparalleled, generosity for the relief of the poor, the inadequacy of all such voluntary efforts has been fully experienced to relieve the constantly increasing sum of human suffering." As to the actual condition of the more wretched portion of the population, he cites the evidence of Mr. Symonds, the Government Commissioner for examining into the condition of the hand-loom weavers. That gentleman states that " the *wynds* in Glasgow comprise a fluctuating population of from 15,000 to 30,000 persons. This quarter consists of a labyrinth of lanes, out of which numberless entrances lead into small square courts, each with a dunghill reeking in the centre. Revolting as was the outward appearance of these places, I was little prepared for the filth and destitution within. In some of these lodging-rooms (visited at night) we found a whole lair of human beings littered along the floor, sometimes fifteen and twenty, some clothed and some naked; men, women, and children huddled promiscuously together. Their bed consisted of a layer of musty straw intermixed with rags. There was generally little or no furniture in these places; the sole article of comfort was a fire. Thieving and prostitution constitute the main sources of the revenue of this population.   No pains seem to be taken to purge this Augean pandemonium—this nucleus of crime, filth, and pestilence, existing in the centre of the second city in the empire.   These wynds constitute the St. Giles's of Glasgow, but I owe an apology to the metropolitan pandemonium for the comparison.   A very extensive inspection of the lowest districts of other places, both here and on the Continent, never presented anything one half so bad, either in intensity of pestilence, physical and moral, or in extent proportioned to the population."   Mr. Alison says these observations perfectly coincide with what has fallen under his own notice, and immediately he proceeds to reiterate his testimony to the " splendid progress and magnificent liberality of the citizens of Glasgow."   From all this evidence I conclude that, as regards the great mass of the people, there is no reason for congratulation upon the progress of wealth, virtue, or happiness.   The mercantile middle class become opulent through the use of cheap substitutes for labour, but the labourers sink in the scale of social existence.   "It is doubtful," says Mr. Mill, the political economist, " if all the mechanical inventions yet made have lightened the day's toil of any human being."   But there can be no doubt that large fortunes have been made by the use of those inventions.   In the acquisition of wealth the nation has made great progress, but in that distribution of it which seems best calculated to impart moderate comfort on the one hand, and to abate the pomp of superior position and insolence of riches on the other, the science of modern times is at fault, while the selfishness connected with it revels for the present in unabated triumph.

CHAPTER VIII.

PRESENT CONDITION OF THE PEOPLE—MORAL.

We have now seen something of the actual condition of the poorest and lowest classes in towns; and though it would be a most mistaken judgment to confound the whole mass of the working classes with these unfortunates, I think it would be even more erroneous to suppose that, taken as a whole, the great bulk of the people have shared in what are commonly considered to be the benefits of modern improvement. Mr. Macaulay, with something like an air of contemptuousness, intimates that public discussion has produced an excess of sympathy for the working classes. He says, " The press now often sends forth in a day a greater quantity of discussion and declamation about the condition of the working man than was published during the twenty-eight years which elapsed between the Restoration and the Revolution. But it would be a great error to infer from the increase of complaint that there has been any increase of misery." Such inference, however, need not depend upon " discussion and declamation :" it may be based upon distinct statements of facts. Besides, if there be declamation upon the side of complaint, there is even more upon the side of congratulation. Declamation, indeed, is much more often resorted to in these days by public men who pronounce panegyrics upon the progress of opulence, than by writers who lament over the advance of poverty and crime. Two men, holding the highest office that a sub-

ject can hold in England,* have, within a few years,
visited Glasgow, and both of them have declaimed in very
complimentary terms upon the commercial enterprise and
industry of that city, and upon the consequent advancement of wealth, exhibited in the splendid entertainments
they received, and the rich community that surrounded
them.   Neither of them said one word of the poverty and
depravity which festered beneath the wealth which they
complimented.   But what says Mr. Alison, who speaks
from official experience ?   " It is no doubt true," he
says, " that in Glasgow and Edinburgh from six to four-
teen hundred mechanics are to be found who attend
lectures on scientific subjects with pleasure and advantage.   Humanity has much reason to rejoice at such
assemblages ; but it is not less true that in each of these
cities thirty or forty thousand workmen exist who have
hardly any enjoyments but those of the senses, and who,
so far from being refined in their habits by the education
which they have received, and the means of further instruction which they enjoy, are more addicted to the
grossest intemperance than any people except the Swedes
and the Norwegians in Europe.   Amongst the educated
weavers of Glasgow three times the number of public
houses are to be found, in proportion to the population,
that exists in London or Paris.   In no city of the empire
*has the progress of vice been so rapid, or the demoralization
of the labouring classes so extensive.*   In 1808 five criminals
stood their trial at the spring assizes ; in spring 1828 *one
hundred and fifteen* were indicted, of whom no less than
seventy-five received sentence of transportation.   The
great majority of these unhappy persons had received a
good education ; and this remarkable increase of crime

---

* Sir R. Peel and Lord J. Russell.

took place at a time when the diffusion of instruction was
more general than at any former period. Serious crime
in Lanarkshire was in 1840 advancing at the rate of 52
per cent. every three years : in other words, it doubles in
about five years and a half, while population doubles in
about thirty years ; so that crime is increasing six times
as fast as the numbers of the people. And so extraordinary and alarming has the progress of crime for the
last thirty years in this part of the island been, that it
appears from the Parliamentary Reports that the criminal
committals have increased from 89 annually in 1810 to
3176 in 1837, a rapidity of increase probably unexampled
in Europe at this time." It has been seen that Mrs.
Somerville congratulates the country that crime has become less frequent as well as less atrocious, and that the
moral disposition of the age appears in the refinement of
conversation. Mr. Alison, on the other hand, alleges
that " in England it has been completely established, by
the evidence laid before several Parliamentary Com-
mittees, that the education of the lower orders has had
no effect whatever in checking the progress of crime. It
has altered its direction in many instances, and substi-
tuted inroads on property for personal violence ; but if
the nature of the offences has become less atrocious, the
number of the criminals has been immensely increased,
and their character more completely depraved. A Chief
Justice of England in the reign of Edward IV. boasted
of the bold and manly qualities which distinguished the
English highwayman : but it would be difficult to find
any grounds for national exultation in the character of
the thieves who are daily transported at the Old Bailey."
Indeed, so little does this criminal judge sympathise with
Mrs. Somerville's views of the tendency of modern progress to diminish evil and lead to human perfectibility,

that he seems to fear a dissolution of society from the vices which " advancement " brings with it. " The causes of depravity," he says, " in the advanced stages of society are so numerous, and the seductions of vice in crowded situations so powerful, that reason may frequently be led to despair of the fortunes of the species in such situations, and philosophy to look upon the decay of political bodies, like that of individuals, as preparing the regeneration of mankind in more youthful forms and from purer sources." Take the testimony of another judge, the late Recorder of London, in his address to the grand jury of the 26th of November, 1849. " The calendar," he said, " contained charges of murder, manslaughter, of shooting at the person, of attempting to drown, sending a threatening letter, and rape, and some of them were of the most aggravated character, for he found there was one charge against a son of attempting to shoot his father, against a father for committing an atrocious offence upon the person of his own daughter, and many other cases of a similarly heinous character." In his commentary upon these matters, the judge, who was a man of no inconsiderable experience, proceeded thus :—" Indeed, he lamented to say that his experience in that court compelled him to state his opinion that there was no appearance of any improvement in the morals of the large population over which the Central Criminal Court had jurisdiction. Various endeavours had been made by the legislature with that object : the punishments for different offences had been revised and altered ; in some cases the penalty for a particular offence had been mitigated, and the sentence of transportation had also been strictly carried out ; but still it seemed that these proceedings had been ineffectual, and that no satisfactory result had been obtained with regard to the diminution of crime by the efforts of the

legislature." *   When public writers find such statements made upon such authority, are they not justified
in making complaint, and is it not something too much
to say that, notwithstanding this complaint, it would be
a great error to infer that there had been an increase of
misery ?

As for Mr. Mackay's assertion that the last seventy
years have been more prolific of improvement than the
preceding seven hundred, we may set against *his* authority that of Mr. Urquhart, a member of the House of
Commons, who some years ago delivered lectures on
pauperism, and taught that the condition of the common
people of England had been best in those ages which the
enlightened Mr. Mackay regards with a modern and nice
abhorrence.   Mr. Urquhart quotes a great deal of evidence, which he thus sums up :—" I think I have now
established my case, that, from the time of Hengist down
to that of William III., barring those great convulsions
which mark and are concluded in the epochs of the wars
against northern invaders, for the Crown or against the
Crown, the people enjoyed great comfort and prosperity.
It was not only that the land was well cultivated and
well peopled, and the people contented, but, in the words
of Clarendon, their prosperity was ' the envy of all sur-
rounding nations, and unparalleled by any people at the
same period in Europe.' "   It is necessary for the reader
here to bear in mind the distinction between the people,
considered as a great community, and the mercantile and
money-dealing class.   *Their* star was, no doubt, in the

---

* I find in the House of Commons' debate of the 19th of February, 1850,
the Secretary of State for the Home Department gives the authority of
the Recorder of London for a precisely opposite opinion to that given in
the text.   I can only say that I have faithfully copied the words of the
learned gentleman.

ascendant when William of Orange undertook the regeneration of the Saxon liberties of our country in his peculiarly honest and generous manner; but, as regards the welfare of the mass of the common people, I am not able to perceive that it was augmented by the practical application of Dutch philosophy; nor is it in my power to comprehend that, in order to cure the bigotry and blockheadism of the policy of James II., it had become necessary to trample upon honour and fidelity, and to bring a coldly ambitious foreigner into the seat of England's kings. How admirably does a distinguished author and critic of our own day describe *that* consummation of the tragedy of 1649 :—

> " The axe that strikes the king lays order low—
> In every limb old Reverence feels the blow ;
> Law, Faith, Love, Honour, Grace, are trampled down,
> In the same bloody quagmire with the crown.
> The awe of ages poison'd into hate,
> Fierce leaps the rabble hoof on all that 's great—
> Till vulgar rage, expert Ambition's tool,
> Dies out, and some cold scoundrel grasps the rule."

Mr. Urquhart holds the theory that even the cultivation of the land has in some districts deteriorated since ancient times. It is, he says, " impossible to walk many miles in any direction without finding traces of cultivation on soil not under culture to-day. Where forests have been, or in lands that now lie waste, the openings of pits are still seen whence chalk has been dug for the fields ; and there is not in Hampshire a field which could be benefited by chalk, where such a pit is not to be found, from time immemorial. There was culture where none is found to-day ; and there is nothing cultivated to-day that has not been cultivated of old. There is not a village in Hampshire that does not trace back its origin to Saxon times—indeed, this may be said of the whole of England ; and there are boroughs still retaining the name, where the vestige of every function connected with the establishment is out of date, even of legal memory." No doubt cultivation has shifted its ground ; but I cannot agree in the opinion that there is no land cultivated at present which was not cultivated in the olden time. Agriculture, like every other kind of industry in England, has, it may fairly be supposed, made immense advances in the lapse of time, and more especially during the present century. The defect with which our age is chargeable is certainly not that of neglecting to improve what is improvable by industry, and capable of being made profitable ; but it lies in that change of habits which causes the wealth, whether of agricultural or any other business, to accumulate in heaps, while the condition of the working people either deteriorates or remains stationary. The result of the new activities which have sprung up is, that the slower and poorer sort of people have been completely left behind. In former days the progress which society made was a progress of the whole mass. It was like the cloud described by our great modern poet,—

" Which moveth altogether if it move at all."

But in our days the bonds of society are loosened ; the selfish tendencies of our nature have obtained a greater freedom of action ; the brotherhood of society is less and less recognised ; and each individual uses his powers, natural or artificial, to advance himself, without regard to the interests of his neighbour. Thus we have, in manufactures, rich proprietors and depressed operatives, and, in the country, we have improved agriculture with a peasantry which exhibits no trace of improvement.

CHAPTER IX.

CONDITION OF THE PEOPLE—ITS POLITICAL DANGER.

In Sir Walter Scott's diary, under date November 24th, 1826, he writes thus:—" Breakfasted at Manchester; passed on, and by dint of exertion reached Kendal to sleep; thus getting out of the region of the stern, sullen, unwashed artificers, whom you see lounging sulkily along the streets in Lancashire. God's justice is requiting, and will yet further requite, those who have blown up this country into a state of unsubstantial opulence at the expense of the health and morals of the lower classes." Such was the judgment of a man who brought as much kindness of heart to bear upon public questions as any other who ever undertook the discussion of them—a man also who had much more practical knowledge of life, in all its varieties of fortune and rank, than is generally possessed by those who take a part in the discussion of public affairs. Since his day the evil which he lamented has grown and spread, and is no longer confined to the manufacturing districts. The mercantile spirit has been driving out every other spirit from England during the years which have elapsed since 1826; and now it is proclaimed, as it were, from the very house-tops, that the land must be dealt with upon mercantile principles, and that any other sentiment with regard to it is absurd. But a few years ago the gentleman who then filled the office of prime minister * expounded to the parliament the moral

* Sir R. Peel, 10 June, 1845.

and social grounds which made the application of mere
mercantile principles to the occupation and cultivation of
land not only undesirable, but highly to be deprecated.
Even he, however, has since been among the advocates of
that absorbing commercialism, against which he then
raised his warning voice; and, instead of trying to avoid,
the nation seems to be blindly inviting, that judicial visitation which loomed darkly upon the prophetic soul of Sir
Walter Scott. If any one could match with him in
earnest feeling for the practical good of all classes, it was
—a very different man in many respects—Dr. Arnold,
of Rugby. Observe, however, what he said in the full
tide of that " progress " and " improvement " which
chiefly develop themselves in commercial activity for
commercial ends:—" I would," says he, " give anything
to be able to organize a society for drawing public attention to the state of the labouring classes throughout the
kingdom. Men do not think of the fearful state in which
we are living; if they could once be brought to notice
and to appreciate the evil, I should not even yet despair
that the remedy may be found and applied, even though
it is the solution of the most difficult problem ever yet
proposed to man's wisdom, and the greatest triumph over
selfishness ever yet required of his virtue. . . . It seems
to me that people are not enough aware of the monstrous
state of society, absolutely without a parallel in the history
of the world; with a population poor, miserable, and
degraded in body and mind, as much as if they were
slaves, and yet called free men, and having a power, as
such, of concerting and combining plans of risings which
makes them ten times more dangerous than slaves. And
the hopes entertained by many of the effects to be wrought
by new churches and schools, while the social evils of
their condition are left uncorrected, appear to be utterly

wild." The publication of Dr. Arnold's earnest views, which appeared to far more advantage, as it seems to me, in his familiar and frank communications to his friends, than in anything he had prepared specially for public instruction, might have opened the mind of the English nation—if anything could have done so—to the dangers of the mercenary career in which it has embarked. But the disease was too strong for such correctives.

> " Here wisdom calls, 'Seek virtue first, be bold:
> As gold to silver, virtue is to gold.'
> There London's voice, 'Get money—money still;
> And then let virtue follow if she will.' "

I am satisfied of the truth of the observation with which he concludes, that it is a wild and almost a fanatic notion that churches and schools will effect the necessary amendment required, while the social evils of the people are left uncorrected. A people crushed into poverty by competition, which has been fostered to the grossest excess, are not in a situation to reap the benefit of schools and churches. There is a class of persons who take no small credit to themselves for relying entirely upon the efficacy of ecclesiastical institutions to cure every national evil, while they actually encourage the encroachments of commercialism upon all the long-established feelings, usages, and privileges of the national community. Such people I regard as the unconscious pioneers of Romanistic error and abuse. Practical good sense and good feeling, and " pure religion breathing household laws," appear to be alike neglected by these votaries of mere ecclesiastical authority and system.

Dr. Arnold did good service in drawing the practical distinction which all statesmen ought to have present to their minds between the abstract truths of political economy and the social circumstances which bear upon the condition of the people independently of considerations of national wealth. "I doubt not," he says, "the ability of those writers (on Political Economy), or the truth of their conclusions as far as regards their own science; but I think that the *summum bonum* of their science and of human life are not identical, and therefore many questions in which Free Trade is involved, and the advantages of large capital, &c., although perfectly simple in an econo- mical point of view, become, when considered politically, very complex, and the economical good is very often, from a neglect of other points, made in practice a direct social evil." There is a tendency in modern politicians and in all theorists to look at extremes, and thus to ex- clude themselves from the middle way of practical truth. Latterly it has become the fashion of the partisans of economic philosophy to accuse those who differ from them of "Communism" or "Socialism." The sting of this lies in the circumstance that certain lazy and dissolute persons in various countries have banded themselves together under the name of "Communists" or "Socialists," while from their practices it is evident that their object is to invade the principle of property—to rob the industrious, and to revel in vice. Apart from scolding and abuse, a rational view of the distinction between Political Economy and Com- munism may be taken from a "liberal" journal of esta- blished reputation. "The essential principle," says this authority, "in all the different systems that go by the generic name of Communism or Socialism is—industry exercised in co-operation, and common property in the fruits of industry. . . . Political Economy is the science of the principles and operations concerned in the exercise of industry, and the formation of wealth. . . . In Politi- cal Economy the question is whether competing or leagued industry can create the larger amount of produce in proportion to population, and whether competing or leagued industry can the better keep the ratio of production ahead of population.   In polity the cardinal question is whether the motives of industry can be the better stirred under competing or leagued labour. . . . In competing labour each strives to get for himself the largest share of produce or its representative emolument, and the principle is violated whenever numbers league to obtain large aggregate produce divisible among the co-operators."*   With regard to the rival principles of competition and co-operation, my opinion is, that society requires the modified action of *both*, and that the wise politician should guard against the predominance of either.   It appears to be generally admitted that the great progress of competition in modern times has rendered the obtaining of a livelihood a more difficult struggle to all the unpropertied classes than it formerly was.   Has this been inevitable, or, if not, where is the benefit of the change as regards the great bulk of the people ?   Had our modern "progress" led to a greater ease of life—to more freedom from painful labour, and from anxiety in the task of obtaining the means of existence—had it given to the people more leisure for the improvement of their minds, and for rational enjoyment, then the benefit and the blessing of this "progress" might have been readily acknowledged. But if the result be not this, but the contrary—if the more we have advanced in the competitive system— whether in the competition of machines with manual labour, or of foreign with home labour—the more arduous has become the struggle of the multitude to obtain the means of existence ; then we may be permitted to entertain very strong doubts that our "progress" has been

---

* *Spectator*, September 15, 1849.

that of patriotic wisdom. If, under a less severe system of competition, England became a great and rich country —if without this universal struggle—without this *maximum* of labour and *minimum* of profit—our nation grew to the highest position among the nations of the earth, would it not be wise to consider whether the newer is the better way ? Is it not reasonable to suppose that some radical error in our political or social system must exist when concurrently with our mechanical improvements, and the increase of our scientific knowledge, has been the increase of the difficulty to live, and the augmentation of the struggle of our industrious population to obtain those comforts—

      Queis humana sibi doleat natura negatis.

If our mechanical improvements and our discoveries in chemistry had been brought into action more for the general benefit, and with less view to individual profit, the struggle and the difficulty to live would have been less, for nature has not been less bounteous than of old. But our improvements, however they may have operated indirectly, have directly, and in the first instance, been used for individual gain, and I fear it must be said for the labourer's loss. Every mechanical substitute for labour has been used—not to mitigate human toil, but to compete with the labourer, and to reduce the rate of his remuneration. Unquestionably this is an evil to the correction of which it is not easy to see one's way, but hitherto our politicians have not appeared to perceive—at all events they have not admitted—that it is an evil at all. To me it seems that there is a value in the system of competition, and a value also in the opposite system of co-operation. Some degree of rivalship is needful to call the energies of men into action, and some degree of co-

operation, from other motives than those of self-interest,
appear to belong to our duty to our neighbour. The
tendency of modern philosophy has been to give every
encouragement that legislation can give to the selfish
principle, and to throw the nation almost entirely upon
the agency of rivalship and competition. Of this we see
the result in the increased inequalities of condition, in the
augmented luxury of some classes, and the painful privations
and debasement of others. More especially we see it in the
uncertain, feverish state of various branches of industry,
and the exceedingly augmented difficulty of the unfriended
labouring man to obtain an honest livelihood. It is, I
think, unquestionable that the resources of the British
empire—its wealth—its enterprise—its scientific skill—its
power of providing the necessaries and comforts of life,
have increased in a larger proportion than its population,
but it seems equally indisputable that the bulk of the
population finds more difficulty in obtaining the means of
subsistence than it formerly did. From this I infer that
we have carried our competitive system too far, and that,
whatever else we may have achieved by it, we have failed
to secure for the people at large a fair share of the advantages with which Providence has blessed our country.

Finally, there are some other things to be considered
besides that advantage of either the working or the employing classes which comes under the description of
wealth, or any improvement of a man's material circumstances. It is fit that even the statesman should think
of the moral and domestic feelings of the people, and
should hesitate to encourage any description of industry
which, however calculated to augment wealth, is unfavourable to the domestic happiness of the poor. Manufacturing industry has been torn from the abode of the
poor man, and his family must follow it to the rich man's

manufactory or warehouse, where they become attendants
on the power of the mighty steam-engine.   And what is
the consequence at the poor man's hearth ?—

> ———— " Domestic bliss
> (Or call it comfort by a humbler name),
> How art thou blighted for the poor man's heart !
> Lo ! in such neighbourhood from morn to eve
> The habitations empty ! or, perchance,
> The mother left alone,—no helping hand
> To rock the cradle of her peevish babe ;
> No daughters round her, busy at the wheel,
> Or in despatch of each day's little growth
> Of household occupation ; no nice arts
> Of needlework ; no bustle at the fire,
> Where once the dinner was prepared with pride ;
> Nothing to speed the day or cheer the mind ;
> Nothing to praise, to teach, or to command."

Such is the effect which the modern manufacturing system
has had upon the households of the poor ; and though I
do not see how this could have been altogether prevented,
I do see that there ought to be more reluctance than
there is to make the nation more and more dependent on
a system which affords so little hope, and presents so much
danger, to the great bulk of the community.

———•———

CHAPTER X.

CRIMINAL OFFENDERS.

In the month of June, 1850, a very elaborate statement was furnished to both Houses of Parliament of the number of criminal offenders in England and Wales in the year 1849. This statement occupies more than sixty folio pages of closely-printed tables, going into the most minute classification of offences, and their localities. These tables are difficult to read, and, when read, rather overwhelm than inform the mind. They are, however, preceded by a valuable Report, prepared at the office of the Secretary of State for the Home Department, by Mr. Redgrave, which affords a kind of synoptical history of the amount of criminal offences in England and Wales during the last fifteen years. In the last ten years, it appears, there have been great fluctuations in the numbers committed for trial. Between the years 1842 and 1845 the variation exceeded 22 per cent. The commitments, however, in 1849 remain of nearly the same amount as in 1840; and, on a comparison of the last five years with the five years preceding, there appears a decrease of more than 4 per cent.; a result which will appear more favourable when the probable increase of population is taken into account.

If, however, we go back before 1840, we find that the increase of commitments, as compared with that period, is very manifest; the five years 1845-49 showing

an increase of above 20 per cent. upon the five years
1835-39.

The commitments from the end of 1834 to the beginning of 1850, for all sorts of offences, were as follows :—

1835	. . .	20,731	
1836	. . .	20,984	
1837	. . .	23,612	
1838	. . .	23,094	
1839	. . .	24,443	
			——— 112,864 in five years.
1840	. . .	27,187	
1841	. . .	27,760	
1842	. . .	31,309	
1843	. . .	29,591	
1844	. . .	26,542	
			——— 142,389 in five years.
1845	. . .	24,303	
1846	. . .	25,107	
1847	. . .	28,333	
1848	. . .	30,349	
1849	. . .	27,816	
			——— 136,408 in five years.

The decrease of commitments in 1849, compared with
1848, extends over twenty-six out of the forty English
counties. It applies to both agricultural and manufacturing districts, but is more marked in the latter, as
might have been expected from the tendency of legislation, which has led to more distress and want of employment in the agricultural than in the commercial and
manufacturing parts of the kingdom. While, upon the
aggregate of the two periods of five years 1840-44 and
1845-49, there is, as has been shown, a decrease of commitments for crime, it appears there has been an increase
in some counties, and even in those which show a marked
decrease of offences when the year 1849 is compared with
1848. Upon the five years the increase of crime in Middlesex is 17 per cent., in Surrey 18 per cent., in Devon

17 per cent., in Dorset 8 per cent., in Hants 4 per cent. Cumberland, Northumberland, Durham, Bucks, Cambridge, Huntingdon, and Rutland also show an increase. As regards the classification of crimes, it appears that, notwithstanding the general decrease in 1849, there is an increase in the malicious offences *against property*. This is a symptom which deserves the consideration of political philosophers and statesmen. Among such offences, wilful burning, and the maiming of cattle, show more increase than the others. This implies a state of savage exasperation in the rural districts, which requires the hand both of correcting and ameliorating government.

The following passage on the philosophy of crime is to me not very intelligible ; but as it has been communicated from the Secretary of State's office to Parliament, I am willing to believe there is something in it which others may comprehend more fully than I do :—"The offences of simple theft and fraud," says this official paper, " of which indictable crime is so largely composed, owe their increase or decrease greatly to circumstances which from time to time affect *the general welfare* of the community. Other offences—as, for instance, murder and attempts to murder, *the uniform recurrence of which appears incidental to a particular state of society*—are not, or are in an exceptional degree only, directly affected by such general causes ; and the offences against the person, of which these crimes form a part, have been shown (in former tables) not to have been simultaneous in their fluctuations of increase or decrease with the offences against property."

I now come to the most repulsive part of the task of him who undertakes to give a fair account of a nation such as it is. One would gladly draw a veil over the record if it were possible ; but as no account of a country could be complete without the statistics of its crime, I must not hesitate to transcribe from the official document the hideous catalogue of the offences of the kingdom. The Government compiler, nothing daunted by the effect of such a process, has presented these offences in masses of five years' accumulation. It must, therefore, be recol-

Total Commitments for Crime in Fifteen Years.

	Five years 1835-39.	Five years 1840-44.	Five years 1845-49.
Murder	315	347	365
Attempts to murder, wounding, &c.	739	1,157	1,173
Manslaughter	1,024	1,053	980
Concealing the birth of infants	224	306	331
Offences against nature	403	561	542
Rape and abuse of children	296	506	567
Assaults with intent to ravish	652	690	663
Bigamy	215	354	399
Assaults	5,616	5,824	5,228
Other offences against the person	75	87	70
Burglary, housebreaking, and sacrilege	4,041	6,241	5,517
Breaking into shops and warehouses	1,030	1,562	1,325
Robbery and assaults with intent to rob	1,874	2,306	1,969
Other violent offences against property	89	165	147
Cattle, horse, and sheep stealing	2,466	2,984	2,187
Simple larcenies	78,391	98,169	98,361
Embezzlement	1,384	1,805	1,812
Receiving stolen goods	3,465	4,059	3,587
Fraud	2,225	3,000	2,868
Other offences of simple theft	119	202	260
Arson and other wilful burning	294	519	708
Felonious riots and destruction of property	36	140	24
Maliciously killing and maiming cattle	160	176	162
Other malicious offences	142	231	134
Forging and uttering forged instruments	404	781	783
Coining and passing counterfeit coin	1,718	2,047	1,946
Offences against the game-laws	647	655	656
Sedition, riot, &c.	231	1,241	256
Breach of peace and riot	2,870	2,676	1,699
Keeping disorderly houses	693	945	526
Other offences not included in any of the foregoing classes	1,026	1,600	1,163
Total	112,864	142,389	136,408
Yearly average	22,573	28,478	27,282

lected that to bring this monster of multiplication to its
average yearly dimensions a division by 5 is necessary.
The average, however, is less than the actual amount of
crime in 1849, though the crime of that year was less than
that of the year preceding. (See table at p. 101.)

The actual number committed in 1849 was 27,816;
of whom 6786 were acquitted and discharged, 21,001
were convicted, and 29 were detained in custody as
insane. Of those who were convicted, 66 were sentenced
to death, but of these only 15 were executed. The sentences of transportation and imprisonment in 1849 were
as follows :—

        Transportation :—
            Life   60
            Above 15 years   31
            15 years and above 10 years   .   .   .   255
            10   ,,   ,,   7   ,,   .   .   .   933
            7 years 1,565
                                                                              ———
                                                                              2,844
                                                                              ———
        Imprisonment :—
            2 years and above 1 year   548
            1   ,,   ,,   6 months 2,485
            6 months   ,,   3   ,, ... 4,817
            3   ,,   ,,   2   ,, ... 3,272
            2   ,,   ,,   1   ,, ... 2,722
            1 month and under   3,916
                                                                              ———
                                                                              17,760

Thus it appears that, out of 21,001 persons convicted
of crime in England and Wales in the year 1849, no less
a number than 17,212 had committed offences of so
light a character, according to the philosophy of our present laws, that imprisonment for periods varying from one
year to one week was deemed sufficient punishment.

Of the persons convicted in 1849, one in every 318 was
sentenced to death, and one in every eight to transporta-

tion ; but, taking into account all the serious offences for which persons were convicted, the sentences of three-fourths were imprisonment for periods of six months and under, of one-half for three months and under, and one-third were for two months and under.

If we take the sentences in masses of five years each for the last fifteen years, it will display the altered character of criminal punishments :—

	Five years 1835-39.	Five years 1844-40.	Five years 1844-49.
Sentenced to death	1,627	368	282
Transported for life	2,623	990	353
,, above 15 years . . .	23	172	140
,, 15 years and above 10 years	3,085	3,333	1,503
,, 10 years and above 7 years .	2,002	6,433	4,670
,, 7 years	10,864	8,677	7,998
Imprisonment above 3 years . . .	0	3	0
,, 3 years and above 2 years .	72	73	15
,, 2 years and above 1 year .	1,775	2,395	2,208
,, 1 year and above 6 months.	8,007	10,977	11,075
,, 6 months and under . .	48,334	66,524	70,904
Whipped, fined, and discharged . .	2,859	2,983	1,871
Total number sentenced . .	81,091	102,928	101,019

This account shows a very marked decrease in the severity of sentences since the quinquennial period 1835-39. It cannot be added that this more merciful treatment of criminals has led to a diminution of crime. The more atrocious crimes, for which sentence of death was passed, were more numerous in 1849 than in any year since 1843. Since 1841 no one has been executed in England except for murder, but there were more executions in 1849 than in any year since 1844. The following is an account of the crimes which occasioned sentences of death to be passed, from the end of 1841 to the beginning of 1850 :—

	1842.	1843.	1844.	1845.	1846.	1847.	1848.	1849.
Murder	16	22	21	19	13	19	23	19
Attempts to murder, with wounds	3	9	1	4	9	4	6	12
Cutting and wounding maliciously	..	1	..	..	..	..	..	..
Unnatural offences . .	12	18	15	15	17	14	18	18
Burglary, with violence .	18	22	4	8	5	5	7	10
Robbery, attended with wounds	5	23	14	2	8	9	3	3
Arson of dwelling-houses, persons being therein . .	2	2	2	1	4	..	3	4
High Treason . . .	1	..	..	..	..	..	..	..
	57	97	57	49	56	51	60	66

" Of the 19 persons convicted of murder in 1849," says the Report, " 15 were executed, the crimes of several being marked by circumstances of peculiar atrocity. Five of these persons were females—one for the murder and robbery of her mistress; one for the murder of her husband by poison, who was also charged with, and confessed, the murder of her two adult sons, and the attempted murder of a third ; one for the murder of her infant by poison, suspected to have been the eighth or ninth similar offence ; another for the murder of her husband by poison; and the fifth was (with her husband, who was also executed) convicted of a deeply-laid plan of murder and robbery. Of the other males, one was convicted of murder, who was also charged with a second murder, and the attempted murder of two other persons, in furtherance of extensive forgeries and fraud ; one was convicted of the murder of four persons, and robbery ; one of the murder of his mother; one of the murder of his child ; one of the murder of a young girl, supposed from motives of revenge ; another of the murder of a female, the motive not being made apparent ; and three of separate cases of murder in connection with burglary and theft."

This fearful history belongs to a year marked by revived activity in foreign commerce, by unprecedented
cheapness of the necessaries of life and of many of its
comforts, by an abundant harvest, by unwonted attention
to measures of sanitary improvement, by the opening of
many new churches, and the increased zeal of those who
are charged with the business of education. Unfortunately, the activity which was the parent of all this good,
extended also to things evil, and added the foregoing
shocking summary to the previous annals of crime.

Of all the atrocities which came under judicial investigation in 1849 the most remarkable was that of the husband and wife mentioned in the Report as having been
executed together for a deeply-laid plan of murder and
robbery. The names of these people were Manning, the
husband being an Englishman, and described as a commercial traveller; but the woman was a foreigner, a
Genevese, and had been a lady's-maid in some English
families of distinction. She was said to have some pre-
tensions to a masculine cast of beauty, and she seems to
have possessed more than masculine energy in the conception and execution of crime. She appears to have
despised her husband, who was a weak and commonplace
profligate; and to have loathed her paramour, a mean
and sensual Irishman, whom she deliberately killed that
she might possess herself of his property. This woman
and her husband lived in a small house in a low part of
London, which lies to the south-east of London Bridge.
There her paramour O'Connor, a gauger in the Customhouse Docks, occasionally visited her, and she also
visited him at his lodgings, where she was well known.
Having resolved to murder him, she foresaw the expediency of providing means for disposing of the body after
his life was taken. With her husband's assistance, there-

fore, she dug the man's future grave under the hearth-stone of her kitchen, and provided a store of quick-lime to bury along with the body for its more speedy destruction. The man who was to be murdered saw this preparation for his remains as it proceeded, but supposed that it was something necessary for the drainage of the house. When all was ready he was invited to dinner, on pretence that he should meet some young woman from the country whom he had a desire to see. It appears that when the time came he hesitated whether he should go to dinner or not. But his fate prevailed. There was no young woman from the country, nor any dinner prepared in the house ; but full preparation had been made for him nevertheless. He was asked to go down to the kitchen to wash his hands before dining, and as he descended the stairs, the woman, walking behind, having a pistol loaded with ball, shot him through the head. While he lay groaning, the husband (who, in confessing this, coolly remarked that " he never much liked him ") attacked him with a crowbar, and broke in his skull. He was then put in the grave which had been prepared for him, and all was covered up. The dead man was missed, but no one save his murderers knew what had become of him. The woman who killed him made, in the mean time, several visits to his lodgings, pretending to expect his return, while she employed herself in robbing his coffers of money, and securities for money, which she knew he possessed. As soon as she had got all she could, she sold the furniture in her house, sent her husband off upon some fool's errand, put a quantity of portable property into boxes which she left at the station of the Brighton railway, and then, with her money and her securities, fled to Scotland, leaving the partner of her crime to shift for himself, without any portion of the plunder and in complete ignorance of the course she had taken. The departure of the Mannings from the house strengthened the suspicion that they had something to do with the disappearance of O'Connor. The police made their examinations ; and as it occurred to one of them that the stones of the kitchen had been recently re-laid, it was thought worth while to make some examination of what was beneath. They had not proceeded far when a part of the dead body was discovered. The frightened husband had by this time fled from London. Warrants were issued against both husband and wife ; and the electric telegraph having been put in requisition, she was almost immediately seized in Edinburgh, where, under a false name, she was trying to dispose of certain " railway scrip "—part of the plunder of O'Connor's lodgings. She betrayed no fear nor any other form of weakness. In her case, the demon power, which nerved her for the commission of her dreadful crime, did not desert her in the hour of her detection. Her wretched husband was seized in Guernsey endeavouring to drown his recollection and his terror with deep draughts of brandy. They were tried together in London. They had separate counsel. *His* defence was, that *she* did the murder ; and hers, that she did not do it, and had no motive to such a crime. They were both found guilty ; and no one had the slightest shadow of a doubt that they were both concerned in the murder. When the woman was called upon, as usual, to state if she could show any reason why sentence of death should not be passed upon her, she made a brief speech, full of energy and not destitute of pathos, in which she complained that in her trial she was not only personally but nationally wronged, since she was not an Englishwoman. It had, however, been previously determined, upon legal investigation, that, having married an Englishman, she had lost all distinctive rights as a foreigner. After his sentence the husband confessed the whole revolting history; but she remained firm, suffered much from terror of death towards the end, but did not express her suffering in words, and confessed nothing.

The criminals were ordered to be executed together at the top of Horsemonger-lane gaol, on Tuesday morning, the 13th of November, 1849. Such was the wild and gross curiosity of the multitude to witness this dreadful scene of a husband and wife dying on the scaffold together for murder, that the crowd in front of the gaol began to assemble the evening before around the platforms which had been erected in order to afford spectators, who were willing to pay for the privilege, a better view. The circumstances of the night preceding the execution and of the early morning were so remarkable that I give here an account from one of the journals of the day, as an illustration of what *could* happen in London in the enlightened and civilized era of 1849 : —

" Had matters been suffered to proceed as was at first contemplated, some very serious loss of life must have happened. But, fortunately, the authorities interfered; the dangerous platforms were removed, and barriers were erected in the most effectual positions to prevent the mob from swaying backwards and forwards and becoming unmanageable. Above all, there was a force of 500 police in position on the ground. All these arrangements, which proved most effective, were made on Monday evening, in ample time for the immense streams of people— men, women, and children—that began pouring down towards the scene of the execution as midnight approached. The current of human life, once set in that direction, never ceased to flow until the morning sun was well up in the sky ; and the sea of up-turned faces, all gazing to one dark dismal-looking object—the scaffold—proclaimed that the moment was at hand for carrying into effect the extreme sentence of the law. The hum of their blended voices, mingled together and swelling on the ear throughout the long dark night, told distinctly what had brought them there. The public-houses in Blackman-street and the neighbourhood were filled with customers, many of whom had been up all night ; touters from every corner invited to seats commanding a view of the execution ; every house was lighted, and shops of all kinds were open ; and hundreds of itinerant basketmen were crying ' Manning's biscuits ' and ' Maria Manning's peppermints ' for sale. A mob composed of the lowest rabble had collected in Swan-court and under the drop, where squibs and crackers were flying through the air, and every low cry and oath was to be heard. As morning dawned, the manner in which the assembled multitudes had massed themselves together was sufficiently striking. Taking up their station on the carriage-way, in front and rather to the westward of the entrance of the gaol, were the dregs and offscourings of the population of London, the different elements that composed the disorderly rabble crew being mingled together in wild and unsightly disorder, the " navvy" and Irish labourer smoking clay pipes and muzzy with beer, pickpockets plying their light-fingered art, little ragged boys climbing up posts, and standing on some dangerous elevation, or tumbling down again, and disappearing among the sea of heads. From that great seething mass there rises a ceaseless din of sounds and war of tongues—voices in every note, shrill whistles, and slang calls. The clatter and uproar of this Babel never ceased for a moment. The sight of the drop (a huge, gaunt, and ominous-looking structure), raised on the flat roof of the gaol, and increasing by a hundredfold the gloomy and repulsive aspect of the whole building, failed to put the least check on the uproarious tendencies of the mob. Now it was a fainting fit, then a fight, and again the arrest of a thief; but there was always something to keep up the popular excitement. Even the dreadful sight of two human beings—husband and wife— hurried into eternity for the crime of murder, failed to solemnize for one moment or to check perceptibly the disgusting levity of the crowd. Packed up within the barriers erected by the police, they were powerless for mischief, and could easily be controlled. On the outskirts of this great mass of human beings were grouped, in smaller numbers, a very different class of people, who had paid their two or three guineas to gratify a morbid curiosity, and who, from the fashionable clubs at the west end, and from their luxurious homes, came to fill the windows, the gardens, and the housetops of a few miserable little houses, in order to enjoy the excitement of seeing two fellow-creatures die by an ignominious death upon the scaffold. The best view of an execution at Horsemonger-lane gaol is to be obtained from the tenements at the west end of Winter-terrace. There the more respectable parts of the assemblage took up their position, and watched the proceedings with opera-glasses levelled. There was an impression current that the execution would take place at eight o'clock, but that hour came and went, and there seemed to be no note of preparation sounded. Two men were loitering lazily near the drop, but beyond that there was nothing visible. At last nine o'clock struck, and shortly after the dreadful procession emerged from a small door in the inner side of a square piece of brick-work which rests on the east end of the prison roof. To reach this height a long and steep flight of stairs had to be ascended ; and it is only wonderful that Manning, in his weak and tottering state, was able to climb so far. When the procession appeared above, the thousands of spectators who were gazing at it with upturned faces immediately watched for the appearance of the wretched creatures doomed to die.   Manning came first, supported by two men and accompanied by the chaplain, who read to him the appointed service of the Church.   As he ascended the steps leading to the drop his limbs tottered under him, and he appeared scarcely able to move.   He first turned his face to the east, apparently reluctant to eye the gaping crowds assembled to watch his last mortal agony.   A gleam of sunshine fell upon his features while in this position, and showed that the pallor of his countenance still continued.   When his wife approached the scaffold he turned more round, with his face towards the people, while the hangman proceeded to draw over his head the white nightcap and to adjust the fatal rope.   In the mean time the female prisoner had reached the drop, mounting the steps which led to it with a firm, but, owing to the bandage on her eyes, not a rapid step, and, when at last placed under the fatal beam, standing as fixed as a marble statue.   The male prisoner had by this time recovered his firmness to a certain extent, and, turning to his wife, he shook hands with her in token of a final farewell.   The executioner then drew the nightcap over the female prisoner's head, and, all the necessary preparations having now been completed, the scaffold was cleared of all its occupants except the two wretched beings who stood upon it doomed to die.   The chaplain of the gaol at this last moment, deeply solicitous for the welfare of so great a criminal standing on the brink of time without having confessed her guilt, once more approached, and asked Mrs. Manning if she had anything that she wished to say to him. She replied, ' Nothing, but to thank you much for all your kindness.' He withdrew deeply disappointed, and, when he left, the husband and wife again approached each other and shook hands ; having done so, they finally resumed their positions. In an instant the hangman withdrew the bolt, the drop fell, and the sentence of the law was fulfilled. They died almost without a struggle, and the bodies, having been allowed to hang for an hour, were cut down, and in the evening buried within the precincts of the gaol. The mob during this terrible scene exhibited no feeling except one of heartless indifference and levity. Not a single yell or cry of execration could be heard ; scarcely a hat or cap was raised while the drop fell ; and the bodies of the murderers had hardly ceased to oscillate with the momentum of their fall before the spectators were hurrying in large numbers from the spot.

" On the separation of the crowd the effects of its presence began to be manifested. At the corner of Swanstreet numbers of powerful men were seen lying on the pavement in a state bordering on insensibility, and quite helpless from the crushing to which they had been subjected. As the ground became cleared in various places, hats, bonnets, shawls, shoes, and other articles of dress, were thickly strewed on the ground, which had the appearance of having been the scene of some frightful struggle. Even before the appearance of the culprits on the scaffold, persons of both sexes were dragged out from the compact multitude by the police, by means of ropes, so seriously injured that they were obliged to be taken to the hospital, where many of them still remain. One person, hoping to relieve his chest from the pressure of the crowd against some iron railings, placed one leg between them, when the crowd swayed to one side, and his thigh was fractured. After having been dragged out, he was conveyed to the hospital on a stretcher. Whilst the crowd was pushing between two of the barricades nearest New-ington-causeway, several parties made an attempt to get out. Amongst the number was a young woman who fell down insensible, and was trodden upon by the mob. She was found to be so dreadfully injured that she could not speak. She was removed to Guy's Hospital, and died there on Wednesday morning. Near the same place a young man was forced down amongst the crowd, and was likewise injured to such an extent as to render it necessary for him to be taken to Guy's Hospital, where he still remains in a very dangerous condition. It was fortunate that the authorities adopted the precautions they did, in placing huge barriers in different parts of the neighbourhood of the prison. Never was such a mass assembled on a similar occasion, and when the culprits appeared on the drop the rush was terrific. Hundreds are indebted to the police for the preservation of their lives."

Allowing for a certain redundancy and oceanic swell of descriptive eloquence, peculiar to newspaper records of horrors, there is still enough in this account to make a considerate man ponder with sadness, if not alarm, upon the state of that under-current of society in an overgrown metropolis which becomes visible upon such occasions. At any stage of a country's history or condition, such a manifestation would have in it something fearful; but it is particularly so when contrasted with the excess of lux-urious refinement which prevails at the very same time, not only in Courts and palaces, but in much nearer neigh-bourhood to the classes who exhibited their tastes and habits at the execution of the Mannings. In the same journal from which the above account is taken there is a descriptive paragraph respecting the Lord Mayor's dinner at the Guildhall of London, which took place three days before the notable scene in front of Horsemonger-lane gaol. Let us turn away for a moment from *that* view of society to look at *this* :—

" The business-room of the Court of Aldermen was converted into a mirrored reception-room. The windows at the end of the room were made the openings to a large conservatory filled with trellised columns, up which clambered vines in full bearing and rare-foliaged creepers. The floor was laid out in a pattern of rich mosaic. A marble fountain threw a stream of water into the air, with a cooling effect ; groups of choice flowers were massed around ; aviaries with birds of bright plumage and sweet song occupied each corner ; and richly-coloured lamps threw a picturesque light on the whole."

Such are the luxuries which exist in the near neighbourhood of a population so brutal as that which crowded to the execution of the Mannings ! The magistrates day after day proceed from the investigation of the fray, to the indulgence of the feast, but they are not startled. Habit has dulled their sensibilities ; and, besides, to think of anything beyond the matter in hand, is a trouble which they do not deem it necessary to take.

Another of the cases alluded to in the official Report is that of Rush, the Norfolk farmer—a dogged, shameless, remorseless, unwavering villain, as unlike Manning as one murderer can be to another. He was licentious, crafty, and resolutely atrocious. Although past middle age, and having children grown up, he lived at his farm with a young person who had been a governess in his family, and who had become his mistress. Having compelled this woman to forge some instruments relative to the land he held, which instruments, if valid, would have made it his own, he determined to murder those whose signatures were forged, so as to make the direct evidence of his fraud impossible. After drinking tea with his paramour he went forth alone in the dusk of the evening, and, arriving at the house of his landlord, Mr. Jermy, a magistrate of the county, he met him as he walked out of his own door after dinner, and shot him dead. His son, rushing from the dining-room to the door at the noise, received the contents of the second barrel of the murderer's weapon, and also fell dead. Having either reloaded his gun, or being provided with another, he now entered the house. The men-servants were frightened, and fled to the back of the house to escape and give an alarm. Mrs. Jermy, the wife of the younger victim, coming down stairs in terror, but not knowing the extent of the calamity, was fired at next, and so severely wounded that she lost her arm. Her maid, more faithful or more courageous than the men-servants, flying to the assistance of her mistress, was also shot, and severely wounded. Both mistress and servant survived, however, and the latter, who recognised Rush, notwithstanding a disguise which he wore, positively identified him as the murderer when he was tried. Rush, having dropped some papers to intimate that the house was surrounded, no doubt to deter any one from following him, walked home, after some time went to bed, and was not seized till the next morning. From first to last, he seemed to rely on his own cunning and courage for escaping the penalty of his frightful crimes, and not only denied his guilt, but acted with sturdy effrontery, and some rude skill, the part of a man who was confident of showing that other persons, and not he, would have to answer for the murders which had been committed. At his trial he chose to conduct his own defence, with a kind of brutal confidence in the powers of chicane, which wearied and disgusted even the most patient and most experienced in such affairs. His tedious cross-examination of the witnesses showed him to be destitute of all sense and feeling applicable to the circumstances in which he stood, and exhibited only dogged resolution to pursue his own course, however offensive to others, and imprudent for himself. He was without hesitation found guilty ; and the judge, in passing sentence, failed not to mark, by somewhat unusual terms of indignation, his sense of not only the enormous guilt, but the gross and shameless effrontery of the prisoner. He was executed in the presence of an immense crowd in front of the gaol called Norwich Castle. He died as he had lived, exhibiting no emotion of fear, nor sense of contrition, but to his latest breath trying to deceive. The magnitude of his crime and the bold atrocity with which, all alone, he committed it, cause the case of the murderer Rush to hold a conspicuous place in the annals of criminal offences.

The number of capital convictions in each year since 1841 has already been mentioned. The executions of offenders have been as follows :—

In 1842	.	.	9	In 1846	.	.	6
1843	.	.	13	1847	.	.	8
1844	.	.	16	1848	.	.	12
1845	.	.	12	1849	.	.	15

—making 91 persons who publicly suffered death upon the scaffold in England and Wales in the eight years between the end of 1841 and the beginning of 1850. These were distributed over 31 English counties, and two in Wales :—

Bedford	.	.	.	1	Derby	.	.	.	4	Lincoln	.	.	.	3
Berks.	.	.	.	2	Durham	.	.	.	1	Middlesex	.	.	10
Bucks	.	.	.	1	Essex	.	.	.	1	Monmouth	.	.	2
Chester	.	.	.	3	Gloucester	.	.	1	Norfolk	.	.	.	2
Cornwall	.	.	2	Kent	.	.	.	2	Northumberland	.	4
Cumberland	.	.	1	Lancaster	.	.	9	Nottingham	.	.	2
Devon	.	.	.	1	Leicester	.	.	1	Salop	.	.	.	1

Somerset . . . 2	Surrey . . . 4	Worcester . . 1
Southampton . 1	Sussex . . . 2	York 9
Stafford . . . 7	Warwick . . 3	Brecon . . . 2
Suffolk . . . 3	Wilts . . . 2	Glamorgan . . 1

The most singular incident in the English statistics of murder for some years past is the increase in the proportion of females who have been accused and convicted of this highest of crimes. The table of commitments for murder, having reference to the sex of the accused, stands thus—

	Males.	Females.	Total.
In 1845	41	24	65
1846	42	26	68
1847	38	34	72
1848	42	34	76
1849	42	42	84

Going further back, and taking the commitments for murder in masses of three years, the account stands thus:—

Five Years.	Males.	Females.	Total.
1835–39	223	92	315
1840–44	221	126	347
1845–49	205	160	365

This steady increase for fifteen years in the number committed for murder can scarcely be attributed to mere accident. It seems to indicate a change in the character of society, at least in the classes in which violent and shocking crimes are generally committed, and is perhaps one of the most fearful symptoms that could be adduced of the growing depravity of the social state, which unfortunately is concurrent with our improvements in commerce and general civilization.

The foregoing particulars are taken from the returns made to the Secretary of State's office by the officers of the assize and sessions courts. They are therefore wholly apart from summary convictions before police magistrates and justices of the peace, which give rise to the great mass of minor punishments in prisons, bridewells, and penitentiaries. If these were taken into account the number of offences would be multiplied six-fold, or perhaps more. As, however, all the more grave offences are reserved for trial at the sessions or the assizes, the foregoing statements will be found a fair epitome of the serious crime, though not of the social disorder, of this kingdom.

CHAPTER XI.

MANNERS—CONVERSATION.

In no part of the world that I am acquainted with do the more excellent qualities of human nature sweeten and adorn, in any very noticeable degree, the ordinary business or idleness of life. Everywhere we must be content to witness

> " The greetings where no kindness is, and all
> The dreary intercourse of daily life."

And if, in spite of this, we can accept the poet's teaching, and preserve " a cheerful faith that all which we behold is full of blessings," so much the better for our happiness. The world, however, being what it is, it is no great compliment to say of the English people in general, that they have beneath the surface as much virtue, and even generosity, as any other people under the sun. But the more precious ores of their character lie deeply embedded, and it requires circumstances of considerable force and urgency to bring them forth. The ordinary habit of Englishmen, and especially of those who have been, in a certain sense, " educated," and have mixed with the world, is to repress their thoughts and feelings ; and the higher we advance in society, the more common do we find the practice of assuming a light and trivial manner as an ordinary mask. An eminent critic,* speaking of

---

* Francis Jeffrey.

the tone of good society, describes it as " that air of
gaiety and playfulness in which persons of high rank seem
from time immemorial to have thought it necessary to
array, not their courtesy only, but *their generosity and
their hostility.*" I believe this to be, as a matter of fact
and practice, perfectly true. The same critic, upon another occasion, propounds a theory respecting French and
English society, attributing the greater ease of the former
to the equality of rank of French polite society in the
middle of the last century. Under such circumstances,
the peculiarities of individuals were not ascribed to ignorance or awkwardness, but to caprice or peculiarity of
disposition. In England, the critic proceeds to say, " we
have never had this arrangement. The great wealth of
the mercantile classes, and the privilege which every man
here possesses of aspiring to every position, has always
prevented any such complete separation of the high and
the low born, even in ordinary society, and made all large
assemblages of people to a certain degree promiscuous.
. . . . With us, therefore, society, when it passes beyond
select clubs and associations, is apt rather to be distracted
with little jealousies and divisions, or, finally, to settle
into constraint, insipidity, and reserve. People meeting
from all the extremes of life are afraid of being miscon-
strued. Conversation is left to a few professed talkers,
and all the rest are satisfied to hold their tongues, and
despise each other in their hearts." I imagine this somewhat severe picture of society, as he actually found it,
was " drawn from the life," as exhibited at the Whig
literary dinners of Holland House. All people, of all
political colours, however, and especially those whom the
world recognises as " scientific " or " literary," are apt
enough to exchange cold civilities at table, while they
despise each other in their hearts.

It would, however, be a great mistake to suppose that in the present day men of humble condition could obtain access to the society of the rich and great in England easier than in France. And it would be no less an error to suppose that such society is generally marked by more constraint and reserve than the society of the middle class. The constraint experienced by those who have not been accustomed to such society arises from a difficulty, or sense of impropriety, in adopting the unceremonious indifference that reigns around—the polished rudeness, if one may use such a phrase—the easy unconcern, which goes straight to the point, without the ceremonies that formerly were considered polite, and which still remain, in some measure, with the middle classes. In a great house most of the ceremony is left to the chief butler and the groom of the chambers. *They*, indeed, are very consequential personages, but they are paid for taking the trouble to be so. With the gentlefolk as much pride remains as ever, and disdain the most ineffable for every feature of vulgar pretension; but all is cool, easy, and smooth. Lord Byron, in his scoffing way,* has given as faithful an account, as anything written in that spirit could be, of life as it passes in the country-house of an English notable who receives company. And thus he winds it up :—

> " But all was gentle and aristocratic
>   In this our party ; polish'd, smooth, and cold
> As Phidian forms cut out of marble Attic.
>   There are now no Squire Westerns as of old ;
> And our Sophias are not so emphatic,
>   But fair as then, or fairer, to behold.
> We have no accomplished blackguards like Tom Jones,
> But gentlemen in stays, as stiff as stones."

---

* Don Juan, canto xiii.

Sidney Smith, the most notorious and the cleverest scoffer and sneerer of his day, complained that the momentary lords of the earth would receive his statement about cathedral patronage " with derision and *persiflage* —the great principle which is now called in *for the government of mankind*." Soon afterwards he enters into a mock defence of Lord Melbourne, then prime minister, whose manner, even upon important occasions, was frequently that of careless indifference, whatever his inner thoughts may have been. "Our Viscount," says Sidney Smith, " is somewhat of an impostor. Everything about him seems to betoken careless desolation ; any one would suppose from his manner that he was playing at chuck-farthing with human happiness; that he was always on the heel of pastime ; that he would giggle away the great charter, and decide by the method of teetotum whether my lords the bishops should, or should not, retain their seats in the House of Lords. All this is the mere vanity of surprising and making us believe that he can play with kingdoms as other men can with nine-pins. Instead of this lofty Nebulo—this miracle of moral and intellectual felicities—he is nothing more than a sensible, honest man, who means to do his duty to the sovereign and to the country. Instead of being the ignorant man he pretends to be, before he meets the deputation of chandlers in the morning he sits up half the night talking with Thomas Young * about melting and skimming ; and then, though he has acquired knowledge enough to work off a whole vat of prime Leicester tallow, he pretends the next morning not to know the difference between a dip and a mould. In the same way, when he has been employed in reading Acts of Parliament, he would persuade you that

---

* The minister's private secretary.

he has been reading ' *Cleghorn on the Beatitudes,*' or
' *Pickler on the Nine Difficult Points.*' Neither can I
allow to this minister (however he may be irritated by the
denial) the extreme merit of indifference to the consequences of his measures. I believe him to be conscientiously alive to the good or evil that he is doing, and that
his caution has more than once arrested the gigantic projects of the Lycurgus of the Lower House. I am sorry
to hurt any man's feelings, and to brush away the magnificent fabric of levity and gaiety he has reared; but I
accuse our minister of honesty and diligence; I deny that
he is careless or rash : he is nothing more than a man of
good understanding and good principle, disguised in the
eternal and somewhat wearisome affectation of a political
roué." I have transcribed this passage, because it is
a most lively description of that sort of affectation which,
in a greater or less degree, is so common in English
society, and because the description itself is a striking
illustration of that scornful and airy mirthfulness which in
Sidney Smith was joined with a witty genius and a keen
sense of the ludicrous.

An author of very different temperament from the Rev.
Sidney Smith complains that, in the present time, there
is " a light, jesting, flippant, unkind mode of talking
about things and persons, very common in society, exceedingly different from wit, which stifles good conversation, and gives *a sense of general hostility rather than
sociability*—as if men came together chiefly for the purpose of ridiculing their neighbours, and of talking slightly
about matters of great concern." *

Upon this point of conversation, as distinguished from
what Dr. Johnson used to call " good talk," we have

---

* Friends in Council, part ii.

some noticeable remarks from Mr. H. Taylor, whose grave and graceful prose is only less to be esteemed than the sweet wisdom of his verse. He says that conversation is an exercise dangerous to the understanding when practised in any large measure as an art or an amusement. He then goes on to describe the conversationist of modern society. " To be ready," he says, " to speak before he has time to think; to say something apt and specious— something which he may very well be *supposed* to think, when he has nothing to say that he really does think; to say what is consistent with what he has said before; to *touch topics lightly, and let them go,*—these are the arts of a conversationist, of which, perhaps, the *last is the worst*, because it panders to all the others. Nothing is searched out by conversation of this kind; nothing is *heartily believed*, whether by those who say it, or by those who hear it. It may be easy, graceful, clever, and sparkling, and bits of knowledge may be plentifully tossed to and fro in it, but it will be vain and unprofitable; it may cultivate a certain micaceous, sandy surface of the mind, but all that lies below will be unmoved and unsunned. To say that it is vain and unprofitable, is indeed to say too little; for the habit of thinking, *with a view to conversational effect*, will inevitably corrupt the understanding, which will never again be sound or sincere." * I think this is deeply true; and any one of experience may have observed that the readiest and (to the crowd) the most agreeable conversationists to be found in society are persons for whose mental or moral qualifications little respect can be entertained. But as some men are said to be of an easy temper, because they have not substance enough in them to be ruffled, † so of others it may be said that

---

* Essay on the Rich and Great.   † Edmund Burke.

they have not matter enough in their understanding to be liable to that " corruption " of which Mr. Taylor speaks. In short, the people, such as one ordinarily meets, are as incapable of good conversation as of singing Greek verses to a lyric accompaniment. With such persons, when a man has nothing to say which he really does *think*, because such matter would be unsuitable, he may escape the awkwardness and the chill of silence by some remark calculated to dissipate dulness, and to preserve the spirits from sinking into torpidity. Again, it may be said that life cannot be a continual study of wisdom, though it ought never to degenerate into mere folly. The man who can think only in that superficial way which serves the turn of a conversationist, is not indeed worthy of much consideration; but we should not undervalue the power of throwing aside the severer habits of reflection, and tossing the ball of lighter thought in animated talk. But the truth is, that conversation such as Mr. Taylor describes—that is, easy, graceful, clever, and sparkling conversation, with bits of knowledge tossed to and fro in it—is, if not very rare, at least not very common, even in the circles of the highest pretension. There is plenty of lightsomeness, plenty of sarcasm ; but gracefulness, cleverness, and bits of knowledge, even of the superficial kind, are only to be met with on fortunate days or nights. The conversation one too often hears, and the manner which accompanies it, are not merely vain and unprofitable, because wanting in depth and earnestness, but directly and unquestionably pernicious, because fraught with a sneering spirit which feeds pride, and puts humble truth out of countenance.

> " And there are smiles by shallow worldlings worn,
>   To grace a lie, or laugh a truth to scorn."*

---

* Lago Varese, by H. Taylor.

Mr. Eliot Warburton, in his book called 'The Crescent and the Cross,' describes a visit to the island of Delos in his usual picturesque and striking manner, and adds,—" The island has been very little visited, and there appears to be a wide field for research among its varied relics. Our party was a large one, and consisted moreover entirely of English, a circumstance which, I know not why, is always fatal to research, or even to reflection: *a scoffing spirit inevitably prevails*; and whether on the mountain of Parnassus, or in the valley of Jehoshaphat, our countrymen seem to think that everything is unreal except themselves and their sandwiches: this is the very triumph of objectivity."

I do not know what "the triumph of objectivity" means, but, for the rest, I think Mr. Warburton has justly described the ordinary outside habit or affectation of the English: a lightsome indifference—a kind of disdainful carelessness which they do not really feel—is aimed at by almost all who desire to assume the tone of high society.

The present Lord Chief Justice of the Queen's Bench, who succeeds in everything he attempts, and who, before he assumed the ermine, had attained the position not only of a Cabinet Minister and a Peer of Parliament, but also of a popular author, achieved his literary success by a happy attention to this prevailing taste for contemptuous gaiety of manner. Although in his capacity of politician he was an advocate of popular influence, and always contended that great weight should be given to the wisdom and the will of the multitude, yet in his capacity of author, when writing the life of Lord Eldon, he says, " The recent victory of Salamanca, a renewed cry against Popery, and *a plentiful harvest*, which had, as usual, given the people a high opinion of the wisdom of the government," &c. The government of 1812 was a Tory government, which accounts for the learned lord's peculiar opinion of the wisdom of the people in thinking well of it on that occasion, and for his method of expressing that opinion.

The jesting, flippant, and contemptuous tone of remark is very frequently applied to the habits and circumstances of the speakers themselves. Men seem to regard themselves as the sport of a fate which they despise. They who have run the round of fashionable dissipations, sneer at the insipidity of civilized life. They will not take the trouble to set an example of better conduct. They will not themselves substitute good sense, moderation, cordiality, and politeness, for the pomp, ceremony, affectation, and vainglory of which they are conscious, but they go on with the crowd, and sneer at what the crowd is doing. They talk of " stale civilization," ridicule those who are " pinioned at dinner-tables," " stuck up in ball-rooms," or living in a round of formal ceremony and " utter respectability," while an humbler, more genuine, and more simple life than this, is no less scorned, if it be unaccompanied with great expense, or the ability to be greatly expensive.

One prevailing folly of all English society above the lower range of the middle class, is the desire to push themselves forward, and to gain what they consider a higher social footing. The ambition of private life in this way is most absurd, painful, and ridiculous. Hospitality is to a great extent perverted by it, and the ease and pleasure of social intercourse diminished if not destroyed. People who give entertainments do not consider how they may make others happy, but how they may make themselves appear of consequence. To have some guest of higher rank than usual, or to display something more magnificent than their general acquaintance can pretend

to, or to exhibit a greater crowd in their rooms than
others can attract—this is their strange ambition, rather
than to enjoy a happy evening with their friends. To
triumph, not to please, is their object; and if they obtain
their triumph, there is, I believe, in general, not much
care whether it has given pain or pleasure to others.

A critic already quoted (Jeffrey), after describing the
plague of *ennui* with his accustomed clearness and vivacity,
proceeds to say that there is another "curse of the
happy" which has a range more wide and indiscriminate.
"This is the desire of being fashionable—the restless
and insatiable passion to pass for creatures a little more
distinguished than we really are—with the mortification
of frequent failure, and the humiliating consciousness of
being perpetually exposed to it. Among those who are
secure of 'meat, clothes, and fire,' and are thus above
the chief physical evils of existence, we do believe that
this is a more prolific source of unhappiness than guilt,
disease, or wounded affection; and that more positive
misery is created, and more true enjoyment excluded, by
the eternal fretting and straining of this pitiful ambition,
than by all the ravages of passion, the desolations of war,
or the accidents of mortality. This may appear a strong
statement, but we make it deliberately, and are deeply
convinced of its truth. The wretchedness which it produces may not be so intense, but it is of much longer
duration, and spreads over a wider circle. It is quite
dreadful, indeed, to think what a sweep this pest has
taken among the comforts of our prosperous population.
To be thought fashionable—that is, to be thought more
opulent and tasteful, and on a footing of intimacy with a
larger number of distinguished persons than they really
are, is the great and laborious pursuit of four families
out of five, the members of which are exempted from the

necessity of daily industry.   In this pursuit their time, spirits, and talents are wasted, their tempers soured, their affections palsied, and their natural manners and dispositions altogether sophisticated and lost."   This was written many years ago; but I do not perceive that the " march of intellect " of the last decade has at all diminished 'this social or anti-social insanity.   It is really as unaccountable to me as any extravagance within the walls of Bedlam, that persons who are in other respects clever and reasonable, should take the trouble they do to get into company where they are certainly not appreciated, and perhaps despised.   To see men of science pursuing knighthoods, and ribbons, and decorations—men of literature anxious to rub their skirts to dull dukes or leaden lords—artists of genius running after patronizing princes who suffer them to approach and no more—members of parliament propitiated by tickets to a state ball —professional men who scarcely allow themselves an hour of domestic recreation, having their houses lighted up for nonsensical and expensive routs, and their rooms crowded with people whose faces or names they do not know ;—to see all this, and the pompous, hot, heavy dinners—the parade, the waste, the prodigality of expense, the poverty of sense, cheerfulness, and cordiality—is certainly enough to abate one's pride in the social philosophy of England, whatever we may say of the energy, enterprise, ability, and perseverance of the people in affairs of business.

Enough, however, for the present of deprecatory criticism.   The faults I have adverted to chiefly apply to persons and things without the range of the family circle. Within that sacred line, I am persuaded that there is in England more virtue and affectionateness, more fidelity and truth, as well as more manliness, gentleness, grace, honour, loveliness, and domestic worth, than the world elsewhere can show. Nor must I omit to say that even they whose affectation and superciliousness I have thought it right to condemn, require only the impulse of some great occasion to exhibit great qualities worthy of the land from which they spring. The dawdling military fop of St. James's-street, when taken to the field of battle, shows not only a courage which nothing can appal, but a cool endurance amid circumstances of distraction and dismay, of which perhaps a quicker sensibility would be incapable. And so of the rest. The man who habitually affects contempt, would peril his life, in any case of emergency, for those to whom on ordinary occasions he never thinks of offering a kind or respectful word. We are a people whose hearts are better than our manners, and whose follies, however thickly they may encrust the surface, have not, I think, penetrated so far as to corrupt the affections, or debase the understanding.

CHAPTER XII.

RICH AND POOR.

So far as general literature goes, and so far as public de-
bating and remonstrances in public journals may be relied
upon as evidence of a prevailing sentiment, there is no
want of public consciousness of the great social evil of the
time.   I mean the separation between rich and poor—
the dissympathy of classes, and that mutual disgust which
appears to threaten some sort of violent revolution in society at no very distant period.*   But I think it worthy
of especial note, that, while this danger is rung into the
ears of the reading classes month by month, week by
week, and even day by day, the *practice* of society under-
goes no change.   The tendency to isolation of classes,
which arises out of circumstances, and out of the habits
which have been acquired, is too strong to be affected
by essays, novels, newspapers, and reviews.   Institutions
for scientific and literary teaching by lectures, at the
cheapest possible rates, are established ; parks for the
recreation of the lower orders are planted ; even clubs,
upon something like the aristocratic model, are established, where conveniences and luxuries are supplied at
low prices : but all this seems to be unsuccessful.   It is

---

* A recent publication of M. de Lamartine informs the world that the
danger of this kind which did exist in England has passed away under
the influence of our great improvements of late years. I know no one
who utters more splendid nonsense than M. de Lamartine.

a sort of copper-lace imitation of genuine finery, which actually feeds the fatal contempt of the rich English for those who cannot afford all that money will purchase. What one wants to see is not the aping of the habits of the rich by the less wealthy in a cheaper and coarser manner, but a mutual and hearty recognition of the differences of condition—a kind and cordial condescension on the one side, and an equally cordial, but still respectful, devotedness on the other. But this, as I have said, appears to makes no progress. The vulgar attempts at imitation and rivalship to which I have alluded, only widen the breach, and render the return to a healthier and happier state of things more hopeless.

It is difficult to say which side has been most to blame for the change which has taken place in English society in regard to the social position of rich and poor ; but now that the change *has* taken place, and that a reform has become needful, there can be little question that the rich have more in their power than the poor have, to bring about the better understanding which is so desirable. But the difficulty is to persuade the rich to take the necessary trouble for such an object. The mischief has been in progress for a long time, being indeed an ordinary incident of advancing civilization, but it proceeded with extravagantly accelerated pace at the time that riches were so rapidly accumulated in this country, under the stimulus of abundant paper money, aided by a large government expenditure. A description of this has been given by a writer of more vigour than refinement of style, who, notwithstanding the occasional exhibition of frantic political animosities, has made some useful contributions to contemporary history. " Amidst the artificial rise in all commodities," he says, " and the expenditure of the money borrowed by the Government, fortunes were rapidly accumulated, and an appearance of prosperity created among the middle classes totally unlike anything that had appeared before.   One of the worst effects of this was a total change of manners among these classes — a reckless profusion — a disdain of homely and prudential living — and a disgusting and soul-degrading aping of aristocratical manners and ways of life, pernicious in the highest degree.   At former periods the abundance of diffused weath had caused symptoms of this malady to appear in England ; but it now spread like a pestilence, and changed all the wholesome usages of society.   Education was totally changed.   Forgetting that the business of life must be carried on by men and women, with the partial exception of a very few indeed of the very highest rank, a rage for showy and superficial accomplishments seized upon the middling classes of society.   All the useful arts of life were to be despised and thrown aside as vulgar and degrading.   Common sense seemed to have fled the land.   Quackery and affectation spoiled everything.   All young men were to be linguists and fine gentlemen ; and all young women, musicians, painters, and heroines of novels.   The pianoforte and the pencil and colours found their way into the farm-house and the back shop ; and from that hour the really useful domestic sciences became obsolete.   What the middle classes had ceased to learn they could not teach, and a domestic revolution was effected, the uncomfortable effects of which we are feeling at this hour.   The manufacturing system, by taking thousands of young females from their homes, and shutting them up amidst the heat, ignorance, and vice of those demoralised dens called ' factories,' completed the work ; and domestic comfort, as it formerly existed in England, is unknown.   The parlour tables are loaded with degraded and silly novels and albums, and

still more contemptible music-books; whilst ignorance of
the real arts of life, affectation, recklessness, vice, and
dishonesty, too often occupy the rest of the house. Such
are the effects of essentially vicious systems. Their
diseased ramifications reach every class. They afflict society as the 'dry rot' does the mansion—sparing nothing,
and affecting everything, from the garret down to the
cellar, until a nation becomes one corrupt and crawling
mass of degradation, vice, affectation, ignorance, misery,
and mischief." * Although this may be regarded as a
somewhat coarse and exaggerated picture of the great
changes which took place during the first fifteen years of
the century, yet it has much truth in it. The great mass
of the middle class who were born or brought up during
that period have but little notion of the simplicity and
frugality of life that previously existed. If any tradition
of the comparative humbleness of their fathers' and grand-
fathers' condition have reached them, such traditions are
regarded with a feeling the very opposite of respect. They
have, in their own opinion, advanced beyond that condition, and they are ashamed of it. I wish there were good
reason for believing that virtue and happiness had advanced along with habits of expense and refinement, but
I cannot see that it is so. I rather believe that society is
feeling at this day "the uncomfortable effects" of that
extraordinary progress, and the peculiar direction afterwards given to it by the monetary policy of the legislature. The abundance of money and the gradual depreciation of the currency from the beginning of the century
to 1815 were no doubt the causes of an extraordinary
diffusion of wealth. The reward of industry never before
had been so great; and even they who but held firmly

* Doubleday's 'Financial History of England.'

what they possessed at the beginning, seemed year by year to grow richer, because they could year by year dispose of their property for more of the current money. The new distribution of property caused by the government loans and the expansion of currency was sealed, as it were, in the hands of the then owners by the restoration of a gold currency in 1819. From that time the great disposable wealth of the country was no longer in the hands of the landed proprietors; and from that time the influence of great capital has been in operation, not merely to assist, but in a great measure to compete with, the interests of labour. Ever since that period labour has had an up-hill fight in Great Britain, and hitherto it has been beaten. I do not find it specifically denied by any class of politicians, that since that time the rich have been growing richer, and the poor more poor. I have indeed found it directly asserted in the House of Commons by members of the Government, during this year, 1850, that at no former period of our history were the great mass of the people better off than they are at present; while the direct contrary of this was maintained by men of undoubted ability, honesty, and experience, on the other side ;* but even then, no question was made of the fact, recalled in very striking terms to the attention of the House, that the result of modern legislation had been to make the rich richer, and the poor more poor.

It is certainly true that since the close of the war in 1815, and more especially since the Parliamentary Reform Act of 1832, the middle, or mercantile, class have made great encroachments upon aristocratic power and influence, so far as concerns legislation and the

---

* See particularly the debate on Mr. H. Drummond's motion, March 12, 1850.

action of government. It is doubtful whether, socially, the aristocratic classes have permitted that advance into their domain which politically they have not had the skill or the energy to prevent. It seems to me, however, that there can be no doubt of the total failure of the working class to accomplish any advance at all. They have allowed themselves to be made the instruments of the middle orders, or men of business, who were seeking for political power. The working people have been led away by the delusion of accomplishing political changes, from which practically *they* could derive no advantage; and they have failed to seek the social benefits—the security for employment at reasonable wages—the fair share that honest industry and orderly obedience to the law may well claim in the advancing wealth of the country—*that* they have failed to seek, and not only have they thus neglected their own advantage, but they have, as it seems to me, contributed to their own injury, by giving countenance to a policy of which the object is to cheapen the produce of labour—in other words, to reduce the remuneration of the labourer. If the labourer were more a consumer than a producer, this would be prudent policy; but as the labourer is more a producer than a consumer, the policy is manifestly inimical to his interests.

At all events, whether the view I take of the effect of the policy, tending to make the produce of labour cheap, be a correct one or not, I apprehend there cannot be much doubt of the fact that something is very wrong in our political or social systems, and that the people at large do not share, as it is desirable they should, in the advantages which some classes possess. An eloquent writer, who admits that much more wretchedness was occasionally suffered in former days than is ever experienced now, proceeds to speak of the present time in the following terms:—

" What we say is unparalleled in the history of the world is the *co-existence* of so much suffering in one portion of the people, with so much prosperity in another; of unbounded private wealth, with unceasing public penury; of constant increase in the national resources, with constant diminution in the comforts of a considerable portion of the community; of the utmost freedom consistent with order ever yet existing upon earth, with a degree of discontent which keeps the nation constantly on the verge of insurrection; of the most strenuous efforts for the moral and religious improvement of the poor, with an increase of crime unparalleled at the same or perhaps any other period in any civilized state. So habituated has the nation become to the constant contemplation of this extraordinary combination, that a large part—especially of the thinking portion of it—has come to regard it as unavoidable—as the necessary consequence of our advanced national years and old-established civilization; and they deem it as vain to fret against it as against the variableness of our climate, or the churlishness of a large portion of our soil. But a little reflection must convince every candid inquirer that this is not the case, and that the notion that public prosperity and private misery, public poverty and private opulence, external peace and internal feuds, general growth and individual decline, necessarily must exist together, is essentially erroneous. Experience, indeed, too clearly shows how invariably the ceaseless agency of human corruption educes evil out of good, as the opposite springs of human improvement bring good out of evil; and therefore we may always expect to find numerous social and political misfortunes springing up out of the very blessings which have been most ardently desired, and, to appearance, can bring only general felicity in their train.

But it is evident that there is in our present state something more than this—something which demonstrates the existence of *a great and latent evil*, which poisons, for a large part of our people, all our prosperity, and converts the fruits of industry into the apples of Sodom." *

I must repeat that this strong impression of the inefficacy of the wealth of the nation, under present circumstances, to save the people from the last miseries of poverty, is not confined to any one class of politicians. A writer in an eminent periodical, which supports the most extreme views of the political economists, tells us that—" in a country like this, including both England and Ireland, with its precarious harvests, its fluctuating demand for manufacturing labour, and, above all, with a population which has been allowed, or rather encouraged, to multiply without forethought or restraint, and to grow up without any education that could enable it to see either the perils by which it is surrounded, or the means of escaping them —it is absolutely certain that, but for extraneous relief, thousands upon thousands must annually die miserably, under the very eyes of the legislature, and of the wealthy individuls by whose want of judgment, neglect, or instrumentality, much of that destitution and helplessness has been created." † The philosopher who writes thus, is of opinion that the poor man's notion, that if he is willing to work he is entitled to be fed, is, *when submitted to the test of reason*, a clear absurdity ! As it happens that when a man does not get food he is apt to die miserably whether he be poor or rich, it is necessary to inquire how a writer who thinks the poor man's notion that he ought to be fed an absurd notion, should feel any compunction at the

---

* Alison, 'England in 1815 and 1845.'
† Edinburgh Review, October, 1849.

alternative of his miserable death before the eyes of the
wealthy. His scruples arise from considerations of political logic. It seems he would be willing enough to let
the people die, but for one consideration, which squares
not with his views of the fitness of things—namely, that,
since the most atrocious crimes cannot receive a greater
punishment than that of death, it seems inconsistent that
mere improvidence, and multiplying more rapidly than
prudence warrants, should be punished with the pain-
fullest of deaths—to wit, that of starvation! Such is the
form which sympathy for our fellow-creatures takes when
" submitted to the test of reason," and moulded by the
principles of modern political economy.

But the destitution of the lower orders is as great in
other matters as in those which concern the support of the
body, and the want of due sympathy is not confined to
those who take their creed from the harsh school of the
Political Economists. An earnest clergyman of the metropolis, expatiating upon the great peril of ignorance,
and the absence of all moral and religious training, in the
children of the poor, thus pours forth his complaint:—
" The wealthy and the great see no danger. Men walk
in Grosvenor-square, and cannot believe there is poverty—
converse with shopmen in Bond-street, and cannot understand how the lower orders can be ignorant—cherish little
dame-schools as pet amusements on their estates in the
country, and smile with incredulity when, in remembrance
of the innocence which dwells around their own doors,
they are told of vice, profaneness, and heathenism in
happy England. Alas! it is the superficial acquaintance
with the things that are going on around them that will
prove their ruin. The complacent and self-satisfied air
with which they look upon the little good that they do in
a contracted sphere, cheats them into a belief that therein

is to be found a representation of the whole country. The hereditary landlord of vast territorial possessions, as well as the wealthy capitalists in the funds; the fox-hunting squire, and the city merchant; the noble lord of the House of Peers, and the little shopkeeper in the country town turning his honest penny at the counter—all of them are equally asleep, in a self-satisfied idea that the education of the people is abundant, that we have done all that is necessary, and that he who attempts to do more in the way of teaching than is now done will only do injury, not benefit, by raising the lower orders to their own level, and so destroy the necessary variations of society. Thus many might be mentioned, if it were decorous to give names, who, having once made a standing order to their banker to pay a certain sum for the support of schools, wash their hands for ever of the subject of education. They treat it as a thing of a guinea subscription, rather than as a principle affecting the well-being of the country. Their vision is bounded by the local wants of their parish or their estate, and they cannot imagine that there is a national want which must be met by a national supply. Such persons we meet daily in society. Their narrow minds seem to have no idea of the grasp of this great subject. They smile at the comments which the clergy make when speaking in sermons of the spiritual destitution of the people; they turn aside with loathing and vexation at the very sound of a school for the poor. And yet these are the men who serve upon grand juries at the assizes, and bring in true bills against poachers, felons, and murderers; or, as magistrates, levy a county-rate for the lunatic asylum or the gaol, or as legislators sit in the House of Commons and vote away thousands of the nation's money for poor-law commissioners, not seeing that half such expenditure bestowed upon education would save their labour and their time, and produce a happier and a better people." *

So much for the relative condition of rich and poor, their sympathy with, and their knowledge of, each other at the present time. In the country these things go on much better, and there is some familiar acquaintance between the owners of much wealth and the owners of very little. In cities it seems impossible that the separation and estrangement of classes can go much further. But even in the country, low prices and low wages produce gloomy discontent and a destructive spirit. In a House of Commons debate already referred to† it was stated by a county representative to be a common remark with the labourers now that they did not see why there should be such a difference between the rich and the poor ; and he confessed he could not answer the question implied by that remark. The same honourable member also called upon the House to observe the colossal fortunes that were rising up among a starving people. "When," said he, " Mr. Pitt created the legacy-duty, he thought it absurd to provide for a legacy-duty on properties above a million ; but now not a year passed away that persons did not die possessing fortunes of upwards of a million— fortunes so enormous that in Mr. Pitt's time it was impossible to suppose they could ever be made." Such is the uncontradicted statement made in Parliament at a time when, to cheapen the price of produce, and, by necessary consequence, to lower the remuneration of the labouring producer, seems to be thought by many intelligent men in England the wisest policy that can be pursued.

---

* Rev. W. J. E. Bennet on Crime and Education.
† Debate, March 12, 1850.

CHAPTER XIII.

THE BLUE BOOKS.

It appears to me that the minds of our politicians in these days are too much engrossed by details. Prudent people take pains to impress upon young members of Parliament that they must make themselves acquainted with facts ; and this is very good advice up to a certain point, but the study of principles is even more important than the acquisition of facts. The details of public business now laid before Parliament are so voluminous, so various in their subjects, and so vast in their extent, that he who tries to get all this matter into his mind will have room for but little else, and may so encumber himself with knowledge as to weaken or deaden his powers of reflection. If a man be gifted with a mind capable of great things, it is lamentable to see it made a mere storehouse of particulars, which it is sufficient that under-secretaries and chief clerks should know. I indeed admit that politicians, as well as poets, should " comprehend the vast and attend to the minute ;" but I observe that very sedulous attention to the minute—especially in politics—takes away the power and the disposition to study and comprehend the vast, and therefore it is that, while I would exhort political men not to dissipate their minds in vague speculation, I would no less earnestly caution them against occupying themselves too much with the mere drudgery and small details of public business.

I have heard a man of parliamentary eminence remark that Sir Robert Peel had the Blue Books by heart. This may have been creditable to his industry, but not, I think, to his statesmanship. The Blue Books are very insufficient furniture for the heart of a statesman. The kind of attention necessary for a mastery of these details is, in some respects, injurious to the mind. Its nobility is impaired—its discursive and soaring tendency is destroyed. Perhaps, if the attention of Sir Robert Peel to minute statistics had been less fixed, his adhesion to principles and political friends had been more firm. By continually looking upwards, as Arnold remarks, our minds will grow upwards—admiration and enthusiastic reverence for excellence impart to ourselves a portion of the qualities we admire. An opposite effect is produced by continually looking downwards upon minute details and complex computations. Thus it is that men who have begun with the arguments and the sentiments which embrace the highest objects of national pursuit, and have been led by the highest aspirations of national glory, come at last to propound to an assembled senate that the great object of legislation and government should be to enable the people to buy in the cheapest markets, and sell in the dearest. Nor is this the worst. The " ever-dwindling soul " sinks from mean contemplations to mean devices; and statesmen who have studied Dryden in their better days, forget that pithy lesson of his, which is especially applicable to political life,—

" For little souls on little shifts rely,
    And coward arts of mean expedients try :
    The noble mind will dare do anything but lie."

Again, we are to consider that all men who hope to effect great things should guard themselves not only against idleness, but also, and quite as carefully, against

excessive occupation.   Dr. Johnson has well said, that,
where all men work, there will be no intellectual improvement.   " All intellectual improvement arises from leisure,
and all leisure arises from one working for another."   One
of the great evils of public life in the present day is that
it admits of so little leisure; and the reason of this is
that public men of note are expected to be masters of details, and to devote a large portion of their time to the
investigation of minute particulars.   Wordsworth, who
stands at the opposite pole in literature from Samuel
Johnson, proclaims, in noble verse, that it is neither in
the despotism of the battle-field, nor in the drudgery of
political study, that the grand science of government is to
be mastered :—

> " 'T is not in battles that from youth we train
> The governor who must be wise and good,
> And temper with the sternness of the brain
> Thoughts motherly, and meek as womanhood.
> Wisdom doth live with children round her knees:
> Books, leisure, perfect freedom, and the talk
> Man holds with week-day man in the hourly walk
> Of the mind's business: these are the degrees
> By which true sway doth mount; this is the stalk
> True power doth grow on; and her rights are these."

Now, our modern statesmanship, whatever merits it may
possess, appears to be much wanting not only in greatness
of view, but in simplicity and affectionateness.   The
science which is cultivated is the science of gain; and the
goodness and grandeur of thought, which in former times
gave beauty and dignity to the public pleadings of leading statesmen, seem out of place in discussions wherein the
wisdom of the heart is not recognised as a branch of political wisdom.

I have seen somewhere a glowing panegyric upon
Edmund Burke's letters on a Regicide Peace, attributed

to Sir James Mackintosh, and worthy, I think, of his
candour and eloquence. The passage is remarkable, and
will give you the *beau ideal* of a great political mind,
fitted to the circumstances of a civilized, free, and intelligent people. These letters, we are told, " are amongst
the most distinguished works even of their author:—possessing the same vast reach and comprehension of view—
the same unbounded variety of allusion, illustration, and
ornament, drawn from every province of nature and
science—the same unrivalled mastery over language—
the same happy power of relieving the harshness of political dispute by beautiful effusions of sentiment, and of
dignifying composition by grave and lofty maxims of
moral and civil wisdom—the same unlimited sway over
the human passions, filling us at his pleasure with indignation, with horror, or with pity. There is nothing ordinary in his view of a subject He is perhaps, of all
writers, the one of whom it may be said with the strictest
truth that no idea appears hackneyed in his hands, no topic
seems commonplace when he treats it. When the subject
must (from the narrowness of human conceptions, which
bounds even the genius of Burke) be borrowed, the turn
of thought and the manner of presenting it are his own.
The attitude and drapery are peculiar to the master."
This description places before us the lineaments and
action of a really great public man. The genius which
inspired Burke is not a thing to be imitated ; but regarding it with reverence and admiration, the politician will
certainly fall into juster and nobler views than he is likely
to gather from the most painful study of the details of
Blue Books.

While it must be acknowledged that it is almost impossible to pay more respect than ought to be paid to sound

and well-digested information, yet it is to be observed, that of late years there has grown up in the minds of politicians a somewhat exaggerated estimation of mere knowledge of facts and circumstances. Now experience does not teach that in any field of human action—in the courts of law, or in the practice of physic—in the schools, or in the senate—the man possessing the largest amount of mere information is the ablest man. Mr. Macaulay, who has been upon some occasions a very unscrupulous eulogist of mere acquirement, has a passage in his history of James II., which portrays in a striking manner its comparative inadequacy in practical affairs. " There is," he says, " a certain tact, resembling an instinct, which is often wanting to great orators and philosophers, and which is often found in persons who, if judged by their conversation and their writings, would be pronounced simpletons. Indeed, when a man possesses this tact, it is in some sense an advantage to him that he is destitute of those more showy talents which would make him an object of admiration, of envy, and of fear. Sydney was a remarkable instance of this truth. Incapable, ignorant, and dissipated as he seemed to be, he understood, or rather felt, with whom it was necessary to be reserved, and with whom he might safely venture to be communicative. The consequence was, that he did what Mordaunt with all his vivacity and invention, or Burnet with all his multifarious knowledge and fluent elocution, never could have done." This passage is not without Mr. Macaulay's habitual exaggeration for the sake of heightening the effect, but it exhibits a happy discrimination and *decision* in the delineation of character. Unquestionably the intellectual instinct which he describes is, much oftener than is generally supposed, the gift which makes a man of ability in the world's business. In politics or private business knowledge is useful only in proportion as men have energy, tact, and readiness to make use of it, and, in the absence of these qualities, no acquaintance with minute particulars, however various or extensive, will lead to eminent usefulness.

CHAPTER XIV.

MARRIAGES, BIRTHS, AND DEATHS.

If nature had anything to do with official returns and
" blue books," the reports of the Registrar-General of
England might well be called *lusus naturæ*. The last
three annual reports have indeed been becoming fine by
degrees and beautifully less, and the very last presented
to Parliament, in the year 1849, and relating to the affairs
of the year 1847, is only a series of arithmetical tables
without note or comment. Whether previous theories
were not sustained by the experience of 1847, or the
Registrar-General had found some other channel than
that of an official report for pouring out the miscellaneous
riches of his mind, I cannot tell. The Report for 1846,
presented in 1848, is, 1 venture to say, the most singular
melange that ever was laid upon the tables of the Houses
of Parliament, containing not only a very copious supply
of such details as a registrar of births, marriages, and
deaths might be expected to furnish, but also a torrent of
information upon general politics, statistics, crops, corn
laws, medical theories, meteorological influences, potatoes,
political economy, public revenue, the state of trade,
foreign affairs, Irish distress, sanatory measures, and the
fluctuations of human affairs, whether in towns, where
merchants most do congregate, or in the country, " procul
discordibus armis."

As the liberal gentleman said in the House of Commons, after he heard Lord John Russell describe the

ministerial scheme of Parliamentary Reform in 1831, such announcements " take away one's breath;" but there are many facts in the Registrar's Report, which, so far as they may be depended upon, are of great interest and importance, and the more prominent of them, bearing upon the ostensible subject of the Report, I shall proceed to abstract. The Registrar is particularly erudite on the subject of marriages, and, to avoid mistakes, he states in one line the number of marriages which have taken place for some years past, and in another the number of persons married. I think, however, it may be taken for granted that the latter will always be found precisely the double of the former; for though one has heard of such things as three-cornered duels in Ireland, I certainly have not heard of any marriage in England in which more or less than two were concerned as principals. The following table contains, in brief compass, the record of the events most interesting to families, which took place in the seven years 1840—1846 in England :—

Years.	1840.	1841.	1842.	1843.	1844.	1845.	1846.
Marriages . . .	122,665	122,496	118,825	123,818	132,249	143,743	145,664
Births	502,303	512,158	517,739	527,325	540,763	543,521	572,625
Deaths	359,687	343,847	349,519	346,445	356,933	349,366	390,315
Excess of Births registered over Deaths . . .	142,616	168,311	168,220	180,880	183,830	194,155	182,310

The Registrar is of opinion that " the fluctuation in the marriages of a country expresses the views which the great body of the people take of their prospects in the world." It is in order to maintain this thesis that the extraordinary variety of information, already alluded to,

has been brought forward.   The argument is, however,
more elaborate than important, and more curious than
satisfactory.   No one will deny that, other things being
the same, a period of general prosperity will probably
abound more in marriages than a period of a contrary
character.   But no array of figures, or accumulation of
facts, will persuade an intelligent man, who considers
with an attentive eye the current of life in which he is
placed, that marriage is uniformly, or even for the most
part, founded on a calculation of ways and means.
Perhaps it would be much better for the independence
and well-being of society in the United Kingdom if it
were.   But the Registrar-General rides his hobby upon
this subject at a very great pace, and seems to persuade
himself that marriages in general are determined by the
state of trade, the price of wheat and of consols, and the
call for money to set labour in motion.   After setting
forth the progress of these several matters from 1841 to
1846, he comes to the conclusion that, " under these
circumstances, 50,000 more persons married in 1845 than
in 1842."   Referring to the accounts of criminals committed, he draws the conclusion that, as the marriages increased, the crimes decreased progressively down to 1845,
but they began to rise in 1846 as the marriages fell off.
This deduction would be more satisfactory if it harmonised
with the facts; but, according to the Registrar's own
tables, the marriages of 1846 exceeded those of 1845.
He finds that there have been great fluctuations in the
amount of marriages since 1780—" the fluctuation has
generally extended over six years, has commonly followed
a similar course, and has almost invariably attended
speculations in trade."   The Registrar is very philosophical on the subject of fluctuations in general, and intro-
duces a theory of waves which I do not think has been

heard of at the sittings of the Royal Society. " These fluctuations," he says, " these periodical seasons of activity and repose, of success and misfortune, occur not only in manufactures and commerce (as well as in marriages) but in the more placid pursuits of the agriculturists—

> Agricolas ! quibus ipsa, procul discordibus armis,
> Fundit humo facilem victum justissima tellus :

who have also their distresses and good times.   From all we have seen for a century, the tide of affairs has set in waves ; any extraordinary advance has always been followed by a reflux ; in vain is it bid ' Be still,' for it is one of the conditions, and perhaps means, if not of the ex- istence, at least of the progress of society ; which, amidst all its perturbations, moves steadily up and down on the shores of time—under the dominion of a power that makes nations advance or recede, and under laws which can only be discovered by long, accurate, analyzed observation. As statistical science and education advance, the severity of seasons of distress—whose general course can be cal- culated—will be diminished by mutual aid, and provision will be made in prosperity against their recurrence, as the losses of shipwreck, fire, and life to society are miti- gated by the various kinds of insurance.   Knowledge will banish panic."   The last is a pithy sentence, but not con- firmed by experience.   It is generally believed, that in the last thirty years knowledge has made very great pro- gress, but from 1824 to 1848 Great Britain has suffered more from commercial and monetary panics, than in any threescore years of her previous history.

The births in 1846 (572,625) exceed any number ever before registered (for one year).   The males were 293,146, the females 279,479.   Of these 19,735 boys, and 18,794 girls appear to have been born out of wedlock.   Of

528,690 married women 523,313 gave birth to one child,
5349 to twins, and 27 to " triplets," while 1 woman had
4 living children. Of 38,230 women who bore children
out of wedlock 37,934 bore a single living child, 293 had
twins, and 3 had " triplets."

On the subject of births the Registrar-General is as
curt and concise, as on that of marriages he is redundant
and discursive. He gives no information, statistical,
medical, or miscellaneous, to guide the conclusions or
gratify the curiosity of the obstetric amateur.

He makes amends, however, upon the more melancholy,
though not more serious, subject of deaths. The number
in 1846 was 390,315, of which number 198,325 were
males, and 191,990 females. The number of deaths
registered in 1846 exceeded the registered number of the
preceding year by no less than 40,949, the rate of mortality having been higher than in any of the eight preceding years. The excess in 1846 arose in the latter
half of the year. In general it appears that the quarter
ending in September exhibits the smallest number of
deaths; that ending in December comes next in the
series, though that quarter and the quarter ending in
June approach very near an equality; but the quarter
ending in March is by far the most fatal of all. Tem-
perature in winter seems to have much more effect on the
duration of life than is, I think, generally supposed. The
Table inserted in the next page relates to London and the
winter quarters of 1845 and 1846. The excess of deaths,
however, in the latter part of the year appears to indicate
that the respite afforded to invalids by the mildness of
the winter of 1846 was but short. The report of the
quarter ending September, 1846, contains some striking
facts as to the comparative salubrity of town and country
life. It says: " At the last census the population of

Weeks.	Mean Temperature of the week.	Deaths, 1845.	Mean Temperature of the week.	Deaths, 1846.
1	37	1320	40	1038
2	40	1089	40	942
3	40	990	41	1003
4	39	976	48	874
5	32	970	47	878
6	33	963	43	888
7	29	1082	36	858
8	31	1097	44	907
9	37	1097	51	894
10	29	1079	47	829
11	29	1034	44	874
12	33	1132	38	832
13	47	1115	42	988

Anglesea was 38,105, the deaths in the last quarter were 160 ; the population of Gateshead was 38,747, the deaths in the same quarter 473 ; the population of Abergavenny and Newtown 77,000, the deaths 378 ; the population of Sheffield 85,000, the deaths 1039. Again, the population of the seven Welsh districts was 273,000, the deaths in the last quarter 1465 ; the population of Manchester and Salford 263,000, the deaths 3149. The population of the six districts of the south-eastern division was 218,000, the deaths in the last quarter were 1458 ; the population of Liverpool was 223,000, the deaths in the same quarter 2946."

Calculations have been made, based upon the returns of deaths for the seven years 1838—44. From these it appears that the annual deaths in the town districts of Manchester, to 1000 males living, are 37 ; in the extra-metropolitan parts of Surrey, 19 in 1000. The annual mortality of boys under five years of age is 48 in Surrey, and 148 in Manchester, to 1000 living.

The deaths registered in the *seven* years 1838—44, from a population of 163,856 inhabiting the town sub-

districts of Manchester, were 39,922. The population of
the extra-metropolitan districts of Surrey is 187,868, and
the deaths in the same period were 23,777.

The population of Surrey exceeded that of Manchester
by 24,012, yet in seven years 16,145 persons died in
Manchester over and above the number of the deaths in
Surrey. The manufacturing towns of England generally
present a similar result, as compared with the rural districts. The Registrar-General, though full to the brim
of that modern wisdom which flourishes in crowded towns
as much as human health decays, confesses that nothing
effectual has been done in those towns to put a stop to
"the disease, suffering, and death in which so many
thousands perish." The improvements, he says, chiefly
of a showy, superficial, outside character, have not reached
the homes and habits of the people. The house and
children of a labouring man can only be kept clean and
healthy by the assiduous labour of a well-trained, industrious wife, as any one who has paid the least attention to
the subject is aware. This is overlooked in Lancashire,
where the woman is often engaged in labour from home.
The consequence is, that thousands not only of the
children, but of the men and women themselves, perish of
the diseases formerly so fatal, for the same reasons, in
barracks, camps, gaols, and ships.

A member of parliament, of more notoriety than *vous*,
was wont to complain very vehemently that England was
governed by nobles and country squires, and announced
the object of his political ambition to be that of causing
England to be governed by the intelligence of the manufacturing towns. Now, as the Registrar-General does
not attribute the unhealthiness and redundant mortality
of these towns to their superior genius for government—to
that quick and feverish intelligence which " o'er informs

its tenement of clay," and wears it out, but to dirt, dissipation, and bad habits, it would perhaps be as well if this loud legislator could induce the town-bred statesmen to try their 'prentice hands upon their own immediate localities before undertaking the government of the whole empire.   It would be rather a reproach to them if, while making themselves competent to direct the destinies of States, they should have so neglected the dirt of their streets as to make life languid and precarious, and death frequent and premature.

The Report of the Registrar, presented to the Home Office at the end of July, 1849, relates to the year 1847. In that year the registered marriages were 135,845 ; the births 539,965 ; and the deaths 423,304.   According to this Report the marriages were thus distributed :—

By *special* licence	14	
By licence	17,032	
By banns	84,863	
Superintendent-Registrar's Certificate	1,968	
Not stated	16,999	
	120,876	{ Total of the Established Church.
Roman Catholics	2,961	
Other Christian denominations . .	7,483	
Superintendent-Registrar's office . .	4,258	
Quakers	83	
Jews	184	
	135,845	

These may be all the marriages *registered*, but no one can believe that there were but 83 marriages of Quakers in England in 1847, or but 184 marriages of Jews, the population of both Quakers and Jews amounting to many thousands.   Again, when we consider the multitudes of Irish who crowd the worst parts of all our great towns, can it be supposed that the Roman Catholic marriages in a year in England are under 3000 ?

It appears that the quarters ending in March and in September do not so abound in marriages as the other two quarters of the year; and the quarter which ends the year is that most generally chosen for the commencement of matrimonial life. The numbers, as furnished by the Registrar-General, are as follows :—

Years.	Quarter ending March 31.	Quarter ending June 30.	Quarter ending September 30.	Quarter ending December 31.
1845 . .	31,417	37,111	35,070	42,066
1847 . .	27,480	35,197	32,439	40,729

In 1847 the numbers were :—

Of bridegrooms registered as widowers . .	17,564
Of brides registered as widows . . .	11,602
Of marriages of bachelors with spinsters . .	112,576
,, ,, widows . .	5,705
,, widowers with spinsters . .	11,667
,, widowers with widows . .	5,897
Of men not of full age who married . .	5,566
Of women not of full age	18,118

It is a remarkable, and not at all a creditable fact, that out of 135,845 marriages registered in 1847, 42,429 of the men who were married, and 61,877 of the women, could not sign their names to the marriage-register !

In all England, the births registered in 1847 were 539,965. The following is an account of births in various localities differently circumstanced :—

		Population in 1841.
London	68,331 . .	1,948,369
Lancashire	72,315 . .	1,698,764
Yorkshire (West-Riding) .	43,366 . .	1,176,514
Yorkshire (whole county) .	56,244 . .	1,584,116
Devonshire . . .	15,489 . .	537,270
South Wales . . .	17,780 . .	529,364
Staffordshire . . .	21,471 . .	528,867
Part of Surrey . . .	14,852 . .	398,537

Population in 1841.

						Population in 1841.
Norfolk	.	.	.	.	12,560 ..	405,124
Part of Kent	.	.	.		14,210 ..	447,115
Durham	.	.	.	.	13,776 ..	326,043
Berkshire	.	.	.	.	5,529 ..	190,372
Northamptonshire	.	.	.	6,614 ..	199,208
Leicestershire	.	.	.	.	6,979 ..	220,304
Cumberland	.	.	.	.	5,737 ..	178,038
Cambridgeshire	.	.	.	6,231 ..	169,638
Hertfordshire	.	.	.	.	5,152 ..	162,394
Huntingdonshire	.	.	.	2,000 ..	55,565
Rutlandshire	.	.	.	.	711 ..	23,151

Of illegitimate births in the year 1847, the total number in England was 36,125.* Total population in 1841, 15,914,148.

The following are the returns from the same places, already selected for comparison with reference to the population, according to the returns of 1841 :—

					Population in 1841.	Illegitimate Births in 1847.
London	.	.	.	.	1,948,369 ..	2,702
Lancashire	.	.	.		1,698,764 ..	5,477
Yorkshire (West-Riding)	.		1,176,514 ..	3,047
Yorkshire (whole county)	.		1,584,116 ..	4,030
Devonshire	.	.	.	.	537,270 ..	758
South Wales	.	.	.	.	529,364 ..	1,271
Staffordshire	.	.	.	.	528,867 ..	1,409
Part of Surrey	.	.	.		398,537 ..	598
Norfolk	.	.	.	.	405,124 ..	1,295
Part of Kent	.	.	.		447,115 ..	872
Durham	.	.	.	.	326,043 ..	812
Berkshire	.	.	.	.	190,372 ..	438
Northamptonshire	.	.	.	199,208 ..	395
Leicestershire	.	.	.	.	220.304 ..	531
Cumberland	.	.	.	.	178,038 ..	629
Cambridgeshire	.	.	.	169,638 ..	442
Hertfordshire	.	.	.	.	162,394 ..	368
Huntingdonshire	.	.	.	55,565 ..	80
Rutlandshire	.	.	.	.	23,151 ..	30

* A decrease of 2404 upon the return for 1846.

It will be seen from these selections how very irregular are the proportions of illegitimate births to the population in different localities. Lancashire and Norfolk seem the most rife with this offence. As regards the latter, it would be satisfactory to have a separate return for the city of Norwich, which, notwithstanding it is the seat of episcopacy, has by no means a spotless reputation in respect to popular virtue of any kind. London seems to fare well in the account, not perhaps on account of more virtue, but of more promiscuous vice. Cumberland is bad as compared with Cambridgeshire ; and Devonshire appears virtuous in comparison with Staffordshire and South Wales. The more exclusively rural the population, the less seems to be the proportion of illegitimate births. In these districts, however, legitimacy of birth is but too frequently secured by marriage, after the moral necessity for it has become obvious.

The total number of registered deaths in England in 1847 was 423,304. I shall again select for comparison the districts already enumerated :—

	Population in 1841.	Deaths in 1847.
London	1,948,369	59,131
Lancashire . . .	1,698,764	68,765
Yorkshire (West-Riding) .	1,176,574	32,311
Yorkshire (whole county) .	1,584,116	42,860
Devonshire . . .	537,270	10,574
South Wales . . .	529,364	13,052
Staffordshire . . .	528,867	16,672
Part of Surrey . .	398,537	12,447
Norfolk . . .	405,124	8,364 *
Part of Kent . . .	447,115	10,417
Durham	326,043	9,100
Berkshire . . .	190,372	4,211

* This small proportion of deaths is unaccountable. I suspect some mistake.

	Population in 1841.	Deaths in 1847.
Northamptonshire . . .	199,208	4,486
Leicestershire	220,304	4,990
Cumberland	178,038	5,191
Cambridgeshire . . .	169,638	4,203
Hertfordshire	162,394	3,493
Huntingdonshire . . .	55,565	1,414
Rutlandshire	23,151	489

It will be seen that Lancashire, with a far less numerous population than London, exhibits a much greater
number of deaths.   On the other hand, the West Riding
of Yorkshire, which contains the manufacturing districts
of that great county, does not exhibit more than a just
proportion, as compared with the whole of the county.
South Wales, Staffordshire, and Devonshire, with their
nearly similar populations, show remarkably different
amounts of deaths.   Cumberland, with only nine-
elevenths of the population of Leicestershire, shows a
considerably greater number of deaths ; not, I am persuaded, because mountains or sea-coast air is insalubri-
ous, but because habits of deep drinking very much
prevail, not only among the lower, but among the middle
classes also of that county.

I have no great confidence in the accuracy of the numbers returned to and by the Registrar-General ; but there
is more reason to expect them to be accurate in the record
of deaths than in that of marriages or births ; for I believe
it is a necessary preliminary to interment, that a certificate
shall be produced from the District Registrar of the
death having been duly entered in his books.

CHAPTER XV.

SIR ROBERT PEEL.

IT had been sometimes said, before the lamentable death of that eminent person, as it has been frequently said since, that he was emphatically *the* man of his age. Believing this to be true, I commenced these letters upon the present condition of England with a short history of the political career of one who was so closely identified with the prevailing national tendencies since the close of the great struggle with France in 1815. At the period to which I refer, Sir Robert Peel was in the enjoyment of health and strength, of great political influence, and almost unbounded personal prosperity. I wrote as one might be supposed to write who believed the interests of his country to be deeply involved in the restoration of the policy which, from 1832 to 1842, Sir Robert Peel, with varying spirit, but upon the whole so ably and so effectually, supported—that policy which he afterwards abandoned, and which he still continued to assail. I wrote from the fulness of antagonistic feeling, and even in a spirit of resentment. The awful calamity which has since occurred has obliterated all such feeling. Justice and fidelity command that a writer upon contemporary matters should state his honest convictions concerning one whose knowledge, ability, and position, gave him so great an influence over public affairs; but the humblest person who feels he may fairly use the freedom of the press to arraign in terms somewhat indignant the conduct of an eminent public man while in the enjoyment of life, prosperity, and power, may think himself of sufficient importance to check his hand when a sudden and painful death has laid low the lofty object of his former enmity. I shall proceed to describe Sir Robert Peel with, I trust, the impartiality of a historian, and with no hostility of spirit. That hostility did exist, but it is buried in his grave.

It is true that Sir Robert Peel was the leading man of his time in England—the man whose individual character embodied and reflected the character of the age in which he lived. If this were a great age, the admission would imply the highest compliment. If this were an age of heroic devotedness to great principles—of severe virtue— of rich and romantic genius—of mighty achievement in arts, or arms, or eloquence—the panegyric implied in this admission would be complete. If, on the other hand, the age be essentially unheroic—if it be an age of compromise and of artifice—an age more prolific of prudence than of elevated feeling—an age in which generous enthusiasm is dead, and in which the value of all things is more than ever estimated by their power of procuring wealth, or of affording amusement—if this be the character of the age, then to say that this or that man is its leading type or representative, may be to confess a truth without implying a compliment.

The most popular of the public journals, which is naturally encomiastic of an age in which it has been so successful, said, when Sir Robert Peel died, that "a great age had lost a great man." Immediately afterwards, as if conscious that this not only was, but would seem to be, a doubtful proposition, unless the public could be indoctrinated with some new views of that sort of character with which the quality of greatness might be associated, the journalist proceeded in a strain which a writer, mean-

ing to be popular, would, I apprehend, have scarcely
ventured upon in any age but this, when the foundations
of all things are unsettled. "Sir Robert Peel, it is said,
besides many smaller violences to the consciences of his
followers, twice signally betrayed them—twice he broke
them up—and we now behold the result in a smitten and
divided party * * * But were his acts right or wrong?
Our own answer shall be without hesitation or reserve.
They were among the most needful and salutary acts that
ever were given man to do. *Grant that Sir Robert Peel
compassed them unfairly, and it must at least be admitted
that he had a fine taste for glory, and prized the gifts of
heaven when he saw them.* But is it possible that a man
should do such deeds, and a whole life full of them, and
yet do them basely? To confess that, were indeed a
keen satire on man, if not a presumptuous imputation on
his Maker. *But perhaps there is some semblance of a
truth in it.* Take, then, the long list of earth's worthies
from the beginning of story to the present hour, and let
us *be candid with them.* It will not be easy to find many
of that canonized throng whose patriotism has not been
alloyed with some baseness, who have not won triumphs
with subtlety, deceived nations to their good, counter-
mined against fraudulent antagonists, or otherwise sinned
against their own greatness. But when we have employed
towards other men the candour imposed upon us in the
case of Sir Robert Peel, we find these imperfections
rather a condition of humanity than a fault of the individual. Nearly all great things, even the greatest of them,
have been done in this earthly fashion. * * * Some sort
of doubleness is alleged, and some sort must be conceded,
though it may not be easily described. * * * The age
wherein we live is *interested* in vindicating the character of
its own statesman. Be he double or single, Sir Robert

Peel was the type and representative of his generation. We have lived in a period of transition, and Sir Robert Peel has guided us safely through it. England has changed as well as he." *   To estimate properly the value of the panegyric, it is only necessary to consider the moral character of this explanation and defence of it. Man is weak and defective at all times, and individual frailty has disgraced periods when public spirit was in its noblest condition. It has been, however, reserved for the present time to attempt to palliate, if not to justify, those infirmities which in former times were thought worthy of reproach, even though they might be admitted to be an almost unavoidable condition of human life. Let us compare the foregoing ingenious defence of some degree of baseness, and some sort of doubleness of character, with a very few words of Lord Bacon. "It will be acknowledged," he says, "*even by those that practise it not*, that clear and round dealing is the honour of man's nature, and that mixture of falsehood is like alloy in coin of gold or silver, which may make the metal *work the better*, but it *embaseth it* : for these windings and crooked courses are the goings of the serpent, which goeth basely upon the belly, and not upon the feet. There is no vice that doth so cover a man with shame as to be found false and perfidious." †   To say that whatever the character of Sir Robert Peel may have been, the age is interested in defending it, because he was the type and representative of the age, is as much as to say that there is an interest paramount to that of truth and justice. Now, though most men in their secret minds do in fact prefer some other interest to that of truth and justice, still no such thing is to be taught as a doctrine. It is an infirmity

---

* *The Times*, July 4, 1850.   † Essay of Truth.

and a vice, which even they who sink under it generally have had the grace to condemn.

In the posthumous notice taken of Sir Robert Peel in the House of Lords, the Duke of Wellington praised him as it might have been supposed such a man would, if he praised at all. He did not judge him like the popular journalist, but he found the materials of his panegyric in qualities which had certainly not been *generally* recognised in the character of Sir Robert Peel. " I never knew a man," said the illustrious Duke, " in whose truth and justice I had a more lively confidence, or in whom I saw a more invariable desire to promote the public service. In the whole course of my communication with him I never knew an instance in which he did not show the strongest attachment to truth ; and I never saw, in the whole course of my life, the smallest reason for suspecting that he stated anything which he did not firmly believe to be the fact." Yet the venerable Duke could not have been ignorant – though he may have forgotten it at the moment—that no man was so much in the habit as Sir Robert Peel was of giving different accounts of the very same thing at different times. Take, for instance, his account of the operation of the Corn Laws upon the condition of the people in 1839, and compare it with his description of the very same thing in 1846. If he was always careful to speak the exact truth as it appeared to him at the time, truth must to his mind at sundry times have taken extremely different shapes.

Lord Brougham, in speaking of the deceased statesman, seemed to be impressed chiefly with a sense of the sacrifices he had made. " Differing," he said, " as we may differ, on the point whether he was right or wrong—disputing, as we may dispute, on the results of his policy— we must all agree that to the course which he firmly be-

lieved to be advantageous to his country he firmly
adhered, and that in pursuing it he made sacrifices, compared with which all the sacrifices exacted from public
men by a sense of public duty, which I have ever known
or read of, sink into nothing."

Upon this point of sacrifices Lord Stanley made a very
remarkable observation, which will be found in the following extract from the speech which he was unexpectedly
called upon to deliver in consequence of the notice taken
of Sir R. Peel's death in the House of Lords :—" I never
was one of those who attached unworthy motives to a
course of conduct which I cannot but deeply lament.   I
believe that in that step which led me to differ from him,
he was actuated by a sincere and a conscientious desire
to obtain that which he believed to be a public good.
Mistaken as he was in that view, I am satisfied that upon
that occasion, as upon all others, the public good was the
leading principle of his life ; and that to promote the welfare of his country he was prepared to make, and did
actually make, every sacrifice.   *In some cases those sacrifices were so extensive, that I hardly know whether the great
and paramount object of his country's good was a sufficient
reason to exact them from any public man.* * * * we are
deprived of the services of that great, powerful, laborious
intellect—of that unflinching diligence—of that unsparing
application of all his best talents—his health, his strength,
and all his great powers to the interests of his country.
* * * No one will deny to my lamented friend the
praise of having been an able, an assiduous, and a conscientious servant of his country."   This is discriminating
praise, spoken at a time and on an occasion when any
other tone than that of praise, would have been unbe-
coming.   But in the House of Commons, the favourite
scene of the departed statesman's exertions, his eulogium

was no less ably pronounced by Lord John Russell, who had so long been his opponent, but who had in later years been much indebted to his assistance. "In speaking of that great man," he said, "it is impossible not to lament that hereafter this House will no longer be guided by that long and large experience of public affairs, by that profound knowledge, by that oratorical power, by that copious and yet exact memory, with which this House was wont to be enlightened and instructed and guided. * * * There can, I think, be no doubt that, however history may deal with the wisdom of the course that he pursued, it will be admitted that on two great occasions, when he held power undisturbed, and apparently almost without a rival, and when he proposed measures to this House which shook, and after a short time subverted the government, he did so from those motives of deep love to his country which ever distinguished him."

Rightly to appreciate these passages, we must take them as parts of funeral orations, pronounced while every heart was affected with surprise, pain, and sorrow, at the abrupt and deplorable event of Sir Robert Peel's death. Every one felt that England had been, by the cruel accident of a moment, deprived of a man of the greatest capacity, learning, industry, and eminence. The spirit of criticism was paralyzed by grief and pity; and it was, indeed, no time for public orators to hint at faults. But if, even at the distance of a few months from the sad event of his death, such were the general judgment upon Sir Robert Peel; if still, taking him as he was, with his merits and his faults, he should be spoken of with such strong expressions of unqualified regard and esteem, by men of the greatest eminence in the senate, in the liberal professions, in the mercantile world, and in the press, I should not shrink from expressing doubts of the reason-

ableness and justice of judgments so encomiastic, I
should be inclined to account for them by a vitiated state
of the general mind, so far as regards public affairs; by
a want of heroic attachment to high principle; by the fact
that we have at present upper classes of society at once
disdainful and mean, and middle classes worshipping what
is safest, or what seems so, in the present busy dance of
things, rather than what is permanently just and honourable, and therefore safest in the end.   Lord John Russell
refers to two great occasions on which Sir Robert Peel
proposed measures that shook the party, and after a short
time subverted the government, to which he himself belonged.   The measures thus alluded to were those of
which he had previously been the leading opponent.
Why, then, did *he* propose them? why abandon the
opposite policy which he had so long extolled?   Was it
pure love of country, as Lord John Russell says it was?
Even if it were, it will probably be admitted that it was
equally from love of country that he had previously taken
exactly the opposite course.   At one time or other, then,
his love must have been an exceedingly erroneous love.
It is, indeed, not easy to understand how mere love of
country should prompt to the adoption of theories diame-
trically opposite, and that, not at distances of some years,
when the actual circumstances of the country might have
changed, but suddenly, and within a few weeks.   Does
not, then, historic truth seek some hypothesis better calculated to explain the unquestionable inconsistency?
May it not be that, with all Sir Robert Peel's powers and
accomplishments, his riches, his erudition, his taste, his
parliamentary skill, he was yet wanting in that moral
courage which will stand against any odds for the sake of
right?   Or, perhaps, he had no distinct perception of
what was morally right in matters political, divorced from

what seemed practically to conduce to present safety. And being thus minded ; seeing what he had upheld as right ; attacked by men of great activity, energy, and popular following ; and having an overweening disrespect for his own political party, in comparison with what he thought his own more enlarged views and superior abilities ; galled, moreover, as he no doubt was, throughout by their want of *perfect* confidence in himself, while deficient of means and courage themselves to take the lead, he deemed it the more practicable policy to yield to opponents, and he did yield accordingly.   Instead of trying to infuse some heroism into his own party ; instead of showing the people at large that *their* interest was concerned in the maintenance of Conservative principles, he accepted the cry of organized agitation as the voice of the people, and, right or wrong, to *that* he submitted as to the voice of Deity.

It is remarkable that, since the country has lost Sir Robert Peel, the extreme democratic party appear determined to claim him as their own, and to associate his name with their endeavours to subvert, in even a more extensive degree than they have yet been subverted, the ancient ruling influences of this country.   Since his lamented death I have seen the walls of a metropolitan borough placarded with electioneering bills, which described Sir Robert Peel as " the great founder of the system of free trade," and which called upon the people to testify their regard *for him* by returning to parliament a person who pledged himself to support every democratic extravagance, and every violence to existing institutions, which has yet been dreamt of in the brains most fertile of such projects.   These politicians have convenient powers of forgetfulness ; and, though Sir Robert Peel was a public man for forty years, they have no memory of anything he did, except in the last four of them.   I

have seen a public letter from Mr. Cobden, formerly of
the Anti-Corn-Law League, in which he quotes, for the
admiration of the people, a passage from Sir Robert
Peel's speech of the 29th June, 1846—that passage in
which he spoke of the good-will with which he hoped his
name would be remembered " in those places which are
the abode of men whose lot it is to labour and to earn
their daily bread by the sweat of their brow, when they
should recruit their exhausted strength with abundant
and untaxed food, the sweeter because no longer leavened
with a sense of injustice."   Mr. Cobden quoted this, not
that the people might derive therefrom a lesson of the
inconsistency of even the most eminent men—not that
they might remark how this eminent statesman claimed
credit for removing what he then called injustice, omitting
altogether the consideration that, if it were injustice, he,
more than any other man, had himself maintained and
prolonged it—not for such a purpose as this, did Mr.
Cobden quote the passage; but in order to make the
people feel what a debt of gratitude they owed to the
deceased statesman.   To me, however, it seemed that it
would have been more *to the purpose* if Mr. Cobden had
quoted another passage of the same speech, namely, that
one in which a very elaborate personal compliment was
paid to Mr. Cobden himself.   I thought so, because I
could not forget that after Sir Robert Peel's conversion
to the policy of repealing the corn laws was avowed, but
before any compliment had been paid by him in parliament to Mr. Richard Cobden, that gentleman did not
express himself as if much affected by admiration of the
new champion of complete free trade in corn.   Addressing
his constituents at Stockport on the 12th December,
1845, and in allusion to Sir Robert Peel's change of
policy, Mr. Cobden said, in his own peculiarly emphatic

manner, " I give him no credit (for I have seen too much of him) for any feeling of remorse on account of the injury his system has inflicted on the country." And again, in the same speech, not at all dwelling upon the gratitude which the people owed him for his change of policy, but, on the contrary, thinking only of the resistance which, up to that time, he had given to the policy which Mr. Cobden approved, that gentleman said of Sir Robert Peel, " it was he who headed that gang of plunderers and monopolists ; he forced himself into the Queen's council, knowing right well that the very cause of the misery in this district was the cause which he came into power to uphold." This was said in the harsh month of December ; but when the warmth of July had arrived, Mr. Cobden proclaimed in the House of Commons that the Right Honourable Baronet was entitled to a larger amount of popular esteem and gratitude than had ever been awarded to any other minister. Now, the opinions of the Right Honourable Baronet, both new and old, happened to be the same in July, 1846, as they were in December, 1845 ; but in the mean time he had, in his place in parliament, and in a very unusual manner, personally complimented Mr. Cobden. Thus it is that such leaders of the people as Mr. Cobden are induced to scatter blame or praise. Blind guides indeed are they, and reckless and impetuous as they are blind.

No one can be more conscious than I am of the great difficulty of accounting for the phenomena of character displayed in Sir Robert Peel's history, or even of describing them accurately. It is rare, indeed, to find such uncommon abilities and such high respectability in every relation of private life, combined with such apparent want of fixed principle in regard to politics, which formed nevertheless the great business of the life of Sir R. Peel. The most

important distinction between him and other eminent men
does not satisfactorily or fully account for this inconstancy
in respect to his views of political right and wrong. That
distinction lay in his unsympathizing nature—in his want
of that warmth and ardour which casts the glow of genius
upon the conclusions of the human reason, and enables a
man in high station to carry the public with him, not by
mere persuasion of their understanding, but by involving
them in the torrent of feeling which he is able to set in
motion. Nay more, there is a *wisdom* of the heart, even
in statesmanship, and without it no statesman, I am persuaded, can be truly great, though he may be very important and very formidable.

In comprehensiveness of knowledge bearing upon public
matters, Sir R. Peel was almost equal to Burke, and in
the finish of academic education he was much his superior;
but how infinitely inferior in imagination, in feeling, in
sentiment, and, in my opinion, even in taste. With regard to the political institutions of his country, Sir Robert
Peel seemed to think they were worthy of respect only as
they were of demonstrable utility, or were approved of
by public opinion for the time being. Mr. Burke regarded them with a sentiment drawn from religion. "We
procure *reverence*," he said, "to our civil institutions on
the principle upon which nature teaches us to revere
individual men; on account of their age, and on account
of those from whom they are descended. This idea of a
liberal descent inspires us with a sense of habitual native
dignity. By this means our liberty becomes a noble freedom. It carries an imposing and majestic aspect. All your
sophisters cannot produce anything better adapted to preserve a rational and manly freedom than the course we
have pursued who have chosen our nature rather than our
speculations, our breasts rather than our inventions, for

the great conservatories and magazines of our rights and
privileges." There are, I know, persons who, in these
days of cleverness and calculation, would say they could
find nothing in such a passage but fine words. I believe,
however, that the sentiment of reverence for political institutions is a very important and very practical political
reality—that a habitual and native dignity of thought in
regard to political action is also an important reality, and
that the idea that our British liberty ought to be a *noble*
freedom, is an idea pregnant with infinite practical advantage. Such, however, was the mental temperament of
Sir Robert Peel, that I believe he had little sympathy
with such realities. What could be demonstrated like a
theorem in mathematics he admitted, because his understanding was clear; what appeared to him to be in accordance with public opinion he submitted to, because he
held *that* to be paramount to any other principle which
determines right or wrong in politics ; but the noble sympathy with what is abstractedly great and good—that
sympathy which makes of a mere statesman a patriot and
a hero—that ardent communion of sentiment which makes
the head of a party the leader of a political brotherhood,
with no other thought but that of standing or falling together—Sir Robert Peel, I believe, had not. His reasoning faculties were powerful, but his affections were cold.
He was wanting not only in firmness of principle, but in
animation and high spirit: he had, however, wonderful
powers of memory, lucidity, plausibility, and an emphatic
elocution which forced its way to the convictions of men
upon whom the higher order of eloquence would have
been lost. Though he was liable to become ponderous,
and over elaborate, yet in general he was very fluent, full
of information, dexterous in the use of it, and, sometimes,
he was happy in a joke. But his speeches, as well as his

character, were wanting in imagination and enthusiasm; his energy was without fire, and his wit had not the charm of brilliancy.

It is time, however, to take a glance at the more prominent points of his history. From a boy he was painstaking and industrious. At Harrow school he gained whatever distinction was there to be obtained; and at Oxford University he took his degree with the highest honours that academical merit can achieve. He entered Parliament very early, and in 1811 voted against the currency theories of Mr. Horner, which afterwards he so conspicuously espoused. He very soon took office as Under Secretary of State, but first became prominent in official life as Chief Secretary for Ireland, where he took the lead of the Anti-Catholic or Orange party. He assumed the same position in England after he became Secretary of State for the Home Department. He refused to continue in office in 1827, when Mr. Canning was made Prime Minister, and he did so on no other publicly-avowed ground than the favour with which that gentleman was understood to regard the claims of the Roman Catholics to what they called emancipation. Yet in the beginning of 1829 Mr. Peel, as leading Minister in the House of Commons, introduced a far more complete and sweeping measure of concession to the Roman Catholics than any of those against which he had from time to time so earnestly, and no doubt so sincerely, protested. He declined making part of Mr. Canning's government, in 1827, because of the abstract danger of acting with a Prime Minister whose opinion was in favour of Roman Catholic emancipation, though the Minister did not intend to bring that measure forward. In less than eighteen months afterwards, having in the mean time stepped over Mr. Canning's grave to the leadership of the House of

Commons, he prevailed upon himself to propose Roman
Catholic emancipation to that House, and, in the teeth of
all his former arguments, maintained that it was politically expedient that the point should be yielded, and the
constitutional exclusion be abolished.*

Nearly ten years before this he had turned round in a
similar manner upon the currency question, by taking the
lead in a measure opposed to his own former views and to
the policy which his father still warmly supported. Sir
Robert Peel the elder was a man of great practical sagacity, who had made an immense fortune in the cotton
manufacture when the profits of it were very high. The
elder Sir Robert had considerable heartiness in his demeanour as a public man; he presented petitions from
men of his own class against his son's measure, and supported them in earnest speeches; he described the measure as " destructive of the commercial interests of the
country," and represented the undue advantage to the
rich and the injury to the poor, which from that measure
were likely to arise : but it was all in vain; Mr. Peel the
son had been of his father's opinion, and had acted upon
it in Parliament, but he had changed to the opposite side,
avowing that he did so " without shame or remorse," and
he persevered in carrying what so many still regard as
the fatal currency measure of 1819.

He opposed the Reform Bills of 1831 and 1832, and
argued that the revolution which they embodied was

---

* Though it may fairly be said that Mr. Peel, having made up his
mind in 1829 that " emancipation" must be granted, could not well
avoid, under the peculiar circumstances of the time, proposing it himself
to the House of Commons; what shall we say of the fact that, although
the Roman Catholic clergy and others in Ireland lost no time in trampling
upon the "securities" provided by the act of 1829, Mr. Peel never once
made the slightest effort to enforce them? He allowed them to be trodden
under foot with an absolute passiveness.

fraught with present injustice and future evil; but when
the Bill of 1832 was carried, he lost no time in declaring
his allegiance to the new arrangement, and in exhorting
his friends to take all possible advantage of it for building
up again the political power which it had so seriously
shaken. This is a part of his policy which received the
special eulogy of Lord John Russell in the very able discourse which the noble lord addressed to the House of
Commons upon Sir Robert Peel's death. After alluding
to the occasions on which that gentleman had shaken the
party, and subverted the governments to which he himself
belonged, Lord John Russell proceeded thus :—

" Of those occasions I shall not speak, but there is one
part of his career in which I was most deeply interested,
and of which perhaps I may be allowed to speak, because
I feel it due to him to pay a tribute that hitherto has not
been paid to his deserts. I allude to the period which
elapsed from 1833 to 1841. After the contest which took
place on the Reform Bill, it was to be dreaded that those
who had opposed that Bill, expecting results from it calamitous to the country, might have retired in disgust from
public contests, and thereby have left the war of classes to
be carried on, which might have inflicted permanent injury
upon this country. I consider Sir R. Peel to have been
the man who prevented such an occurrence taking place.
Although he had opposed the Reform Bill, yet he addressed himself manfully to the situation in which he was
placed. He addressed himself to the country on behalf
of the principles of which he was the most eloquent de-
fender, and brought back again the various powers of the
state into harmony, and showed himself not afraid of
abiding by the verdict of the people on the measure that
had been carried."

Lord John Russell having taken a very prominent part

in carrying into effect a measure so dangerous that it depended—according to his own statement—upon the conduct of the political opponents whom he had triumphed over and offended, whether the measure should or should not inflict permanent injury upon his country, it is very easy to see why *he* should be particularly grateful for the part which his leading opponent took after that measure was passed; but I think it is very questionable whether the friends of the British monarchy, and the more judicious friends of the British nation, will hereafter think that Sir R. Peel took the best course in submitting so completely as he did to the democratic revolution of 1832. I say this, though I am as thoroughly convinced as I can be of any theory of political justice and prudence, that a reform of the representation of the people, and of the mode of electing members of Parliament, not only was necessary in 1832, but had been a great deal too long delayed. In the peroration of his most important speech against the Reform Bill (September 22, 1831) Sir R. Peel said :—

"If, Sir, the people of England, after meditating on these things—on the condition of foreign states—on the signs and indications at home of the probable consequences of this measure of reform, still insist on its completion—their deliberate resolve will, no doubt, ultimately prevail. I shall bow to their judgment with the utmost respect, but my own opinions will remain unchanged. To all the penalties of *maintaining those opinions*—the incapacity for public service—the loss of public favour—the withdrawal of public confidence—I can, and must submit. The people have the power and the right to inflict them, but they have neither the power nor the right to inflict that heavier penalty, of involving *me* in their responsibility—of making *me* an instrument for accomplishing that act, by which we—the life-renters of these institutions that have

made our country the freest, the happiest, the most powerful nation of the universe—are to cut off from those who
are to succeed us the inheritance of what we ourselves
enjoyed."

Of these sentiments I do not approve, because I believe
it is as erroneous to assume that the people have " a right "
to do whatever they will in respect to their own political
institutions, as it is to assume that a human being may do
what he will with his own life.   The political institutions
as well as the life which a man inherits are sacred trusts ;
and they ought to be improved according to the principles
of religion, justice, and prudence ; but they ought not to
be wantonly tampered with or destroyed upon the mere
impulse of will—of will which may be based on ignorance,
and may be inflamed by passion.

But Sir Robert Peel, having said that he would maintain the opinions which led him to oppose the Reform
Bill, ought, I think, to have done so.   No doubt it was
his duty to submit to the law, as soon as it *was* law ; but
he ought as a legislator to have temperately but firmly
protested against the policy of the law, and avowed his
intention of appealing to the people's better judgment, so
soon as that better judgment should return, in order to
remedy the enormous error which, in 1832, was committed.

If it can be supposed that concurrently with such
avowed political views, the circumstances and the state of
public feeling from 1841 to 1845, could have come round,
how glorious might the political work of Sir Robert Peel
then have been !   How much nobler, how much more
useful, to have in 1845 rebuilt the fabric of the popular
constitution of Great Britain upon sound foundations, than
to have fostered the frantic, speculative spirit of the time,
and to have fed the monstrous appetite of the money-
makers to such repletion as brought on the disease of

1847, and the fearful crash of mercantile credit in that fatal year.

*   *   *   *

The policy, however, of submitting to the Reform Bill as soon as it became inevitable, and of making the most of the new Constitution, such as it was, appeared to succeed; and the "Reform" government having become weakened by dissensions, it was overthrown towards the end of 1834. Sir Robert Peel was then at Rome. He was sent for, and quickly returned to be made Prime Minister. He dissolved Parliament, but he failed to obtain a majority in the House of Commons, the Speakership being carried against him in the first division, and he only held office till April, 1835; but these few months ought to be regarded as by far the brightest in his whole career. He fought bravely and ably against a superior force. At that time there was no coquetting with opponents, no yielding to the enemy. He maintained his cause with spirit and with honour, as long as he could, and when he found certainly that the circumstances he had to contend with were too strong for him, he yielded the position to his adversaries. Thenceforward, as leader of a powerful opposition, he maintained the views which he had propounded as a minister. The whole nation applauded the spirited struggle of Sir Robert Peel's first essay as prime minister, and had he continued to maintain the firmness of character which he displayed during that brief career, he would have gone down to posterity with no cloud upon his fame.

But this was not to be his fate, because it was not in his nature. So long indeed as he continued leader of the Conservative Opposition, namely, from the spring of 1835 to the autumn of 1841, he held his ground with great energy and skill, and gradually accumulated the parliamentary strength which at length placed him in a position of extraordinary power. In 1835 the numerical strength of the Conservatives in the House of Commons was 280 ; in 1836, 288 ; in 1837, 310 ; in 1838, 315 ; in 1839, 318 ; in 1840, 325 ; and at last the point was turned in 1841, the Conservatives having increased to 368 as soon as the Whigs declared for a low fixed duty on foreign corn. Sir Robert Peel managed his forces with equal dexterity and perseverance, and in several pitched parliamentary battles he all but won the day, long before his final triumph. In 1837, upon the Church Rate Bill, when 570 members voted, the Whig majority was only five. On the 6th of May, 1839, upon the Jamaica Bill, when 583 members voted, the government majority was equally low, and then Lord Melbourne's ministry resigned ; but as their wives and sisters who held offices in the Royal household did not follow the example, and were supported by the Queen in their determination to remain, Sir R. Peel declined to proceed in forming a new government, and Lord Melbourne and his friends came back again rather to office than to power, to struggle on with their scant majority. They made alterations in the Jamaica Bill to render it more palatable, and increased their majority from five to ten. The very next day, however, in a division upon the education question, when 555 members voted, their majority fell to five ; and in another division upon the same subject, which included a grant of money, within a few days afterwards, the majority went down to two ! These were triumphs for a leader of opposition ; and the offence given by Sir R. Peel, both on the Currency question and the question of Roman Catholic Emancipation, seemed to be forgiven or forgotten. Nothing perhaps so much contributed to this as the steady,

intelligent, and, as it seemed, the sincere and earnest
support which Sir R. Peel gave to the landed interest.
His advocacy of Protection to agriculture had all the
appearance of firm and decided conviction that the policy
was just and sound. His speech of 1839, upon the Corn
Laws, was perhaps the ablest he ever made in the House
of Commons. It was that speech which he concluded by
" peremptorily refusing to throw the protection secured to
agriculture by the existing law, into *the lottery of legislation*, in the faint hope that they might by chance draw the
prize of a better Corn Bill." He did not seem to dream
of the possibility of a system in which there should be no
protection at all. After quoting the glowing descriptions
given by his opponents of the means which foreign countries
possessed of supplying England with cheap corn, he proceeded to say :—" Here, then, would be a boundless prospect of foreign supply. But what chance would domestic
agriculture have of competing with these happy regions ?
*Who would employ capital on domestic improvement when
it could be transferred with such profit to fertilize the rich
wastes of central and northern Europe ?* There we are
told land pays scarcely any rent, labour is at the rate of
fivepence a day. Steam is diminishing every hour the
distances which separate nations, and skill and machinery
will stimulate to an increase of a hundredfold the natural
capabilities of a neglected but most fertile soil. *All this
may be consolatory enough to the manufacturer, but it
should be whispered into his ear exclusively, for it is calculated to fill with dismay the proprietor and occupier of
land at home.*" Who could have imagined that within
a few brief years the man who by these arguments had
risen to the height of power, would tell the House of Commons that he expected the gratitude of the people for
overthrowing that protection to domestic agriculture which

was a tax upon their daily food? Who could have expected that he would in a few years denounce protection
to agriculture as a public injury, and assert that an intelligent and abundant outlay of capital upon the British
soil was the only sure and legitimate method of meeting
foreign competition? Towards the close of his speech of
1839 he alluded, in terms more glowing than he was wont
to use, to the considerations apart from those of political
economy, and, as he truly said, far above it, which determined his mind in favour of Protection. There were, he
said, " *higher considerations* involved than those of mercantile profit, which should lead us to doubt the policy of
making this great country more dependent than it is on
foreign supplies. Admitting that the extension of intercourse, by the reciprocation of benefits and the sense of
common interests is a great guarantee for peace, still we
should not implicitly rely on its efficacy. We should
remember that within our own short experience the insane
ambition of a single man, bent upon our destruction, had for
many years overruled all the impediments which the love of
gain, or the prosecution of peaceful industry among millions
of men, could offer to his reckless course. We should find,
even in the present state of the world, in North America,
in Africa, in Spain, in the Gulf of Mexico, ample proof that
*the interests and influence of commerce will not always ensure
the peaceful arbitration of differences.* Could you prove
to us that the true principles of mercantile dealing required
us to purchase corn in the cheapest market, and to withdraw the capital which has fertilized the inferior soils of
this country for the purpose of applying it to the rich but
unprofitable wastes of Poland—still we should hesitate.
We should remember with pain the cheerful and smiling
prospects which were *thus to be obscured.* We should
view with regret cultivation receding from the hill top

which it has climbed under the influence of protection, and from which it surveys with joy the progress of successful toil.   If you convinced us that your most sanguine hopes would be realized—that this country would become the great workshop of the world—would blight, *through the cheapness of food and the demand for foreign corn*, the manufacturing industry of every other country—would present the dull succession of enormous manufacturing towns, connected by railways, intersecting the abandoned tracts *which it was no longer profitable to cultivate*—we should not forget, among all these presages of complete happiness, that it has been under the influence of protection to agriculture, continued for two hundred years, that the fen has been drained, the wild heath reclaimed, the health of a whole people improved, their life prolonged, and all this not at the expense of manufacturing prosperity, but concurrently with its wonderful advancement." Such were the sound, the sagacious, the high-minded reasonings and convictions, in 1839, of Sir R. Peel, who afterwards stigmatised these landowners, or at least some of them, who remained constant to the sentiments he himself had taught them, as persons who preferred their own sordid interests to the advantage of the public !   Nor can inexperience be pleaded in excuse for his opinions of 1839, if they were erroneous, for in that same year he appealed, in reply to an address from Shrewsbury, to his public services of *thirty years*.   Again, in 1841, when some persons took the liberty of doubting that his real opinions were always fully and fairly expressed, he denied the charge with apparent indignation, and broke forth in the tone of a man against whom an injurious suspicion had been whispered, to the following effect :—" *Take the Corn Laws :* I should like to know who has stood more forward than I have done in defence of the existing Corn

Law ? I should like to know whether any man looking at
these debates can really have a doubt that my desire is
to maintain a just and adequate protection to the agricultural interest ?   Have I not contended for this while I
admitted, and always will admit, that there may be some
details of the present law that require alteration ?"   At
the conclusion of his speech he scornfully and indignantly
reproached the Melbourne and Russell ministry with being
about to dissolve the Parliament on a cry of *cheap bread*,
and with thus " arraying classes of the community in
bitter discord against each other, and stirring up society
to its foundation."   All this was in 1841, but it was
before he had attained to supreme power by the ardent
support of the country party in the general election of that
year. In September he became prime minister, and never
more was "forward in defence of the existing corn-law,"
though he continued for four years longer an advocate of
the principle of protection.

The result of the appeal of the Melbourne Ministry
"to the country" in 1841 was a House of Commons
which, on the first trial of strength (27th of August),
exibited an adverse majority of 91.   The ministers mustered but 269 ; the opposition, headed by Sir R. Peel,
numbered 360.   His point was gained.   He was now
placed at the head of the government, with powerful
majorities in both houses of parliament, full of confidence in his political wisdom, and full of hope in his
administrative skill.   From that moment, however, his
ambition seemed to be turned towards the gaining of the
favour of those whose views and measures he had previously opposed.   In the contests of the Conservative
opposition with the government upon Irish policy, which
had led to some of the closest divisions of the session,
Lord Eliot (since Earl of St. Germans), a man personally

amiable and without that kind of ability which excites
jealousy, had voted with the minority, and against his
party.   Lord Eliot, however, was selected by Sir R. Peel
to fill the office of Chief Secretary for Ireland.   This was
the first symptom of reaction.   It was, however, but little
noticed amid the general triumph of party and the
obvious difficulties of such a general allotment of place.
The session of 1842 showed, however, that the sentiments
towards the landed interest, which appeared to have
actuated Sir R. Peel as leader of the opposition, were
already considerably modified.   In the last great speech
he made while in that position, he claimed credit for
having been always forward in support of the corn law
of 1828 ; but his first recurrence to the subject as minister
was on the 9th of February, 1842, when he proposed the
repeal of that law, and the substitution of another, containing a considerably lower range of protective duties.
I heard the ably-constructed speech in which he introduced this new plan ; and, from the cold and silent attention with which it was received, I doubted whether the
minister had not already lost favour with his party.   The
debate upon it, however, was adjourned to the 14th, and
by that time the Conservatives made up their minds to
give decided support to the measure.   The Whig opposition mustered only 226 votes against it, while the Conservatives triumphed with 349.   The measures of finance,
rendered necessary by the serious defalcations of the five
preceding years, afforded further indications of a tendency
towards carrying into practical effect the theories of the
politicians who called themselves liberal.   An income-
tax of 7*d.* in the pound, for three years, was proposed,
though to any such financial expedient on the part of the
Whigs Sir Robert Peel had previously offered decided
opposition.   It was carried expressly on the condition

that it was a temporary financial expedient, rendered
necessary by the peculiar exigency of the times, and by
the impossibility of finding any other less onerous tax
which would bring in the required addition to the revenue.
It came out four years afterwards, however, in a letter
from Sir R. Peel to the burghers of the Prussian town of
Elbing, the outlet of the great wheat-growing valley of
the Vistula, who thanked him for having repealed the
British corn laws, that he had in his own mind certain
views which he withheld from the House of Commons
when proposing the income-tax. He announced to the
burghers of Elbing, in August, 1846, that "the object of
that tax was not only to make good a deficit, but also to
lay the foundation of a more just system of taxation, by
putting an end to duties on many kinds of produce necessary to the comforts of the working classes." When, in
1845, the three years for which the income-tax had been
enacted were about to expire, Sir R. Peel renewed that
tax, and repealed a very large amount of taxation on
foreign produce. A comparison of the Elbing letter with
Sir R. Peel's statements to parliament at the time the
income-tax of 1842 was proposed, suggests doubts of his
ministerial candour as perplexing as those which arise
from any other event in his history as a public man.
Amongst the early measures of this session of 1842 was
one for admitting the import of cattle, meat, and other
provisions from abroad at low duties. This was a direct
blow at the profits of graziers and farmers, and obviously
led to a diminution of the funds out of which rents of
land are paid. Sir R. Peel, however, consoled the country
gentlemen, who looked dark at the prospect of a heavy
mulct for income-tax, by an assurance that, owing to his
new tariff, they might save as much in the *cost* of their
provisions as they would have to pay in the form of

income-tax! Some of them perhaps remembered that they lived *by the sale* of provisions.

The affairs of the nation, and especially financial affairs, which had worn a very gloomy aspect during the latter years of the Melbourne administration, brightened in a wonderful manner under the Peel government. Confidence revived; money became abundant; funds were easily raised on credit; and in 1844 there arose a fever of speculation in railway undertakings which proceeded gradually to a kind of universal madness, which was at its height in the summer of 1845. This madness the successful minister did nothing to check. On the contrary, he gave encouragement even personally to the extravagance of railway manifestations. He patronised a second railway-line to Manchester, because some half-hour or forty minutes might thus be saved in travelling from the metropolis of the empire to the metropolis of cotton spinning, and declared he would be ready to patronise a third, if a third could be found to shorten the time by another hour. He even went so far as to join in the ceremonial of commencing the works of the " Trent Valley " line, and himself " turned the first sod," amidst much public acclamation. Alas! for those who were thus induced to embark their money in such undertakings. No tongue can tell—no pen describe—the privation and misery which have resulted from the loss of inherited property or hard-earned savings invested in these undertakings, to the *excess* of which the minister of 1845 lent such fatal encouragement! Meanwhile the Anti-Corn-Law League, headed by men of great activity and audacity, and supported by very large contributions from wealthy manufacturing magnates, made great progress in agitating the public mind, and impressing the populace with the most extravagant notions of the injury inflicted

on them by the corn-laws, and of the immense benefits
which would arise from their repeal. The minister did
not venture to propose any measure in order to check this
organised agitation, nor did the landed proprietors appear
to take very particular interest in answering the uproar
which assailed them from the towns. It seemed as if
they considered themselves quite secure in having a
government composed of Sir Robert Peel and his political
friends. Their attention, however, was aroused when, in
November, 1845, Lord J. Russell, who was paying a
visit in Edinburgh, startled the country by publishing a
letter to his London constituents, containing the information that *his* mind had undergone a complete change
upon the subject of protection to agriculture, and that he
had become a convert to the expediency of a complete
repeal of the corn-laws. In a few days followed a similar
declaration from Lord Morpeth. Rumour then arose
that Sir R. Peel was thoroughly frightened, and the *sen-
sation* reached its climax when, on the 4th of December,
the *Times* newspaper deliberately announced that early
in January the Duke of Wellington in the Lords, and
Sir R. Peel in the Commons, would propose a total
repeal of the corn-laws. The journals which had considered themselves in the confidence of the government
gave unhesitatingly a direct contradiction to this statement. It turned out, however, to be true that Sir R.
Peel had made up his mind to overthrow the policy of
which he had so long been the leading champion, but
had not found it possible as yet to persuade more than a
minority of the members of his cabinet to agree with him.
Nor was this very remarkable when it is considered that
only on the 10th of June preceding he had stated to the
House of Commons that " the agricultural question was
one which could not be legislated upon without the fullest

consideration of the interests which had grown up under
a state of law which had existed for 150 years—that
under the protective system there had grown up a relation
between landlord and tenant and labourer which did not
rest on merely pecuniary considerations—that it would
be a great evil if land and its cultivation were looked on
in the light of a mere commercial speculation—that in a
social and moral point of view such a change would be
deeply to be regretted—that it would alter the character
of the country, and be accompanied by social evils which
no pecuniary gain—no strict application of a purely commercial principle could compensate." Such were the
opinions avowed by Sir R. Peel upon the very last occasion that he discussed the corn laws in the House of
Commons previous to his proposal to the cabinet to yield
all that the most extreme of the commercialists demanded.
On the 11th of December the whole cabinet resigned,
and Lord J. Russell was authorised to form a new
government.   After an ineffectual effort and a week's
consideration, the noble lord gave up the attempt, finding
it impossible to assure himself of adequate support from
those who, since August, 1841, had formed the majority
against him.   Under these circumstances the government
was again placed in the hands of Sir R. Peel; and his
colleagues (with the exception of Lord Stanley)—influ-
enced, it is said, by the fear that, if they did not consent
to serve, Mr. Cobden, with his extreme friends, would
have become ministers—rejoined the premier to carry
into effect that revolution in the affairs of the landed
interest which it had been for some years their chief
business to oppose.

Supposing the conversion of Sir Robert Peel to have been
sincere as it was sudden, and to have been founded on
reasonable and creditable grounds, still it must be ad-

mitted, I think, that he had no right to take advantage
of the circumstances which the country had placed at his
disposal when it considered him a Protectionist, in order
to do the work of an adversary of Protection.   The least
he could in justice have done, was to have dissolved the
Parliament, and to have taken his chance with those
whom the country would have returned after being aware
of the change in his opinions.   He did not do this, but
used all the influence he possessed as a Minister to induce
to vote against the Corn Laws members whom he well
knew to have been elected in order to support the Corn
Laws.   This was, I cannot but think, an offence against
public morality and justice which ought to be, and which
will be, remembered against Sir Robert Peel.

Parliament met on the 22nd of January, 1846, and Sir
Robert Peel made the avowal that he could no longer
maintain the Corn Laws.   He made no apology—he exhibited no contrition, nor did he give any satisfactory
explanation of the change in his policy.   He said he considered that under the existing apprehension of famine in
Ireland the Corn Laws could not be maintained ; that if
they were merely suspended it would be impossible to
bring them into force again, when the emergency ceased,
and therefore it was better to surrender them at once.
There was no force in this explanation, because, according
to the law of the sliding scale, as it stood, the duties on
corn would pass away before famine prices were arrived
at, and the ports would be as open (while prices were
high) as the most extreme free-trader could wish.   Moreover, the year 1846 was *not* a year of extreme scarcity in
Ireland.   It is difficult to believe that the explanation
was sincere.   No reasonable man who sifts the circumstances of the time can avoid the suspicion, if not the
conviction, that it was under some feeling of alarm not

fully stated to the public, or with some ulterior object
assiduously concealed, that Sir Robert Peel determined to
yield to the storm of agitation against the Corn Laws
which the manufacturers had raised, and of which it had
appeared that, at last, the leading Whigs were not unwilling to avail themselves. The insincerity of the excuse
for repeal was, as it seems to me, sufficiently shown by the
terms of the repeal measure. By the existing law the
minimum duty on wheat was 1*s.* the quarter, by the new
measure—intended to meet the circumstances of *famine*—
the minimum duty *for three years* was to be 4*s.* A
strange remedy indeed, if the cause for bringing in the
new measure had been fully and fairly stated! And this
was shown when the famine really came, in 1847, for
then the *remedial* measure was necessarily suspended,
and wheat came in at the minimum duty of 1*s.*, just as it
would have done under the old law. In his abandonment
of the cause of which he had so long been the champion,
and in his support of what he had so long resisted, Sir
Robert Peel carried with him 111 members who had previously opposed the repeal. The rest of his force was
made up of those whom he had previously opposed and
defeated. At 3 o'clock A.M. on Saturday, the 28th of
February, 1846, the House of Commons divided upon the
new measure. The united followers of Peel, Russell,
and Cobden mustered 337 votes, and the minority of
Protectionists was 240. Had the 112 Peelites voted as
they had always previously done on the same question,
the Protectionists would have numbered 352, and the
partizans of free importation 225.

Thus was the cause of Protection lost. Of those who
had been elected to defend it 112 were induced, by the
example and leadership of Sir Robert Peel, to go over to
the ranks of its enemies. There can be little question

that, had Sir Robert Peel felt himself bound to abandon office at the time that he felt himself obliged to abandon the defence of the Corn Laws, no such wholesale desertion on the part of Conservative members would have taken place. Lord John Russell was obliged to relinquish *his* attempt to form a Corn-Law-repealing Government in December, because he found that of the Conservative members who had previously opposed the Free Trade policy *he* could not count upon the support of even so many as 20. The question has been much debated whether Sir Robert Peel, after Lord John Russell's failure to form a government in December, calculated upon being able to maintain his position as Prime Minister, notwithstanding the repeal of the Corn Laws. In the succeeding month of June, after he was defeated in the House of Commons on another question, and compelled to resign, he stated that from the beginning of the session he foresaw and expected that result. It is however probable, looking at all the evidence, that, in the statement referred to, he confused after impressions with previous anticipations. At all events there is no reason to believe that either his colleagues or supporters had supposed that the very extraordinary change of opinion and of policy at which they had so conscientiously arrived, would conduct them, within a few short months, to the bleak and barren shore of unplaced Conservative " liberalism," there to pass listless days and nights without either the excitement of opposition or the more substantial gratification of official reward. It was their belief that after the bitterness of death, as regarded the Protectionist system, was over, old interests and old habits would bring things back to their accustomed channel; that Tories would be reluctant to enter into a systematic opposition of the Queen's Government, and that liberal Conservatism would continue to hold place, while the Whig party would be left upon the Opposition benches to ruminate upon the adverse fate which kept them out of office, notwithstanding the adoption of their policy by the country and by the State.

The disgust and resentment of the Protectionists however were more general, as well as deeper and more lasting, than they who surrounded Sir Robert Peel had calculated upon. If under ordinary circumstances those feelings might have died away, they were sure not to do so when the emergency of the case called from other pursuits to the head of the party in the House of Commons a man of such lofty spirit and such indomitable energy as Lord George Bentinck. There can be no doubt that an opportunity was anxiously sought by the Protectionists to transfer the government from Sir Robert Peel to Lord John Russell; upon the principle that public affairs would be conducted in a more honest and intelligible manner than it then was, if Whig policy, such as the Government had adopted, were under the direction of a Whig, with the constitutional control of frank Toryism in opposition. Along with this there was the animating spirit of vengeance. The Protectionists felt they had been betrayed, and longed to punish the Minister whom they believed to be their betrayer. They had to wait for their opportunity till June. Early in the session the Government had introduced a severe measure for the protection of life in Ireland; but the Minister, after the first reading, held it back as if with a presentiment that it contained the materials of his overthrow. The blow was struck on the 25th of June, when the Protectionists, joining the Whig Opposition against the Bill, placed the Peel ministry in a minority of 73. The muster of members was not very great, the number of voters being only 511. The Ministry had 219 votes—the combined opposition 292. Sir Robert

Peel announced his resignation on the 29th in a speech
which was no doubt the sorest, and probably the most in-
cautious speech he ever made.   So long as he is remembered, that speech will rise up in judgment against him.
To compliment the turbulent enemy of the landed interest, and to give the darkest colour of sordid malignity to
the policy of which he had himself been so long the
champion, were the tasks to which on that wretched
occasion he devoted his declamatory powers.   That was
the speech in which he condescended to eulogize " Richard
Cobden" by name, as the man to whose convincing arguments and unadorned eloquence the country was indebted
for the great advantage of the repeal of the Corn Laws,
forgetting however to acknowledge how insensible he had
himself been, up to the very last moment, both to the
force of those arguments and the fascination of that eloquence.   That was the speech in which he said that he
would doubtless " leave a name to be execrated by every
monopolist who desired to maintain protection for his own
individual benefit; but to be remembered also with expressions of good-will in the abodes of men who earn their
daily bread by the sweat of their brow, when they shall
recruit their strength with abundant and untaxed food,
the sweeter because it is no longer leavened by a sense of
injustice."   It does not appear to have occurred to Sir
Robert Peel, that, if the Corn Laws did really " leaven "
the bread of the poor " with a sense of injustice," he
himself had been for a long series of years the leading
perpetrator of that injustice, and therefore some apology
was due from him to the poor, upon whose good-will he
now so readily calculated.   He should have recollected
that he had tauntingly asked but a few years before, " who
had been more forward than he had been in defence of
the Corn Laws, and who could doubt that his desire was

to maintain a *just* and adequate agricultural protection?" Why did he maintain injustice, and say that it was just? Or, if he had only arrived at his new lights upon the subject within a few weeks, why did he not express contrition for his long-continued error, and why did he not refrain from reproachful allusion to those who still continued to hold opinions which he had so long considered and maintained to be just? How shall this be explained but by that "strange infirmity of character which made the whole life of Sir Robert Peel a series of inconsistencies, and has led him to disclaim, repudiate, and forfeit, one after another, almost every opinion, principle, and pledge that he had ever adopted." *

Perhaps it is really true that *inconstancy of mind* was the one great leading defect of Sir Robert Peel as a statesman, or rather, that it was the origin of all the great faults which are justly laid to his charge. At one time, surrounded by a Protectionist party, whose spirits he desired to keep up, he looked at *their* case only, and with it he was totally occupied. He seized upon all its strong points. He was himself impressed by them. He perceived how much might be said on their behalf, and he prided himself upon the forcible expression of the facts and arguments which had presented themselves to his mind. By and by, having become Prime Minister, he found that popular and vehement harangues were made on every side against the policy of Protection. He was responsible for the government. He knew how important it was that the populace should be satisfied. He perceived that they, too, had some good arguments on their side, as well as much vehemence and clamour. As soon as he gave some indication that his mind was changing, he

* *Quarterly Review*, No. 161, June, 1847.

obtained great applause from former opponents, while as
yet his friends did not venture to remonstrate. He found
it personally convenient and comfortable to have thus
lulled opposition. By degrees he brought himself to look
wholly at the stronger and more admissible points of
those arguments which formerly he examined only to confute. His judgment, it may be, thus actually veered
round, not traitorously, but in the sincerity of an incon-
stant mind. The cause which formerly he upheld from
having studied it in the spirit of an advocate only, he
afterwards opposed from having again studied it in the
spirit of an advocate on the other side. The weak points,
which formerly he overlooked, or looked at only to see
how they might be best defended, he afterwards considered
in the aspect of reasons for giving way, and as affording
grounds for attack. If this were the true theory of Sir
Robert Peel's character, it cannot but be admitted that,
however copious his information may have been, or however unquestionable his administrative ability, he was by
mental constitution unfit to be at the head of the affairs
of a great Nation. Undoubtedly it seemed to be his disposition, when he attained official power, to care more for
conciliating adversaries than for confirming and inspiriting
friends. This appears to have been the bent of his mind
even so early as 1819; for Mr. Plumer Ward says, in
his journal of that year—" Walked with Peel. He asked
how I thought we were as to strength in the House? I
said, Very strong. *But,* added he, *shall we have any of
the Whigs?* They mean, I understand, to rally on the
dismissal of Lord Fitzwilliam. I said, I thought that
signified little; that there seemed a great reaction, and
the loyal population preponderated ten to one. True,
said he; but don't you think the public opinion among
the lower orders has undergone a change within these few

years as to the constitution of Parliament?"   He at that
time, it seems, thought Orator Hunt a clever fellow, in
which opinion Plumer Ward did not concur; but Ward
was of that school which would not readily concede cleverness to a manufacturer of blacking for shoes, even had
he possessed real ability and honesty, which Mr. Hunt
assuredly did not. It is to be observed that, whatever
Sir Robert Peel thought, he never indicated as a statesman
that he had the slightest sympathy with any description
or degree of Parliamentary Reform. Until the change
called reform had been actually accomplished, it had
never occurred to him that Manchester or Birmingham
ought to be directly represented in the House of Commons. Of his share in " Reforms," a Whig writer (supposed to be Sir E. L. Bulwer) thus observed in 1838 : —

" It is not for ordinary men to know where to resist,
where to yield, what to guard against as dangerous, what
to anticipate as unavoidable. It is in this—the instinct
and providence of statesmen—that Sir Robert Peel has
evinced such remarkable deficiencies of judgment ; it is
in this that he has shown himself unfitted to save even the
interests of a party, still less to guide the destinies of a
nation. We address ourselves, not to reformers, but to
Conservatives ; and we ask the last, with due admiration
of the honesty and the genius of their leader,—we ask
them if his whole political career has not been a series of
elaborate miscalculations, of eloquent errors, and cele-
brated conversions? He opposed the Repeal of the Test
and Corporation Acts, and declared that the Dissenters
did not regard those disqualifications as a grievance, on
the very night that the concessions were torn from his
grasp by a majority of forty-four. He opposed the Catholic Relief Bill—he brought in the Bill he had opposed !
He never laid a finger on the abuses of municipal Corpo-

rations when in power; he surrendered without a murmur the glory of their reform to his opponents! He might have put down the Irish Orange Lodges with a word; he suffered them to exist till the whole public rose in arms against the nuisance! He might have made his party irresistible, if he had given the franchise to six manufacturing Towns; he foresaw not that timely concession is wise resistance; he was blind to the swell of the stream till his party were swept away by its overflow. The Country was disorganized by the vices of the old Poor Laws, and he declaimed on the blessings of order till half the provinces of England were in a state of prædial agitation. Convulsions in the counties, sedition in the metropolis, were the legacy that his theory of Conservatism bequeathed to his successors. Is such a man, with all his manifold faculties and gifts, the true conservator of a medium policy—the true prophet of events—the tried and experienced pilot in the storm? What demand of public opinion has he anticipated? what innovation checked at its birth? His policy has been to suffer the abuse to accumulate, the cry to deepen, the crowd to gather; and his eloquence will stand forth to posterity as declamations against what had become inevitable, never as warnings of what might have been prevented. Sagacity and foresight—a thorough knowledge of that which is permanent, that which is fluctuating in public opinion— such are the practical qualities that should distinguish a statesman who desires to hold the balance between conflicting parties, and reconcile popular interests with existing institutions." *

There is, however, another theory of Sir Robert Peel's conduct, which perhaps they who knew him in early life,

---

* *Monthly Chronicle*, No. 1.

and again in his latter days, will fall into more readily
than into that which assumes his inconstancy of mind, or
that which imputes to him an absolute want of Statesmanlike foresight. He may have been early taught to
believe, or may have independently made up his own
mind, that there was in this country a gradually-proceed-
ing, and absolutely irresistible, tendency to democratic
institutions, and that even the question of Great Britain
becoming a Republic was only a question of time. He
may have been led to believe, or have independently
formed the belief, that, as such changes must come, the
great duty of a Conservative British Statesman was so to
guide the descending bark of the British constitution,
that it should not be suddenly and violently dashed to
pieces in the waves of popular turbulence. He may,
upon this theory, have considered that to resist certain
measures of a democratic tendency, so long as they might
safely be resisted, was his duty : but as soon as continued
resistance appeared impossible, then to manage and conduct the change himself, and to withhold from democratic
leaders the excitement and momentum of administrative
success, even at the sacrifice of his own consistency, may
have been his deliberate policy, foreseen and determined
upon from the beginning. And this theory receives some
countenance, not to say corroboration, from the remarkable direction given by him, that his family should accept
no honour or distinction after his death on account of the
services which he might have been supposed to have rendered to his country. It is possible that he foresaw or
apprehended an approaching time when the possession of
rank would be dangerous to the fortunes of those who
possessed it, especially when *he* should be no longer present to moderate the storm. He may have felt, therefore,
that his family and the fortunes of his family would in

such a state of things be more *safe* without the elevation of rank.

> " Sæpius ventis agitatur ingens
> Pinus; excelsæ graviore casu
> Decidunt turres, feriuntque summos
> Fulmina montes."

If this, however, were Sir Robert Peel's theory, still I, for one, should not hold him excused. No man, I think, has a right, in a free country, to act with the profound reserve and reticence which this theory implies. No man is justified in going on from year to year, seeming to hope and expect what he has in fact despaired of, and seeming to set at nought consistency and straightforwardness, because he will not avow the profoundness of purpose which would have made all plain. A man who does this sets no useful example, gives no honest warning to his fellow-men ; and, however matchless he may be in his individual capacity, he is wanting in his duty as the citizen of a free community. They had a right to judge as well as he, and he ought not to have withheld even his fears. If it was on such grounds as I have attempted to delineate that Sir Robert Peel sacrificed his consistency, and apparently sacrificed his party, Lord Stanley might, indeed, well say that the sacrifices of his departed friend were so extensive, that he hardly knew whether the great and paramount object of his country's good was a sufficient reason to exact them from any public man.

An able writer, who regarded with a favourable eye the Free Trade policy of Sir Robert Peel, and was therefore less disposed to censure than he would have been at an earlier period of his career, has given to the world the following graphic sketch of the eminent statesman, taken from a Whig point of view :—" Sir Robert Peel has by no means passed blamelessly through public life . . . .

but he is entitled to the credit of having powerfully aided in a peaceable settlement of some of the most perilous questions of the age. He has displayed undoubted administrative ability, great occasional prudence in the management of political affairs, and sagacity in recognising the immediate wants of his time.* This last most statesmanlike quality he owes, perhaps, not more to the vigour and penetration of his intellect than to his unimpassioned temperament. He has necessarily made himself, by a frequent tortuous policy, the object of bitter vituperation ; but we cannot think, questionable as his political morality often has been, that in any of the great events of his life he has been wholly indifferent to the public good. His ambition, we truly believe, was never sordid or dishonourable, though we may also believe it to have been seldom perfectly disinterested and pure. To consult the dignity of his own character and position, and to merit by his public services that posthumous fame which he has professed to be his idol, would appear to have been his chief desire. His patriotism is not an internal and a burning light. He is animated by no refined or abstract love of justice and truth; nor is his vision apt to be clouded or his enthusiasm kindled by any peculiar cherished predilections. A cold and calculating self-respect, an unceasing and solicitous regard for the interests of his character and the dignity of his position, have been the mainsprings of his career." †

There are some features of this picture in which the likeness is exceedingly well hit off, but upon the whole it does not present to the mind's eye a man of so strangely

---

* Compare this with the Whig Sketch of 1838, already quoted from the *Monthly Chronicle*.

† *Examiner*, February 3, 1849.

doubtful a character as the original. It is true that he
had a cold and calculating self-respect—that is, respect
for himself; but that respect did not apparently extend
to his promises to the public or his engagements to his
party. With unexceptionable decorum of private character, and with many excellent qualities which even they
whom he has most seriously offended have not denied, he
was, with his " cold and calculating self-respect," one of
the least personally likeable men that ever sustained a
prominent part in the public life of England. He at all
times indicated, and latterly professed, a desire to stand
alone. He eschewed friendships as fetters on his self-
action, and looked on professed followers as embarrassments.

Let me present another sketch, from a Tory point of
view, which abounds in the exaggerations of a very strong
likeness, and which is the more remarkable because it
was given to the public before Sir R. Peel had openly
abandoned his party and his own previous professions on
the question of the Corn Laws :—" Any one may read on
the floor of the House of Commons, still more than in
the print-shop, the living portrait of the Premier. The
glance sidelong with which he enters the House ; the look
askance at his opponents, the anxious eye with which,
on rising, he regards them ; the shrinking back when a
murmur from the opposite benches reaches his ear ; the
stealing adroitly into a new topic when he finds one un-
palatable ; the abandonment of opinion or associate when
he perceives them to be obnoxious ; the skill with which
he lays out his argument to catch a cheer, the satisfaction
with which he receives it—above all, from his opponents :
these signs mark the adroitness of the debater and the
infirmity of the statesman. When after such an appearance he resumes his seat, amid the cheers of his oppo-

nents and *the silence of his friends*, you have revealed to
you his character and his policy. His character is to
dread attack, and to make any compromise in order to
avoid it : his policy is to shape his views according to the
opinions of those who are most likely to thwart him. The
effect of such a character is to make him adopt the
opinions of others, and to borrow them from those who
are most opposed to him. . . . . If he is on the side of
falsehood, he adopts popular fallacies, defends them with
skill, and relinquishes them when overcome by opponents.
If he is on the side of truth, his influence is stronger, and
it is all mischievous. He espouses truth from conviction,
his reason being clear; he abandons it on pressure, his
courage being weak. He will generally be right in the
outset, and he will maintain what is true. He will
always be wrong in the end, and will be sure to abandon
the truth; but before he abandons his cause he will
betray it, and he will be the worst of traitors, because he
will betray it while he holds the position of a friend." *

It is plain from this that to some of the Tories at least
the abandonment of the Corn Laws by Sir R. Peel was
not so much a surprise as a confirmation of their fears.
It was not to them a sudden betrayal, but the climax of
a course of perfidious inconstancy. Nor is it altogether
improbable that some consciousness in the mind of Sir
Robert Peel, that to a considerable number of his party
he was already an object of suspicion and dislike, may
have precipitated that step which, while it confirmed their
worst suspicions, inflicted irreparable injury on their union
and power. There were, however, many who trusted
him up to the very hour in which it was impossible to
trust him any longer, and whose earnest condemnation of

---

* *English Review*, No. VIII., October, 1845.

the conduct by which he fell was mingled with tributes
of respect to his abilities and personal motives. By one
distinguished critic (a private friend, I believe, as well
as a political associate) it was said that, " differing as we
do from every opinion that he has recently delivered—
disapproving all his measures, and deploring both the
form and substance of his whole course of proceeding—
it is the more due to his character and to our own feelings to declare our entire conviction of the purity of his
intentions—nay, of his good-will to the very interests
which he seems to have sacrificed." *   And again, in
reply to assertions in some quarters that Sir R. Peel
must have had a low personal motive for the depreciation
of the landed interest, the same writer says, " the accusation is not merely wholly groundless—it is absurd.
Sir R. Peel's interests are especially identified with the
land, and his measure is the more anomalous and alarming from being contrary to those personal interests. But
we take higher ground. Sir R. Peel is infinitely superior
to any influence of that low nature. His heart, if not as
stout, is as pure as Mr. Pitt's. He may be deficient in
official candour and frankness—in fidelity to political
friendships—in firmness against political adversaries—in
contempt of the *civium ardor prava jubentium*—in the
wise courage that prefers to meet the storm in the deep
waters rather than in shoals and straits : these defects
may be imputed to him, and they are probably in some
degree constitutional, but his mind was never sullied by
even the passing cloud of any sordid or unworthy thought.
It is an over-cautious and over-sensitive ratiocination
that reduces him to the level—below his spirit and alien
to his taste—of a temporizing utilitarian. If his heart

---

* *Quarterly Review,* No. 156, p. 549.

were as firm as it is pure—if he were as inaccessible to
the delusions and plausibilities of theorists, the hypo-
critical applause of adversaries, the insidious and interested flatteries of the foreign press, and the menaces of
popular agitation, as he is to either passion, corruption,
or any other ignoble motive—*if he could trust himself as
he requires others to trust him*—he might, as we once
hoped he was destined to do, have stayed the revolution,
instead of, as we now fear, rapidly accelerating it." *

It did not appear by Sir Robert Peel's conduct from
1846 to the period of his death that he had profited as
he might have done from such remarks as those, offered
in a spirit of good-will by some of those whose political
alliance he had so rudely severed. The peculiarity and
doubtful nature of his actual position seemed to be ever
present to his mind. In the House of Commons he stood
apart, as if he wished to be considered a power in himself;
but without originating any measure, he gave his aid to
every change which seemed to threaten the fabric of the
old British constitution, and which tended to substitute
the mercantile and money-making spirit, for the old
national spirit, in the conduct of public affairs.

I must now hasten to the last scene of his Parliamentary life, and happily it was one upon which the
mind can rest with a melancholy satisfaction. I do not
refer to the political purpose of his speech, though it
happened to be in accordance with the views of his old
political friends and associates, but to its general tone
and temper. Not containing any elaborate statement of
matters of fact, in which he was considered peculiarly to
excel, it was yet incomparably the best speech he had
made in the House of Commons since 1839. He seemed

* *Quarterly Review*, No. 156, p. 552.

fully master of himself and of his subject ; he spoke not
only with more freedom, energy, and decision than he
had done for some years, but also with occasional touches
of gracefulness and feeling, of which the public had
begun to forget that he was capable. It was on the
fourth night of a remarkable debate on the management
of the foreign affairs of Great Britain—a debate not only
the most striking of the Session, but exhibiting altogether
more capacity for political discussion of a high order than
had been on any former occasion exhibited by the " reformed" House of Commons. Sir Robert Peel rose after
Mr. Cockburn, an eminent *nisi prius* advocate, ardent,
impetuous, and unscrupulous, who attempted in a vehement torrent of language to persuade the House that a
conspiracy had been formed by the Protectionists and the
followers of the Peel policy to overthrow the government,
notwithstanding that these parties differed in almost
everything but their opinion of the way in which the
foreign policy of the kingdom was conducted. I shall
give some extracts from the speech, retaining the reporter's indications of the way in which it was received
by the House. He commenced as follows, and, with
unusual force and brevity of reply, disposed of Mr.
Cockburn's suggestions and demands :—

" However extended in point of duration the debate
has been, and however exhausted the topics that have
been introduced into the discussion, I think that the House
will admit that I should not be acting in conformity with
a sense of duty if I abstained from assigning the grounds
on which my vote will be given. (Hear, hear.) The
hon. and learned gentleman the member for Southampton
(Mr. Cockburn) has demanded a full explanation of the
circumstances under which that vote will be given. Sir,
he shall have that explanation. I have no reserve. The

hon. member has stated that there is a dishonourable conspiracy formed against her Majesty's Government.   Sir,
a more unfounded charge never was preferred.   (Cheers.)
He presumes that there has been some base compromise
between gentlemen sitting on this side of the House, but
holding different opinions upon matters of vital interest.
He is wholly mistaken.   (Cheers.)   There has been no
such compromise.   He talks of there being three courses
to pursue; he tells us there are three combinations by
which office may be obtained.   He says, ' I demand to
know which of these three courses you contemplate ?'
Now is it not possible for the hon. gentleman to suppose
that there may be a fourth ?   (Cheers.)   Is it not possible for him to speculate upon the possibility that men
in this House may intend to give their votes without
reference to political combinations ?   (Cheers.)   Does he
exclude the possibility of that fourth course of action,
which arises from a conscientious conviction as to the
truth ?   (Cheers.)   Is that excluded from his contemplation ?   (Continued cheering.)   May it not be possible
that men cannot subscribe to a resolution which asserts
that a certain course has been best calculated to preserve
peace and to support the honour and dignity of this
country ?   Is it not possible that, without reference to
party or personal interests, men may decline to affirm a
resolution which deals with principles of greater importance to the welfare of this country, for good or for evil,
than has ever been under the consideration of the House ?"

Having thus disposed of a professional orator, whose
fortunes will certainly not suffer any check from his diffidence, Sir Robert Peel proceeded to allude to three points
of great interest connected with his own position, namely :
the support he had given to the Whig government ; the
continued adherence of his mind to the " liberal " policy

which in the latter part of his life he had embraced; and the feeling with which he regarded his old Conservative connexion :—

" Sir, I will not forget, and I need not remind the House, that I have given, or attempted to give, to Her Majesty's Government my support—I will not say my cordial support—during the last four years. (Cheers.) In utter oblivion of the circumstances under which they succeeded to power (a laugh), I have felt it my duty to give them, not an ostentatious, but, because it was not ostentatious, a not the less effective support. (Loud cheers.) I have not the honour and advantage of possessing their personal friendship; I have never been in political connexion with them. I have held no communication with them during the last four years which may not be had by any member of this House, who may be the most independent and the most unconnected with their policy. I have given them my support, because I cordially approved of the policy which they carried into domestic affairs. I think that their policy in domestic affairs has been a liberal and conservative policy. (Cheers.) I have agreed with them, and I repeat it now, with respect to the principle of commercial freedom. (Cheers.) So far from a base compromise having taken place between myself and the gentlemen who sit near me, and whose confidence I have had the misfortune to forfeit, every day that passes convinces me more and more that upon the cordial adoption and the unequivocal adhesion to those principles of commercial policy, the peace and true interests of this country depend. (Loud cheers.) I have said enough, I hope, to prove to the honourable member that for myself as I know, and for others as I believe, there has been none of that base compromise that he supposes has dictated our unanimity on this occasion."

If he had been aware that this was the last time on
which the Providence that rules the destinies of man
would permit him to address the assembly of which he
had been so long the most eminent member, he could
scarcely have taken more pains to say something as
soothing and agreeable as circumstances and his sense of
truth would permit, concerning the various individuals
and parties to whom he had occasion to allude. First
for his old colleague Lord Aberdeen, who still continued
with him, coupled with the party from which he was
separated :—

"I may say that, separated as I am from those with
whom I had once the good fortune to act, that separation
has not made me forgetful of the general and cordial
support which the foreign policy of my noble friend obtained from others. (Hear, hear.) In justice to ourselves—
in justice to the party with whom I then acted—in justice
to this House, I could not with honour acquiesce in any
covert reflection on the policy of my noble friend—the
policy of peace, consistent with our maintenance of the
honour of the country. (Cheers.)"

Next as to the Whig government in general :—

"I wish I could give the motion my support. It would
be more agreeable to my private feelings—it would be
more in consistency with my disposition to support Her
Majesty's Government if I could do so ; but to speak of
that particular affair which led to the vote of the House
of Lords,* the conduct of Government in reference to the
Grecian affair, I cannot, consistently with my conscientious convictions, declare that I think the course which

---

* The debate arose upon a motion affirming a favourable opinion of
the foreign policy of the Government, which the House of Lords had
formally condemned.

the Government has pursued is the course best calculated to maintain the honour and dignity of this country, or to maintain peace with foreign nations.　(Cheers.)"

Then a graceful compliment to the abilities and temper of the Foreign Secretary in particular, of whose policy he disapproved :—

" I have so little disposition—and I say it with truth, for the feelings which have actuated me for the last four years remain unabated (Hear, hear)—I have so little disposition, I say, for entering into any angry or hostile controversy, that I shall make no reference whatever to many of the topics which were introduced into that most able and most temperate speech, which made us proud of the man who delivered it (Loud and general cheering), and in which he vindicated with becoming spirit, and with an ability worthy of his name and place, that course of conduct which he had pursued.　(Cheers.)"

The peroration of the speech consisted of such sound and sober advice upon the principles which should govern the relation of England with Foreign States, as a great politician might willingly leave behind him as his last words of counsel and of warning.　He takes China as a strong example of a foreign country with institutions which we might be very glad to see changed, but which we have no right to attempt to change, and he thus proceeded :—

" Is it wise to live at peace with China and to make allowance for those peculiar institutions under which the people live, and with which we have no concern?　I believe that to be by far the wiser course, the least likely to involve us in trouble and embarrassment—the best calculated to enable us to promote peace, to make commerce prosperous, and to prevent nations with whom we have commercial and international relations from enter-

taining jealousies of us. (Hear, hear.) That I believe to
be the best policy as far as England is concerned. It is
also my firm belief that you will not advance the course
of constitutional government by attempting to dictate to
other nations. If you do, your intentions will be mistaken
—you will rouse feelings upon which you do not calculate—
you will invite opposition to Government; and beware
that the time does not arrive when, frightened by your
own interference, you withdraw your countenance from
those whom you have excited, and leave upon their mind
the bitter recollection that you have betrayed them.
(Cheers.) If you succeed, I doubt whether or no the institutions that take root under your patronage will be
lasting. (Hear.) Constitutional liberty will be best worked
out by those who aspire to freedom by their own efforts.
You will only overload it by your help, by your principle
of interference, against which I remonstrate—against
which I enter my protest—to which I to-night will be no
party. (Hear, hear.) You are departing from the established policy of England—you are involving yourselves
in difficulties, the extent of which you can hardly conceive—you are bestowing no aid on the cause of constitutional freedom, but are encouraging its advocates to
look to you for aid, instead of those efforts which can alone
establish it, and upon the successful exertion of which
alone it can be useful. (Hear, hear.) For all these reasons
I give my dissent, my reluctant dissent, from the motion
of the honourable gentleman. I am determined to take
upon this occasion the course which I have taken upon
every other. I will not evade the difficulty by silence or
absence—I will state the grounds upon which I protest
against the resolution—the carrying of which, I believe,
will give a false impression with respect to the dignity and
honour of this country, and will establish a principle

which you cannot carry into execution without imminent
danger to the best interests of the country. (Loud and
long continued cheering.)"

These were the last words uttered by Sir Robert Peel
in the House of Commons, and perhaps it is well for his
fame that they were the last. They will remain unweak-
ened—uncontradicted, as those equally wise and eloquent
speeches of 1839 and of 1845 upon the Corn Laws have
been—by the subsequent declarations of him who gave
them utterance.

The day after Sir Robert Peel spoke this speech he was
thrown from his horse while taking an afternoon airing,
and so dreadfully injured, that after three days' suffering
he died. One moment he was the greatest man in
England, rich, eminent, popular, in good health and in
great honour ; the next, by an accident, which any of his
own grooms could have mastered, he was a prostrate,
suffering, dying man ! Such is the instability of all that
this life affords.

His character is, and will be, regarded with that respect
which great information, high talents, and unsullied
private conduct must in this country command ; but I do
not think that the permanent gratitude and affection of
the nation will dwell around his name. He was on both
sides of almost every great public question that was
debated in his time ; and though one writes it down with
deep reluctance, yet a sense of truth compels the avowal,
that he appears to have had but little depth of conviction,
or warmth of attachment, on any side of the great questions with the settlement or unsettlement of which he was,
in the course of his long public life, connected. To the
retrospective eye of posterity his way will seem to have
been ever doubtful, and his path perplexed, because his

public aim was not sufficiently clear and lofty. He was
not one of those—

> " Whose high endeavours are an inward light
> That makes the path before them always bright."

In the various and contradictory views which he took, or
appeared to take, of that policy which was best for England, he was either sincere or the contrary. If insincere,
what reproach could be too strong to direct against *such*
insincerity? But if sincere in all these contradictions,
who shall say, contemplating a man so uncertain and in-
constant, not only in youth, but in the maturity of his
days, that he was *a great man?*

CHAPTER XVI.

THE PRESENT TIME.

WHAT is the leading characteristic of the present time in England? I answer, its industrialism—its wealth-seeking spirit. " This age," says a writer in the *Quarterly Review*,* " has been a money-making age. We are bringing no charge against it ; we are only stating a fact, the boast of many, and admitted by all." This spirit is at war with the sentimental, the romantic, and the delicate in thought and in feeling. Moreover, there is a certain morbid intellectuality and a peering mental inquisitiveness in the present time, which are unfavourable to the soarings of imagination or to the profound musings of meditative reason. I speak now of the general taste. We have now, as we have always had, individual poetic minds ; but the multitude do not much relish any such thing :—they are rather for inquiry :—they wish to " hack into the roots of things," and to do so in the most matter-of-fact and mechanical way. " From whatever source this morbidness may proceed," says the critic already referred to, " whether from an excessive indulgence in private judgment and individual caprice, from vanity, from repletion and satiety, or from a critical habit indulged as if we were the end of all things, and had nothing to do except judge those who went before us—from whatever

---

* No. 142, March, 1843.

cause or combination of causes it may have arisen, this morbidness undoubtedly exists to a degree which in many cases makes our bodies an hospital for diseases, our religion a spiritual nightmare, and society a continual sore. We feel our own pulse in hand and foot, and record the progress of our digestion; we know how our affections have been secreted, and do not much object to turn our moral being, with the whole of our experience, inside out to gratify the philosophical curiosity of the passer-by. This morbidness engenders egotism, and egotism with the mass degenerates soon into selfishness, and selfishness is destructive of sympathy." This writer not only considers that the intellectual bias of the present time is a wrong one, but that its moral qualifications are not exactly of the right sort. The age is "deficient in simplicity, in earnestness, in robustness—in that intrepid and impassioned adventurousness which desires, and dares to watch, the great battle of the passions on the broad platform of common life; and in that elasticity of soul which makes renewed vigour the natural recoil from suffering; and a deeper self-knowledge, with a firmer self-government, the chief permanent results of calamity. The social and sympathetic principle has become merged in the selfish instinct. This principle has also been materially impaired by the exclusive character of modern intercourse, and by those arbitrary distinctions which break up society into cliques and sets." An author of a lighter and coarser texture has come, in his way, very near the same views when he says—"The grand principle of action in the present day was developed nearly forty years ago, when one of a family,* the wittiest perhaps that ever lived, and the one which most quickly seized the feelings of their

---

* The Sheridans.

times, asked 'What did posterity ever do for me?' That
is the secret of everything strange that we see around us.
Each man lives for his earthly life alone. He cares not
either for those who come after, or for remote reputation,
or for a world that is to come. In regard to the first, he
thinks that they will take care of themselves, as he has
done. In regard to the second, he says, 'It is a bubble
that, so far as I am concerned, breaks when I die.' In
regard to the third, his ideas are indefinite, and while he
admits that there may be a hereafter, he takes his chance
and says, ' A bird in the hand is worth two in the bush.'"
All this of course refers to the worser sort of those who
think, or to those who do not think at all, but give themselves up to the selfish habits of the world, or to the practice which is called, in the slang language of the day,
" taking care of number one." I doubt whether in any
other age this selfishness has been carried so far, either as a
practice or a principle—I mean, that in practice there exists
more cleverness divorced from any other view save that
of self, and that in the deliberate purpose of men's minds
there is more complete, unmixed adoption of the merely
selfish principle, than there ever was before. I think that
from the halls of the legislature down to the tap-rooms of
public-houses there is less shame in the declaration of
selfishness, less hesitation in the avowal of dissympathy,
as a rule of conduct, than would have been possible in
former times. No doubt the popular teaching of the
doctrines of political economy (perhaps misunderstood, as
its professors say) has had much to do with this ; and
also the open advocacy in the Legislature of a policy that
seeks only profit, without reference to national greatness
or to the nobler feelings of humanity.

In these days so much does the spirit of trade prevail,
that no one almost will listen to the suggestion of any

rule or ordinance for the correction of covetousness or
the control of extortion. Such correction and control
may be safely left, it is said, to competition. Covetousness in one direction is therefore to be the corrective
of covetousness in another direction. The desire of increased business is relied upon as a sufficient preventive of
too much desire of profit. We are not to oppose what is
bad in principle by what is good, but by making the vice
of one, act in opposition to the vice of another. This
being the rule, there is no remedy at all in cases where
the principle of competition cannot be brought into play.
It is in vain to speak of justice and moderation, and the
reasonableness which ought to govern a man even in the
pursuit of gain. These principles are not held to have
anything to do with business. The principle is, that a
man should take as much profit as he can get, so long as
he can get it, and should only abate his demands when
competition compels him to do so. The principle of
honest forbearance, for honesty's sake, and no other, is to
be left out of the question. Such considerations belonged
to a former age. This having become the rule, there is
no available source of redress for extortion where the
remedy of competition cannot be applied. We are to keep
the British farmer from obtaining too much for his corn
by inviting the foreign corn-grower to compete with him ;
but what shall we do when the British innkeeper charges
exorbitantly ? We know the foreign innkeeper, with provisions at much the same rate, charges much more mode-
rately ; but we cannot import innkeepers and their establishments, and as nothing but competition will be listened
to as a check upon extravagant charges, we must submit.
This is but one of a hundred instances which might be
brought forward to show the practical inadequacy of a
merely mercantile remedy for a moral wrong. But it

belongs to the prevailing philosophy of the age to trust to this kind of remedy rather than any other.

The whole map of human life, as it is seen in England at the present day, presents violent extremes of condition —huge mountains of wealth and luxury, contrasted with awful depths of poverty and wretchedness ; but in respect of mental ability, we find immense flats of uniformity — dead levels of respectable talent with scarcely any such thing as originality, freshness, or high creative genius in any department of literature, art, science, or even trade. Perhaps engineering, and some new uses of chemical science, should be excepted. Viaducts, tunnels, and, above all, the electric telegraph, *do* show greatness of thought, so far as it can be shown in such matters, but all the rest is mere activity, and over activity in the old tracks, producing a monstrous crowd of limited respectabilities, and great effects of multitude and combination, but none at all of new and pre-eminent excellence. Emerson, the American lecturer and oration-manufacturer, speaks not amiss when he says that " a general culture has spread itself and has smoothed down all sharp individual traits ; in the absence of heroic characters, a social comfort and co-operation have come in. There is no poet, but scores of poetic writers ; no Columbus, but hundreds of post-captains with transit-telescope, barometer, and concentrated soup and pemmican : no Demosthenes, no Chatham, but any number of clever parliamentary and forensic debaters ; no prophet or saint, but colleges of divinity ; no learned man, but learned societies, a cheap press, reading rooms, and book-clubs without number." So it is indeed in every walk of life—abundance of talent—abundance of industry—abundance of mental activity and acuteness, but scarcely anything of a more exalted character. In everything we are overdone with quantity ;

but of rare quality there is almost nothing. In arts—in science—in the professions—in schools and in colleges—in the Courts of Law, the Privy Council and the Houses of Legislature, we have men whose knowledge and whose talents for the despatch of business equal, if they do not surpass, the knowledge and the business talents of any former time, but they all seem to labour under the weight of accumulated affairs and to be perplexed with a multitude of details. The chain of routine is upon them, and the flight of genius seems to be impossible. Everything seems to resolve itself into trade. Teaching, advocacy, legislation, gunnery, criticism, imaginative literature—all has come down to trade, and no one thinks of stopping while a guinea is to be made by going on. The successful have no leisure, and they who would indulge in leisure must forfeit success. If you do not undertake all, you will not be asked to undertake anything. Even of the intellectual classes one portion is overworked, while another has nothing to do. One is exhausted with over-exertion—another stagnates in hopeless idleness. In country or in town, it is, in this respect, nearly the same :—

> " Oh England ! ' merry England' styled of yore,
> 　Where is thy mirth, thy jocund laughter where ?
> 　The sweat of labour or the brow of care
> Makes a mute answer—Driven from every door !
> The maypole cheers the village green no more;
> 　Nor harvest-home, nor Christmas mummers rare.
> 　The tired mechanic at his lecture sighs ;
> And of the learned, which, with all his lore,
> 　Has leisure to be wise?" *

A pensive complaint this is, but I think the sentiment of it is true. We have become a busier people than we were, but that we have become wiser is, I think, open to doubt.

---

* ' Lago Lugano,' by H. Taylor.

CHAPTER XVII.

THE PRESS.

It is only they who have been familiar with the popular press of England for the last thirty years who can duly estimate the great change which has taken place in its character. It is wonderful how much its violence of tone has abated. The style of newspapers and magazines is much more decorous, but the writing is less vigorous, and, whatever be its ultimate effect, it makes, at the moment of perusal, a less vivid impression. There is scarcely any such thing as passion in the periodical writing of the present day; thirty years ago, or twenty years ago, it was instinct with passion. How trenchant and slashing were the criticisms of magazines and reviews! They were not, indeed, critical examinations, but bold and often bitter attacks upon literary or political adversaries. What outpourings of wrath and poetry, and merciless banter, were found month after month in *Blackwood's Magazine*. What amazing idiomatic strength and what unscrupulous intrepidity of assertion in *Cobbett's Register*. What energy of "liberal" animosity and bitterness of sneering in the *Edinburgh Review*. What showers of personal satire in the *Morning Chronicle*. What volleys of lampoons and parodies in the *John Bull*. All this spirit of somewhat coarse and reckless fun died away about the time of the Reform Bill; and shortly after that crisis of popular discontent and ambitious intrigue in France, which placed Louis-Philippe of

Orleans upon an unstable throne, another and a worse spirit came into fashion. In 1834 a grave and earnest writer in *Blackwood's Magazine* gave the following account of the state of the press at that time :—" The features by which the press—meaning by that term, not the great works which are destined permanently to delight and instruct mankind, but those lighter productions which attract, and are alone read by the multitude—news-papers, magazines, reviews, novels, superficial travels—is now distinguished, are a general democratic and an increasing licentious character. No doubt there are many and honourable exceptions to the rule ; and in the higher branches of periodical literature, addressed to the really educated classes, a vast preponderance of Conserva-tive principles and religious feeling is to be found. But they unhappily form the exception, not the rule. Gene-rally speaking, the press is decidedly democratic, and this is proved to demonstration by the immense circula-tion which the leading papers which have adopted that side of politics have obtained. That it is daily, too, becoming more licentious—that strong and vivid pictures, addressed to the passions and the imagination, incite-ments to sensual indulgence—and that fatal union of genius with voluptuousness, which is the well-known sign of a declining age, have of late become prevalent, is matter of universal observation." No such severity of condemnation could now be justly applied—not, at least, I think, in such general terms—to our popular literature. The fashion of mingling news with ribaldry and gross allusion, has very much gone out ; and if we are no better than we were, we are at least in this respect more decent. I believe there is still a class of cheap periodicals devoted to mere licentiousness, and no doubt they are abominably mischievous ; but, so far as my information goes, they do not get much beyond the most depraved portion of town society, and are chiefly sold in the shops where every other gross impurity that printing and engraving can supply is to be obtained by those who understand or will bring themselves to use the watchwords of those filthy dens. It is, indeed, disgraceful that there should be a certain kind of cheap periodical literature deliberately prepared for the " swell mob " and their mistresses; but it is better that the lees and feculence of journalism should be strained off for them, than that it should be mixed up with that which goes into general use.

The great mischief of journalism in the present day arises from its morbid activity. The tendency of our time seems to be to carry everything to extremes; and in no department of busy life does this tendency expose itself more glaringly than in journalism. The curiosity of the public—whether laudable or vicious, whether rational or absurd—is pampered to the last degree. The public is assumed to have a right to know everything which can by possibility be hunted out and laid open to the public gaze; and though there may be more art and decency in the manner of such exposures than formerly there was, the popular mind is scarcely the less debased by the gratification of its pernicious inquisitiveness. One, who judges of everything by the standard of practical Christianity, in a communication to me upon this subject, says, that it is not possible such pruriency of human curiosity can be gratified, and this emptying out (as it were), *coram publico*, of everything that should rather be kept back from general gaze, or proclaimed only with entire gravity and discretion, should go on as it does, without ending in wholesale contamination of morals and sapping of principles. To look to " public opinion " as the one corrective panacea, is neither more nor less (in

effect) than to expect *men* (being such as one knows them
to be) to reform themselves—the sinners to sit in judgment upon, and be the extinguishers of the sin.   Everything seems to be set about nowadays in the wrong way.

Adverting also to the suspicions which now so generally
arise when deaths out of the natural course, and not
easily to be accounted for, take place, and which are
therefore very fit subjects for investigation by the constituted authorities, the same correspondent says, " Whence
is it that we are become so morbidly suspicious and
inquisitive ?   Why are we always so ready to fear the
worst, if not to adopt the worst construction of every un-
looked-for, calamitous death?   I fear the answer is—
from all persons having their better minds tainted with
an increased and increasing familiarity with wickedness
through the medium of the newspapers.   I do not think
anything can be much more probable than that the
horrible advance (as it would seem) of tampering with
poisons physical has been caused and is daily extended by
this contagion of publicity or *poison moral*.   Thousands
of innocently disposed people would never think of such
evil as they do, if it were not put into their heads by
printed details—week after week, or day after day—of
crimes apparently grown and moulded into regular system
since the ' great improvements in chemical science.'
Suspicion of having taken poison, or having been poisoned,
is quite the order of the day; and the ramifications of
evil surmisings have become as infinite as they are painful.
Under almost any disaster or annoyance in social life
confidence is shaken, proper charity quenched in its
powers of believing and hoping, innocence treated share-
and-share-alike with guilt, and I know not what besides,
all very mainly arising (as it seems to me) from the publicity given to every form of crime.   In this, however, as

in everything else, it is far easier to see the evil than to suggest the remedy; but I am convinced that, for one thing, it is far more important to protest against current notions of the sanatory force of public opinion (a phrase which practically means tyranny of the newspapers) than to prohibit the sale of arsenic."

This opinion will by many be considered " rather strong," even though to some extent they may agree to it; but I wished to show what is thought by some, who do not publish their thoughts, concerning the excesses of journalism in days when the violence of its language, and perhaps also the vigour of its sentiments and style, have in no inconsiderable degree abated. An author who has published his views upon the present condition of society,* states an opinion scarcely less strong than that I have quoted. This age is, indeed, he says, free from fear of the faggot or the torture; but, he adds, "fear of the social circle, *fear of the newspaper*, fear of being odd, fear of what may be thought of people who never did think, still greater fear of what somebody may say—are not these things a clinging dress of torture?" And, again, he complains that we live " in continual fear and danger of the meanest aspects of public opinion." There can be little doubt that not only in politics, but in other questions of general or local interest, the newspaper is a great engine of democratic power, and that it is often directed with less serious and less conscientious views of the responsibilities attached to such direction than every lover of justice and practical freedom could wish.

Besides the fault of ministering too much and too unguardedly to the morbid, or vicious, or frivolous curiosity of the public, there are two other leading errors of jour-

---

* 'Friends in Council,' 2nd series.

nalism in these days which deserve especial notice, though
they lead in the first instance rather to corruption of taste
than to any more serious evil. The one is a habit of
forced jesting and caricature, as if everything in the conduct of society, whether gravely wrong, or only of doubtful
propriety, might fairly be made the subject of joke and
ridicule. No reasonable person will deny that this manner
of criticism may be used now and then with very good
effect ; but that writers of considerable knowledge and
ingenuity should laboriously address themselves, week
after week, month after month, and year after year, to
the task of pleasing the gigglers and grinners of society,
is surely a great degradation and a sad misuse of literary
talent. Perhaps it may be, in a mercantile sense, the
most profitable kind of periodical writing ; but though
poverty be, according to the late Canon Sidney Smith,
"infamous" in this country, I should think it preferable
to the wealth obtained by enacting the part of literary
"Mr. Merryman" to the commonplace crowd, who have
just enough of understanding to laugh at the victim of a
sneer, while, in nine cases out of ten, they miss the instruction which the author may have intended it to
convey. The other error of taste consists in the assumption of a certain sentimentality, half maudlin, half melo-
dramatic ; as if the affairs of life were proper to be ruled
and fashioned like the scenes of a play ; as if some touch
of feeling, expressed in the way most likely to affect a
gallery audience, were as good as any one of the principles of duty to God or man, by which the framework of
society is really held together. I am in some hope that
this toy-shop humanity—this outpouring of sentimental
prettinesses, as a substitute for sound sense, is going out
of fashion ; the sooner the better, for while it lasts it
emasculates the public taste, and unfits it for the recep-

tion of better and more healthful mental food. It is very well on certain occasions to consider the incidents of life, as they may be used for dramatic purposes, and by strong contrasts to bring out some virtue for particular admiration, or some vice for especial abhorrence ; but so long as we treat of the actual affairs of men in the mixed world that lies before us, we should remember that not only in all classes of society, but in almost all individuals, the good and the bad are strangely combined and interlaced the one with the other ; that sensibility the most genuine and tender is no certain test of sound principles in man or woman ; that it is very possible to be amiable without being honest ; and that he who would teach well and wisely must be made of sterner stuff than goes to the formation of him who fits old sentimentalisms to new circumstances, and who seems more desirous that women should cry " Oh, how charming !" than that men should be stirred to useful and honourable action.

The quantity of laborious activity both of mind and body devoted to the business of journalism in England is probably greater than most people imagine. I apprehend, however, that it is chiefly called into action by the circumstances to which it is applied, or the requirements which it satisfies. I mean, that it is not merely a portion of existing mental activity taken from the general stock to be devoted to journalism, and which would accomplish something else if it did not produce daily and weekly journals ; but it is absolutely called into existence by the needs of daily and weekly journalizing, and, for the most part, would not be applicable to anything else. As to the making of reports—the collecting of intelligence— the arranging of various kinds of matter in the most convenient form, and all the more important part of newspaper construction, that of course requires great industry, quickness, correctness, and judgment, which are all supplied because there is a demand for them and a price. But in every part of this construction, although it is required to be as perfect as the circumstances will permit, yet to do it within the time is the main point, and that which is well enough for a newspaper, which must necessarily be done in a hurry, is confessedly not well enough for publications which admit of more consideration and revision. As to the writers of original articles on the events of the day, it is quickness of thought and readiness of expression on paper, which chiefly fit them for their office. There are men who can write, and with great force too, when they must write, but who cannot bring themselves to write to-day that which might as well be written to-morrow. On the other hand, they who write best cannot write off-hand. They ponder the matter, and the thoughts which occur to them they are able to lay up in store, and deliberately to arrange in the best order. Men who give much of their attention to the events of the day, find their reflections thereon to evaporate even faster than those events shift their position and change their colour. Harassing as the work of the daily journalist may appear, and as it no doubt really is, it is that which *primâ facie* appears the greatest hardship of the task—namely, the necessity for writing off-hand—that makes it from day to day a practicable thing. Besides being a grand and standing excuse for all sorts of mistakes, it is the very life of the cause. For the most part, the journalist writes under immediate impulse, supplied either by the news of the day or the remarks of some rival journal, which impulse quickens some spring of utterance, whether by sympathy, indignation, suggestion of supplementary matter, or what not. Let any topic, however, only wait a few days to grow cold, and it would

be recurred to as a sheer task, which the writer would
scarcely have patience to encounter.

But it is known to those who have had long experience
in such matters, that even the leading article writer is
sometimes considerably at a loss for a topic, and yet
write he must, for the journal must have its supply. The
subjects of the day have perhaps been all written upon
already, even to weariness, and there is little to confute—
still less to praise—in rival publications. Yet a subject
must be found, and the journalist must say upon it something which he believes will interest the public. The
necessity of the hour supplies the energy which, but for
that necessity, would never come. Necessity, says the
proverb, is the mother of invention—perhaps with more
accurate analogy we should say that necessity is the
midwife of invention. One often invents in mere fits of
musing as one sits at ease, or saunters about, or hurries
along in a carriage; but to bring forth in speech or in
writing the results of the mind's working — for *that*,
nothing is so effective as the necessity of the hour.

Though the influence of journalism upon the course
of public affairs in this country is no doubt very considerable, the profession of a journalist gives no social distinction, and the occupation is not even avowed, except
to intimate friends. A man is proud of being in good
practice as a lawyer or a physician, though his exertions
are applied only to private disputes or to the bodily ail-
ments of a few persons of no public importance. The
member of Parliament, also, is proud of being a member,
partly because he influences the making of the laws and
the government of the country; but more because the
title of M P. gives him a position in society. The English journalist, who is always occupied about public
affairs, and who certainly both influences and brings into

action that public opinion which all admit to be so
powerful, is almost ashamed to avow what he is, well
knowing that the feeling of society towards journalists is
more that of fear or curiosity than that of respect or
esteem.   As I do not believe with M. Guizot that there
is a theory and a system in everything, which might be
expounded if one diligently applied one's reason to find it
out, I shall not attempt here to account for the little
esteem which English society awards to journalists.   I am
willing to let it remain an unaccountable fact.   The
only reason that ever suggested itself to my mind is one
of rather a homely character, namely, that the business
of journalism is not exercised by men who are rich, or
in the least likely to become rich.   A barrister getting
into practice may come to five thousand a-year and the
rank of a judge.   A physician who is becoming popular
may come to six thousand a-year and a knighthood or a
baronetcy.   The man who only writes what concerns the
public interests of his country, and influences the minds
of hundreds of thousands upon questions which, next to
those of religion, are the most important of all questions,
is by no means likely to arrive at more than a decent
competence, and that only so long as his mental and
bodily powers are equal to his daily task.   The lot of
those who have written most, and most effectively, for the
public press, is to live in obscurity and to die in neglect.
This, however, every man knows who undertakes the
work, and it is therefore for such men not to complain,
but to endure.

The people of England at large have not so much
taste for discussion as for information.   They care more
for the facts, or what they suppose to be the facts, than
for the most luminous reasoning in the world upon those
facts.   On the Continent, and more especially in France,

they can scarcely understand this. Whoever has education enough to read, has more or less of taste for discussion, and is eager to examine both the reasoning and the
style of the leading articles of the journals. In England,
for five men who care about these things, there are five
hundred who take up a newspaper to read the local news
—to ascertain what points have been discussed in Parliament, not what has been the character or ability of the
discussion—to find what has been passing in the law
courts or the police offices—what accidents have taken
place—who has been married, or who has died—what
was the price of stocks yesterday, or of railway shares, or
of beef and mutton at Newgate-market—who gave parties,
and who attended them—what promotions have taken
place in the army or navy, or who have become bank-
rupts—finally, what has been lost or found—what is to
be sold—who want to be hired, and all the thousand
wishes and requirements, hopes, fears, and expectations,
which appear in the advertisements. The proprietors of
journals, who frequently regard them merely as concerns
for making money, know well enough that, though good
writing in the leading articles is an advantage, it is by
no means the principal thing upon which the success—
that is to say, the sale—of their journal depends. The
man of the most extraordinary *genius* of this century was
Mr. Samuel Taylor Coleridge. He was employed by
Mr. Stuart, the proprietor of the *Morning Post* some
fifty years ago, to write for that journal, and he did write
essays on public affairs distinguished by the most splendid
ability. Neither Mr. Stuart, however, nor any one else
considered that much *honour* should attach to the writer
of those essays, for they knew very well that much *profit*
did not. Mr. Stuart says, in the letters which many
years afterwards he published in the *Gentleman's Maga-*

zine, that " It was the earliest and fullest accounts of
public events that raised the *Morning Post* from 350, when
he took it, in August, 1795, to 4500 when he sold it, in
August, 1803, and then no other daily morning paper
sold above 3000.   It was unremitting attention and
success in giving the best and earliest account of occur-
rences that *made* the *Morning Post*, and not the writings
of any one, though good writing is always an important
feature."   " I have known," continues Mr. Stuart, " the
paper served more by a minute, picturesque, lively
account of the ascension of a balloon than ever it was by
any piece of writing."

When this newspaper proprietor speaks of his paper
being " served more," he means simply that more copies
were sold by reason of his balloon ascent report, than by
any piece of political writing.   I have no doubt that his
statement is quite correct, though, at the very time he
refers to, he had the literary assistance of a man of more
surprising genius, and of more command over the most
striking and picturesque forms of the English language,
than any other that ever wrote essays for a daily newspaper.

Mr. Coleridge afterwards wrote for the *Courier* when
the late Mr. Street (who died in great poverty and obscurity) was the editor, and more intimate with persons
of official information and distinction than any other mere
editor of a London newspaper ever was before or since.   In
1816 Mr. Coleridge, referring to that bygone connection,
said, " Had the paper maintained and asserted not only
its independence, but its appearance of it—it is true that
Mr. Street might not have had Mr. A. to dine with him,
or received as many nods and shakes of the hand from
Lord this or that; but at least equally true, that the
ministry would have been far more effectually served,

and that both the paper and its conductor would have
been held by the adherents of ministers in far higher
respect : and after all, ministers do not love newspapers
in their hearts, not even those that support them ; indeed,
it seems epidemic among Parliament-men in general to
affect to look down upon and despise newspapers, to which
they owe $\frac{999}{1000}$ of their influence and character, and at least
three-fifths of their knowledge and phraseology." Here
Mr. Coleridge writes with the irritability of a man of
genius. In the time of the war with France, the great
sale of the *Courier* arose out of the fact that it was not
independent, but the organ of the Government, and the
medium through which the Government made known that
which it was willing the public should know. The paper
was important because it was extensively read, and it was
extensively read because it was known to be the Government paper. No inspiration of eloquence—no reputation
for independence—would have procured for a daily paper
the tenth part of the readers that were obtained by the
reputation of being the organ of the Government, for
nine-tenths of the readers of newspapers are commonplace people who do not know good composition from
bad, and who would not give a rush for either eloquence
or independence, unless haply it had something to do
with the ascent of a balloon or the price of cotton goods.

Among the few things that have been written about in
these days without much exaggeration, the London daily
newspaper takes a first place. The establishment engaged
in a morning daily paper is enormous, and the expense
proportionate. Suppose any one wished to set up a new
morning paper in London, according to the present scale
of public expectation in such matters ;—his first task
should be to provide himself with at least 50,000*l.* in
order to try the experiment. And with the exception of

setting up an Italian opera-house, there are perhaps few speculations which would afford more rapid opportunities of losing that sum, or perhaps as much more. I shall take a momentary glance — I know it must be a very imperfect one—at the *personnel* of such an establishment. First comes the business-manager, who makes the engagements, gives orders to the cashier — answers letters on business—concludes arrangements with correspondents— confers with the solicitor, and does a thousand things besides, all connected, directly or indirectly, with finance. On pressing occasions he must have an assistant. Then comes the editor-in-chief, who rules over all political and literary communications, deciding whether they shall descend to the waste-paper basket, or be exalted to the printing-office. If he have not a quick eye and a ready brain for plucking the mystery out of a MS., Heaven help him! He must have at least two assistants, one to look over and arrange foreign communications, the other to attend to country affairs and the provincial press. These editorial functionaries begin their work about the time that fashionable people finish their dinners. The writers of the articles called editorial or leading articles dwell Heaven knows where. They have no *locus standi* or *sedendi* in the house where the newspaper is put together. Their communications reach the chief editor under seal, and he looks at them and passes them on to the printer, or keeps them back. If Parliament be sitting, there must be from twelve to twenty reporters of Parliamentary speeches, of whom only one works at once in each house. He takes notes for three-quarters of an hour, another takes his place, and he then comes to the office and writes out or "extends" his notes, the printer's devils sweeping away slip after slip as it is ready for the compositor. Frequently from two to three hours are occupied in writing out from the notes of three-quarters of an hour. Besides the Parliamentary reporters, there are some eight or ten in the various courts of justice ; and after all, the mass of *miscellaneous* reporting is done by outlying news-providers, who watch for anything likely to be of public interest, and, writing out several copies of their brief history, carry it to the different newspaper-offices, where, if it be used, it will certainly be paid for at so much per line when the account is sent in at the end of the week. In the printing-office are from forty to sixty compositors, and sometimes more, toiling with amazing quickness of hand and eye at their work throughout the long night. About four o'clock in the morning a number of columns of type are put together within an iron frame, and firmly screwed and wedged into their position, with much noise of mallets. Away goes the huge frame to the press-room below. It is the first side or " form " of the paper, and then begins the clank of the engine, and whir of the rolling press as the impressions are taken off. Meanwhile the work still goes on above, preparing the " inside " or newest news of the paper. Until four o'clock in the morning messengers and expresses are coming with bundles from this place or that—some public meeting in the provinces, which the reporters have written out as they came up in the railway-carriage, with special engine paid for by the establishment—some rout at the West end, of which the " fashionable reporter " has just finished the embellishments—some dreamy member's notes upon his own speech spoken three hours before. At last the time has come when a finish must be made ; for the railway-train that goes out at six A.M. must carry off *to* the country in print the intelligence which has just come *from* the country in MS. Then another frame of type is wedged and bolted up, descends to the press-room, and the huge sheet, already printed on one side, passes once more through the presses and is complete.* But let us again glance at the establishment necessary for all this. We have mentioned managers, editors, writers, reporters, compositors. All these have attendants carrying backward and forward the "copy," the "proof," the "revise," and so on. Then come the pressmen and enginemen and the attendant boys. Then the publisher's office with his attendants. Besides all these, there is a department for receiving and registering advertisements, a cashier's department, and a book-keeper's department, with their various clerks. To crown all, there is a correspondent to be employed and paid in every part of the world from which intelligence of public interest occasionally arrives. Upon the whole, it is very wonderful with what clock-like regularity all this goes on, and how sure the Londoner, or any one on a line of railway within sixty miles of London, is to have the "morning papers" with his early breakfast, if he chooses to order them, conveying to him the latest news that has come from every part of the world. Not long ago there was a paper in Chambers's

---

* The *Athenæum* of May 25, 1850, contains the following abstract of a portion of a paper read at the Institution of Civil Engineers :—

"On the 7th of May, 1850, the *Times* and *Supplement* contained 72 columns, or 17,500 lines, made up of upwards of a million pieces of type, of which matter about two-fifths were written, composed, and corrected after 7 o'clock in the evening. The Supplement was sent to press at 7.50 P.M., the first form of the paper at 4.15 A.M., and the second form at 4.45 A.M. On this occasion 7000 papers were published before 6.15 A.M., 21,000 before 7.30 A.M., and 34,000 before 8.45 A.M., or in about four hours. The greatest number of copies ever printed in one day was 54,000, and the greatest quantity of printing in one day's publication was on the 1st of March, 1848, when the paper used weighed 7 tons, the weight usually required being 4½ tons. The surface to be printed every night, including the Supplement, was 30 acres, and 110 compositors and 25 pressmen were constantly employed."

Journal which gave a very elaborate account of the proceedings necessary to produce a daily morning paper. So
far as I remember it, it was a tolerably faithful statement,
but somewhat drawn out and overdone in its detail of
Parliamentary reporting.

Formerly an account used to be periodically moved for
in Parliament, and published, of the number of stamps delivered to each paper, but that was at length considered
rather too glaring an interference with private business—
(though no such delicacy prevents the incomes of ten
thousand clergymen being year after year advertised to the
world)—and now only the aggregate amount of stamps
issued is laid before Parliament. The following particulars of the number of advertisements published in Great
Britain, and the duty paid to Government thereon, I take
from the *Times* of February 13, 1850 :—

	Number.	Duty.
1830	788,091	£137,915
1831	787,649	137,838
1832	783,557	137,122

(Duty reduced to 1s. 6d. from July 5, 1833.)

	Number.	Duty.
1834	977,441	73,308
1835	1,038,041	77,853
1836	1,173,136	87,985
1837	1,206,680	90,501
1838	1,315,581	98,668
1839	1,351,421	101,356
1840	1,425,387	106,904

The following is given by the same authority as the total
amount of taxation levied upon newspapers in 1847 :—

Stamp on newspapers in 1847	£343,278
Tax on advertisements in 1847	162,734
Duty on paper in 1847	617,245
Total	£1,123,257

The *Times* states its own contributions to the National Exchequer to be at present 95,000*l.* a-year, viz. :—

Duty on paper	£16,000
Stamps	60,000
Advertisement duty	19,000
Total	£95,000

The sum of 60,000*l.* for stamps on papers within the year shows an immense circulation. Take 313 days of publication at 1½*d.* for each paper and its supplement, it would take 30,778 every day to make up 60,000*l.* ; but as the stamp is only a penny when a supplement is not published, and as it is frequently omitted when Parliament is not sitting, the daily average is perhaps a thousand or two more. There are five daily morning papers in London besides the *Times,* and it is generally believed that the aggregate number printed by them all does not exceed that which rumour and my rough calculation attribute to the *Times;* but I know not on what foundation this current belief has been formed. The weekly papers of London absorb such an enormous number of stamps, that the general return of stamps used is no guide to the daily consumption, which also includes evening papers as well as morning.

It seems to be generally admitted that in the production of newspapers, as in that of cutlery and cotton goods, England far surpasses every other part of the world.*

---

* The following is an official return of the stamp and advertisement duty paid by newspapers in 1849 :—

Stamps issued :—

England and Wales . .	66,159,502	penny stamps.
,, ,, . .	10,309,233	halfpenny do.
Scotland	6,288,205	penny stamps.
,, ...	205,000	halfpenny do.

Ireland

In the Report of the Commissioner for inquiring into the state of the Mining Population, presented to Parliament in the session of 1850, he has occasion to speak very strongly of the pernicious effects of an ill-conducted press. He made a collection of low-priced periodicals (1*d.* and 1½*d.* each) circulating in the towns of Wednesbury and Bilston. Of the whole number, amounting to fifteen, *seven,* he says, were written in a good spirit, though containing portions of very inferior novels (published in fragments, after the manner of the French feuilletons), which would be more likely to lower the taste and injure the morals of the young than to convey any sound instruction. *Eight* were written in a spirit of hostility either to the institutions or the religion of the country, or both; five of these are organs of Chartism or Socialism; the other three, though not professing Chartism, approach very near it, and appear to have more in view the dissemination of infidelity, and the discussion of the doctrines of Socialism, which are spoken of with approbation.

The commissioner was informed that all the publications of the latter class (anarchical, Socialist, and infidel) had a considerable and an increasing sale in these districts. Their advertisements show that there are about thirteen cheap periodicals devoted to these views, pub-

---

Ireland   .   .   .   .   6,345,227 penny stamps.
      ,, ...   38,843 halfpenny do.
London newspapers from which newspaper duty was collected, 160.
Number of advertisements, 886,108.
Amount of duty, 66,458*l.*
English provincial papers, 232; duty received, 62,604*l.* 13*s.* 6*d.*, on 834,729 advertisements.
Scotland, 94 newspapers, 240,901 advertisements, producing 18,075*l.* duty.
Ireland, 117 newspapers, 220,524 advertisements, producing 11,026*l.*, at 1*s.* duty.   The British duty is 1*s.* 6*d.*

lished chiefly in London, of which eight circulate in the
neighbourhood already mentioned. The commissioner
adds that he has compared these publications with those
of the democratic and Socialist press of France, conducted
by Barbés, Louis Blanc, Blanqui, Lamennais, &c., and
he finds them identical in their views and arguments.
The English productions of this dangerous class are, he
says, evidently copies in design, and partly in execution,
of the French ones. Indeed, he affirms that the Repub-
lican and Socialist literature of the Continent is plainly
visible in its effect on the tone, the language, and the
doctrines of all the English publications alluded to as
advocates of Chartism and Socialism.

It is very unfortunate that it is only in respect to what
is bad that our working-people have this taste for imitation of the French. The same commissioner, in another
part of his Report, eulogizes the conduct of the French
working-people as compared with the English, dwelling
upon their good manners, frugality, and forethought, by
which they become in time respectable and independent
members of society; while English people, earning the
same wages, are drunken, rude, and reckless, spending
every farthing of their earnings as soon as it is acquired.

There have been at all times, says this commissioner,
a certain class of periodicals of a low grade circulating
among the poor, conveying to their minds the worst doctrines, and inspiring them with a distrust of the institutions of society and a feeling of enmity against those
above them. But the new feature in the present " agitation " is its extreme bitterness of spirit and violence of
language against all classes except the lowest, its crusade
against wealth, its advocacy of infidelity, and its open
adoption of the principles of Socialism.

I cannot think that a Government can be considered to

do its duty towards the people which takes no steps to
prevent such publications from being circulated. The
usual excuse in these days in England for such remiss-
ness is, that the Government *cannot* wholly suppress such
publications, and to attack them without success, or with
only partial success, would make the mischief greater.
This seems to me a weak excuse. If the law be not
strong enough to correct the existing mischief, it ought
to be made so. The subject is of the very highest importance ; and if rulers were as earnest in matters which
concern the morals of the people as they are in matters
which they believe to concern the profits of trade, it cannot be doubted that some remedy would be attempted,
and would be achieved.

The revolutionary and infidel characteristics of a portion of the press, are not, the commissioner says, confined
to the periodicals avowedly Chartist and Socialist in their
tendency, " but many of them belong to those addressed
to classes whose intelligence and whose interests might
be expected to place them above any sympathy with such
writings—such as the highest class of artisans, and the
lower grades of the middle class. They are the more
attractive, because of their earnest tone and manner, and
the cordial spirit of sympathy with what they believe to
be for the benefit and improvement of those for whom
they write. Many also display considerable command of
language and vigour of style, and skill in the exposition
of their views. The bent of mind which they give evidence of, is evidently traceable either to the sceptical
German school or to a predominating intellectual cultivation, without the guide and check of sound religious
teaching. Indeed, it seems to exhibit the result of a
mental cultivation without any guide at all ; and nothing
is more conspicuous in most of these writings than either

the entire absence of all reference to, or the bold denial of the wisdom and authority of, all the great writers of all ages, who have been hitherto regarded as the instructors of mankind. They write as if history and philosophy had no existence ; and, as respects the former, they are also engaged in distorting it, with a view to vilify the upper classes, and especially in misrepresenting or concealing everything in the continental revolutions of the last two years, from which their real causes, their actual progress, their consequences, and the true characters of the actors in them, could be known and understood. They deny the authority of principles and the wisdom of institutions that have received the sanction of ages ; and they call upon the young, the superficial, and the presumptuous, to reason and to act as if nothing had been fixed before them, and as if society were to begin anew with each generation."

It is the opinion of the commissioner (Mr. Tremenheere) that it would be unwise to treat lightly the possible effect of publications of this character, conducted, as they are, with an ability quite capable of making them attractive. He thinks also that a period of *excitement* might bring to light the fact that the poison of them had been widely and effectively disseminated, and the object of its propagators attained in endangering the peace of society.

All this having been officially reported to Parliament, is with due gravity entombed in a blue-book at the public expense, and then forgotten as completely as the subject of any other interment. That this is not wise, the public will doubtless some day discover ; and let us hope it may not be a revolutionary explosion that will awaken them to a sense of previous neglect. I do not know that all Mr. Tremenheere says is to be taken as perfectly accurate. He may be one of those who are more anxious to make an impression by what they say, than scrupulous in satisfying themselves of the strict correctness of their statements.   Be that as it may, he is a Parliamentary Commissioner : and what he officially reports, when it has an important bearing on the condition of the people, should be investigated.   If his statement be found correct, a remedy ought to be applied ; if it be found incorrect, Parliament should guard itself and the public from being misled upon so important a subject.

CHAPTER XVIII.

MODERN SCIENCE.

THE true scientific spirit has been well described by Mr.
Macaulay as " a spirit admirably compounded of audacity
and sobriety." This is the spirit he attributes to Francis
Bacon; and it is a pity he did not speak equally well, on
another occasion, of the great scholar of the same name,
who so long preceded the philosopher. Upon the illustrious monk—the angelic doctor—of the thirteenth century, he seemed to throw a kind of retrospective scorn,
when, in order to extol the ordinary information of the
present day, he said it was greater than that which made
Friar Bacon the wonder of his age. In this remark, a
hearsay and superficial acquaintance with facts is con-
founded with knowledge and science. This is an error
unworthy of an eloquent philosopher, and it is one which
Mr. Macaulay's critical acumen would quickly have
pointed out to general censure had it been fallen into by
another. Who will compare the knowledge of the man
who has read in the newspaper of the discovery of the
planet Neptune, with the knowledge of him whose daring
thought and long laborious calculation ended in the conviction that such a planet existed, though undiscovered?
The difference between that kind of knowledge which
arises merely from casual instruction and heedless assent,
and that which rewards

> " the long laborious guest
> Of Reason, seated on her sovereign hill,"

is so great, that no conceivable extent of the one is worth
the narrowest store of the other. The bold aspiring spirit
that seeks truth for itself, combined with the spirit of
sobriety, which begets patience, modesty, and caution, and
leads the daring discoverer to compare his new results
with foregone learning,—that is something better than
mere knowledge, for it is the spirit which both acquires
knowledge and turns it to the best account.

That which is *popularly* termed a taste for science in
these times, is either the desire to hear the latest news in
the scientific world, and a willingness to attend lectures,
as one goes to a show or an assembly ; or it is the desire
to become acquainted with something that may be turned
to practical account, for promoting convenience, or for
making money. This is what occasions the perpetual
bustle of the " scientific world " in towns. The going to
lectures is a fashion, which many people submit to, though
it is far from agreeable, just as they do to a thousand
other things tedious or unpleasant in themselves, but
suffered with patience, or even eagerly followed, because
it is the reigning mode.

At the same time it is unquestionably true that in colleges, in observatories, and possibly in many a retired
private house, there are profound students searching the
heavens or analysing the earth, or wearing out eye and
brain in calculations of forces and disturbances—attrac-
tions and perturbations :—counting up the almost infinite
repetition of minutenesses too delicate for ordinary observation, or weighing the isolated effects of magnitudes and
distances so stupendous and overwhelming that the ordinary mind grows dizzy when attempting to contemplate
them but for a moment. Of these, some study and die,
making no sign, while others write books, which a few
read, and which a good many purchase, in order to lay

them upon their library tables. I wish to guard against
being supposed to believe, or to wish others to believe,
that the heights and depths of science are not now ex-
plored with the most devoted and persevering care ; but
I have to speak of what is popularly called science—of
that fashion which crowds lecture-rooms, and which deserts the theatres where tragedy and comedy were wont
to be performed, in order to frequent the theatres of
scientific institutes, where gay bonnets are ranged opposite galvanic batteries, and the natural electric light of
ladies' eyes is brought into rivalship with the artificial
light of electro-magnetism.

The sciences which " crowds run to hear," says a
writer in a recent number of the *Edinburgh Review*, " are
natural philosophy and chemistry—it would be more just
to say that the arts springing out of these sciences are
popular, than that the sciences themselves are. The laws
regulating the elasticity of steam at different tempera-
tures—the theory of waves—the idea of polarity—the
doctrine of dia-magnetism, of electro-magnetics, of iso-
merism, or organic types, and much else, find no favour
with such disciples ; but screw-propellers, electric lights,
and new manures are cordially welcomed. . . . . What
was the planet Neptune to the utilitarian public, or that
public to Neptune ? His appearance in the heavens did
not lead to any reduction in the window-tax, or to any
saving in candles." This is very well as against the
utilitarians, but there are plenty in the scientific world of
fashion who affect an interest in " polarity " and electro-
magnetics, and who yawn piteously at the lectures thereon
in the intervals between the experiments. The utilitarians, who openly avow that they care for nothing scientific except it can be turned to some use, are respectable
in their way, when compared with the danglers and

dawdlers who trifle with science as a mode of killing time. If, however, it were merely the wish to be informed on what is interesting in its organization, or exquisite in its action, that led people to lecture-rooms, they might occupy themselves with simpler things than the scientific lecturer generally brings before them. A nettle or a limpet, as the critic of the *Edinburgh* truly says—the meanest weed or the humblest insect—still more a nautilus or a humming-bird, is, after all, at least as curious a thing as gun-cotton or chloroform; and a torpedo or gymnotus is in reality a much more wonderful machine than a voltaic battery.

As it is a prevailing notion that " liberality " in politics is associated with a due respect for science, while Conservatism, or love of the old ways, is accompanied by a bigoted suspicion of modern proficiency, even in chemistry and geology, I am glad to be able to support my own views of the modern scientific public, by authority, of which the political " liberality " cannot be questioned. I therefore proceed to quote the *Edinburgh Review*, which I suppose will be accounted *sans reproche* in all circles of genteel Whiggery. As for the Radicals, though they may not like to be laughed at, they will, I hope, have the sturdy candour to acknowledge that *utility* is the chief object of their veneration, and that the new planet is nothing to them if " the skies looked no brighter for his coming, and if the street lamps are as needful as they were before." The reviewer assures us that "intelligent appreciation, childish fear, childish wonder, a feverish spirit of speculation, and a *strong infusion of cupidity*, are all strangely mingled in the popular estimate of what the sciences are destined to effect for the world. The general faith in science as a wonder-worker is at present unlimited; and along with this there is cherished the conviction that

every discovery and invention admits of a practical application to the welfare of men. Is a new vegetable product brought to this country from abroad, or a new
chemical compound discovered, or a novel physical phe-
nomenon recorded, the question is immediately asked, *cui
bono* ? What is it good for ? Is food or drink to be got
out of it ? Will it make hats or shoes, or cover um-
brellas ? Will it kill or heal ? Will it drive a steam-
engine or make a mill go ?"

Again, we find this lively and shrewd observer describing the effects upon chemistry, of having been so
much followed after, and, as it were, " used up" by the
utilitarians and the fanciers of wonders. " Chemistry
has long come down from her atomic altitudes and electric
affinities, and now scours and dyes, brews, bakes, cooks,
and compounds drugs and manures with contented com-
posure. Electricity leaves her thunderbolt in the sky,
and, like Mercury dismissed from Olympus, acts as letter-
carrier and message-boy. Even mysterious magnetism,
which once seemed like a living principle to quiver in the
compass-needle, is unclothed of mystery, and set to drive
turning-lathes. The public perceives all this, and has
unlimited faith in man's power to conquer nature. The
credulity which formerly fed upon unicorns, phœnixes,
mermaids, vampires, crackens, pestilential comets, fairies,
ghosts, witches, spectres, charms, curses, universal remedies, pactions with Satan, and the like, now tampers with
chemistry, electricity, and magnetism, as it once did with
the invisible world. Shoes of swiftness, seven-leagued
boots, and Fortunatus' wishing-caps are banished even
from the nursery ; but an electro-magnetic steam fire-
balloon, which will cleave the air like a thunderbolt, and
go straight to its destination as the crow flies, is an invention which many hope to see realized before railways
are quite worn to pieces."

Such, then, is the "science" of the crowd in this enlightened age—such the mental superiority of this period
of progress! But was it not always so, more or less?
No. It has been so these fifty years in a less degree,
but not in a greater. In this, as in so many other things,
such an enormous crowd has run after the fashion of
being scientific, that it has become vulgarised and flat-
tened down into the dullest absurdity. Forty years ago,
in the days of Sir Humphry Davy's triumphs, there was
doubtless a great deal of scientific affectation in the
fashionable world, and carriage company crowded to the
Royal Institution, as they do now, to listen to his scarcely
less-gifted successor. But in his day the *fashion* stopped
with the circle which surrounded him, or not far beyond
it; and if May Fair was scientific (on the "off days" of
morning concerts), Finsbury Circus was content to be
domestic and commercial, and Hackney enjoyed its even-
ings with a game of cards or a dance. Not so now.
Every district of the town must have its scientific insti-
tute, and every suburb its courses of lectures. It is
obvious enough that this is up-hill work, and that something more social, concluding with a supper, would be
infinitely more to the taste of the company, if that more
congenial method of passing the time by good luck happened to be the fashion. But what is *the* fashion must
now be followed by the enlightened middle class; and
so, while the thing is new, subscriptions are paid and
scientific lectureships established in every "enlightened"
neighbourhood. But the zeal, being unnatural, grows
cold. It is found that in science, as in poetry, "no one
is great by imitation." Subscriptions fall off, managers
grow weary of their functions, and at last the affair falls
to the ground or into the hands of those who earn their
livelihood by lectures, and who therefore apportion the

supply to the demand, giving an occasional discourse instead of a series (where the fashion has had its run), and reserving their more continuous efforts for new neighbourhoods, where science is only blossoming, and has yet to be matured into fruit.

Of those who undertake to teach science by lectures, it is matter of regret that so very few are competent to the task. As to knowledge, they have generally enough, and perhaps more than enough; but to communicate that knowledge to others—to perceive how much they should attempt to teach, and how they should make it clear to the minds of a miscellaneous auditory—that is a talent which scarcely one in fifty lecturers appears to possess. Science has proceeded so fast of late years, and so many new things, very interesting, but not easily intelligible to beginners, have been brought forward, that professors appear to be ashamed of teaching simple elementary knowledge. When they appear in the lecture-room (I do not speak of all) their object is rather to show off the newest and most difficult branch of their own knowledge, than to supply those they address with the simpler elements of science, which alone they are capable of receiving and retaining. They talk over the heads of their auditory, or, for the sake of dilating upon something which is intelligible to a few scientific friends, they neglect the instruction of nine-tenths of the assembly. I venture to affirm that a very large proportion of those who have heard lectures upon electro-chemistry, and who have seen water decomposed by the galvanic battery or by magnetic force, could not tell of what elements water is composed. The lecturer thinks it beneath him to begin with the A B C of the science, and talks to an auditory who have not yet learned their letters, as if they could read and understand. The art, or gift, of commu-

nicating knowledge with clearness and earnestness is indeed much more rare than the capacity for acquiring
knowledge, even when men devote themselves to the profession of lecturing with the most anxious wish to become
effective teachers; but lecturers actuated by vanity, and
a desire to show how much they know (which is so natural
a weakness that one cannot apply to it much harshness of
censure), can never be of much use in imparting knowledge to the crowd, even though they succeed in pleasing
or surprising for the moment.   I have seen a gentleman
of no mean abilities devote an hour to an exposition of
the newest application of the power of the galvanic
battery, before an audience of whom nineteen-twentieths
then saw galvanic action for the first time in their lives,
and who had no more notion of the nature of the force
familiarly referred to over and over again by the lecturer,
than they had of the kind of cinder of which the moon is
composed—if, indeed, our beautiful moon, which we so
justly admire, and to which so many sonnets have been
addressed, be nothing else than a huge cinder, as I believe
the learned have now decided.

In teaching science to a popular and miscellaneous
assembly, it seems to me that such knowledge should be
imparted as it is most likely can be made use of afterwards by the persons addressed.   On this account, when
mixed popular assemblies are to be lectured to, I should
rather see natural history taught, and the chemical theories
belonging to familiar matters, than the more difficult and
advanced branches of science.   The peculiarities and
classifications of the various creatures which surround us,
their instincts and their habits, what is known of the life
of birds, of fishes, and of insects, must generally be interesting to a popular assembly; for though we may
never be able to answer such questions as that of the fool

in 'Lear,'—" How does an oyster make its shell?"—we may learn humility even from our ignorance; and from what we can learn we may come to take a livelier, and possibly a more affectionate interest, in the creatures which share with us the world wherein we all live. But with regard to the idea of polarity, the theory of waves, the doctrine of dia-magnetism, and such like, though they are of the highest interest to persons whose chief attention is given to science, and though they are deserving of all respect in their proper place, they are, I think, unsuitable for ordinary teaching. The great majority of the assembly will forget almost immediately all they hear on these subjects, because they have nothing in their daily experience to renew and refresh the ideas they have received. This will be found true even in respect of those who understand what they hear upon these difficult points at the time they hear it; but probably there are many in every popular assembly who have not that advantage, when the more advanced views of scientific reasoners are laid before them.

In respect to chemistry, the interest of it would be very much enhanced if one could bring into familiar use the knowledge which lecturers afford, or into familiar application for intellectual entertainment. It is therefore with great pleasure I have seen the announcement of a course of lectures from the most philosophic chemist, and the ablest lecturer on natural science, that our country at present possesses, upon such subjects as the following—"a fire, a candle, a lamp, a chimney, a kettle, ashes."* These seem to me to be the proper subjects for a miscellaneous assemblage, of whom a very large majority will

---

* These lectures were delivered by Mr. Faraday at the Royal Institution in May and June, 1850, and, if their success might be judged of by the crowds that went to hear them, never were lectures more effectual.

most probably never visit a laboratory, but all of whom have something to do every day of their lives with the objects of which they will hear the chemical history. I hope the scientific teachers in less important lecture-rooms than that of the Royal Institution will follow the example set to them at head-quarters, and will choose subjects upon which the majority of their audience will be likely to dwell after the lecture is over. Chemistry teaches of what ultimate atoms material bodies are composed, and in what proportions the atoms are combined in compound bodies. Every one, of the least intelligence, feels an interest in knowing what water is composed of, of what substances sugar is compounded, what things are put together by nature to make a cup of milk, and what are the ingredients, chemically considered, of a leg of mutton. These are things which, if explained over night, will scarcely be forgotten the next day. If the professor would teach the chemistry of the breakfast-table, expounding the wonder that the sugar which is upon it, the cloth which covers it, and the wood of the table itself, are, with respect to their ultimate atoms, very nearly the same, and that the difference between them is the result of a subtlety of structure and combination which our powers of perception or of analysis cannot master, he would be heard with attention by every one. If the boy were told that the diamond which glitters on his mother's finger, and the pencil of black lead, as he calls it, with which he draws figures on paper, are, chemically considered, almost the same thing, and both of them very nearly identical with pure charcoal, would he not immediately become interested in chemical science? And when he was carried onward to observe how much a man's knowledge may be, when compared with ignorance, and how little he can know when compared with the full history of what has been

done for him by the Omnipotent Creator of all things,
may he not thus be taught the two great moral lessons of
self-respect and of humility ?   Expound to him, if you
will, step by step, the intricate action of that exquisite
machinery—which one wonders that human ingenuity
could ever have fallen upon—the machinery which gradually changes cotton-wool into muslin or to lace ; and
then show him the commonest flower of the field, exhibiting
a minute precision of structure, and an admirable even-
ness of texture, which no art could achieve, and of which
no science can explain the process; do this, and will he
not become a religious creature?   Will not his mind
become usefully convinced of the difference between what
man accomplishes by his skill, and what God ordains by
his inscrutable power ?   Will he not find, both in a sentimental and poetical sense, that the meanest flower that
blows can give

" Thoughts that do often lie *too deep* for tears ;"

and also that, in a scientific and a moral sense, it may teach
even him who knows most, that all art, and all ingenuity,
are as nothing compared with the simplest works of the
Almighty.   " Consider the lilies of the field, how they
grow ; they toil not, neither do they spin, and yet I say
unto you that even Solomon in all his glory was not
arrayed like one of these."

The greatest triumph of our day in practical science is,
I think, the Electric Telegraph.   The steamboat and the
locomotive engine are of more general, and of more
stupendous utility, but their triumph over natural difficulty, their mastery over time and space, their novelty
and marvellousness, are all less than that of the Electric
Telegraph.   Many years ago model boats were made to

move through water by wheels at the sides, which owed their motion to clockwork in the interior, and by the same means carriages and puppet-figures were made to move over smooth and level surfaces. The steamboat and the locomotive engine are but the application of the enormous force of steam to effect those motions upon a large scale, and against great resistance, which without steam had been effected upon a small scale, and against a very small resistance. But the electric telegraph, the setting of types as it were, at the distance of hundreds of miles, by means of the electric force carried through continuous wires, is, I believe, as new as it is wonderful. A rapidity in the communication of intelligence is achieved which anticipates time itself. Time is measured by the motion of the earth, but that motion is slowness compared with the motion of the electric fluid. We can announce, from London to the city of Bristol, the demise of the old year and the birth of a new one, while in Bristol the old year has some minutes of existence still left. While Bristol is still spinning round to twelve o'clock, London has not only passed the point, but may have announced it by the lightning telegraph to her western sister, who is a hundred miles behind her. "Progress" can hardly beat this, let what will happen. In this matter we may rest satisfied that science has done her utmost. The force of nature and of art can no further go.

The utilitarian tendency of scientific inquiry in recent times, and a certain materialistic turn of the general mind, seem to have given a rather undue preponderance to the physical sciences, and indeed to have cast into the shade, so far as popular patronage is concerned, the philosophy of the mind, which at former times gave profound occupation to the most eminent thinkers of our country. In the present time it is only what one can see or handle, or

taste or smell, or measure or weigh, that " philosophers "
seem to care for.   What they can boil in a retort, or
roast in a crucible ; what they can break in pieces with a
hammer, or bray in a mortar, or rend into its primary
elements by electrical force, they will industriously attend
to, but if you invite them to examine the processes of their
own minds, and to consider and classify the powers of
perception, reflection, comparison, deduction, and so forth,
without which all their tasting, smelling, boiling, burning,
weighing, measuring, and all other processes, analytical
or synthetical, would be nothing worth—they have neither
time nor inclination for such inquiries.   This, I think, is
to be regretted ; for though nothing can be more painful
than rash speculation concerning the nature and powers
of the mind, yet no philosophy can be complete, or can
have the elevation which philosophy ought to have, if the
faculties by which it is apprehended and judged of, be
left out of consideration.   Upon this point the late Dr.
Thomas Brown, of Edinburgh University, has said with
no less truth than eloquence, that " In the physics of the
material universe there is indeed much that is truly worthy
of our philosophic admiration, and of the sublimest exertions of philosophic genius.   But even that material world
will appear more admirable to him who contemplates it
as it were from the height of his own mind, and who
measures its infinity with the range of his own limited but
aspiring faculties.   He is unquestionably the philosopher
most worthy of the name who unites to the most accurate
knowledge of mind the most accurate knowledge of all
the physical objects amid which he is placed ; who makes
each science to each reciprocally a source of additional
illumination ; and who learns from both the noblest of all
the lessons which they can give—the knowledge and ado-
ration of that Divine Being who has alike created and

adapted to each other, with an order so harmonious, the universe of matter and the universe of thought."*

In the preface to Wordsworth's *Excursion* there is a noble fragment of a poem, in which the Bard touches, as only a great poet can, upon the stupendous mystery of the mind of man, "his haunt and the main region of his song;" and then proceeds to describe, with the energy and music of verse, that same relation which is dwelt upon in the foregoing extract :—

> '' by words,
> Which speak of nothing more than what we are,
> Would I arouse the sensual from their sleep
> Of death, and win the vacant and the vain
> To noble raptures; while my voice proclaims
> How exquisitely the individual mind
> (And the progressive powers perhaps no less
> Of the whole species) to the external world
> Is fitted :—and how exquisitely too—
> Theme this but little heard of among men—
> The external world is fitted to the mind ;
> And the creation (by no lower name
> Can it be called) which they with blended might
> Accomplish :—this is our high argument."

There is one branch of mental inquiry—I mean Political Economy—which has received a kind of popular attention in these days, chiefly, I believe, because it is supposed to point the way to the accumulation of wealth. There is still much question whether this branch of knowledge is sufficiently matured, and sufficiently distinct, to be ranked among the sciences; but since it has regularly appointed Professors in the Universities of Oxford, Cambridge, and Dublin, it were perhaps disrespectful to express a doubt upon the subject. Political

---

* 'Lectures on the Philosophy of Mind,' lecture ii.

Economy has, however, been described in *Blackwood's Magazine* as " a grave confusion of ideas—the formality of nonsense." It has also been called the "one-eyed science," from the partial view which it takes of the interests of mankind. An eminent barrister, who writes a book called ' Sophisms of Free Trade,' prophesies that Political Economy will be a science, but pronounces that it is not one yet. The *Quarterly Review* says it is a science, but a young one ; and proceeds to complain of the arrogant spirit and insufferable presumption of its professors, who dogmatize as if all their propositions were incontrovertible truths, though they cannot agree among themselves as to their leading principles, but accuse one another of error. Sir Robert Peel, in a speech delivered some years ago, wished it might be far from him to " depreciate that noble science which is conversant with the laws that regulate the production of wealth, and seeks to make human industry most conducive to human comfort and enjoyment." Immediately after saying this, however, he proceeded to show how " the brightest luminaries " of that same " noble science " had " failed to throw light on the obscure and intricate question of the nature and amount of those special burdens upon agriculture, which entitle it to protection from foreign competition." Not only, he said, did he not find in their lucubrations any solution of the difficulties, but he found the difficulties greatly increased by the *conflict of authorities.* Adam Smith had propounded a doctrine concerning rent. Mr. Ricardo pronounced that it was erroneous. Adam Smith thought the value of gold estimated in corn would be highest in rich countries. Mr. Ricardo thought exactly the contrary. Mr. M'Culloch cites the *conflicting* opinions of Smith and Ricardo on the subject of the effect of Tithe upon the price of corn ; but Mr. M'Culloch, instead of pointing out which is right, declares that they are both wrong. Colonel Torrens, again, reviews the *doctrines* of Mr. Ricardo, Mr. M'Culloch, Mr. Malthus, and Dr. Adam Smith, together with those of the French Economists at large, and decides that they are all wrong, and that his own *doctrine* is the right one. Such are the illustrations afforded by Sir Robert Peel of the advantages afforded to the world by that " noble science" which he was anxious not to depreciate! He refers to the book of Colonel Torrens as " an acute and valuable work," and in a few sentences afterwards says " the very heads of Colonel Torrens's chapters are enough to fill with dismay the bewildered inquirer after truth." These headings of chapters all have reference to the errors of other politico-economic " luminaries," which the learned and gallant Colonel desired to expose and refute.

I come now to no less an authority than that of the Professor of Political Economy in the University of Oxford, who seems to differ utterly from Sir Robert Peel as to the view which ought to be taken of the " noble science." Sir Robert Peel said that the object of the science is to make human industry most conducive to human comfort and enjoyment. Mr. Nassau W. Senior, of Oxford University, delivers himself as follows :—" What distribution of wealth is desirable in each different state of society? And what are the means by which any given country can facilitate such a distribution?—These are questions of great interest and difficulty, but no more form part of the science of Political Economy, in the sense in which we use that term, than navigation forms part of the science of astronomy. The principles supplied by Political Economy are indeed necessary elements in their solution, but they are not the only, or even the most important, elements. The writer who pursues such investigations is, in fact,

engaged on the great science of legislation; a science
which requires a knowledge of the general principles supplied by political economy, but differs from it essentially
in its subject, its premises, and its conclusions. The
subject of legislation is not wealth, but human welfare.
Its premises are drawn from an infinite variety of phenomena, supported by evidence of every degree of strength,
and authorizing conclusions deserving every degree of
assent, from perfect confidence to bare suspicion. And
its expounder is enabled and even required, not merely to
state general facts, but to urge the adoption or rejection
of actual measures or trains of action. On the other
hand, the subject treated by the political economist, using
that term in the limited sense in which we apply it, is *not
happiness, but wealth.* . . . . . The business of a political
economist is neither to recommend nor to dissuade, but to
state general principles which it is fatal to neglect, but
neither advisable nor perhaps practicable to use as the
sole, or even the principal, guides in the actual conduct
of affairs. In the mean time, the duty of each individual
writer is clear. Employed as he is upon a science in
which error, or even ignorance, may be productive of such
intense and such extensive mischief, he is bound, like a
juryman, to give deliverance true according to the evidence, and allow *neither sympathy with indigence, nor
disgust at profusion, or at avarice—neither reverence for
existing institutions, nor detestation of existing abuses*—
neither love of popularity, nor of paradox, nor of system,
to deter him from stating what he believes to be the facts,
or from drawing from those facts what appear to him to
be the legitimate conclusions. To decide in each case
how far those conclusions are to be acted upon, belongs to
the art of government, an art to which political economy
is only one of many subservient sciences."

Here, then, the Professor plainly enough avows that wealth, and nothing else but wealth, is the subject-matter of Political Economy—that it does not concern itself with the due distribution of wealth, nor with the happiness of the people—that it disavows sympathy with indigence— that it feels no disgust at avarice or profusion, has no detestation for abuses, and no reverence for existing institutions. Such is the Oxford Professor's account of that "science" which Sir Robert Peel said, in his place in the House of Commons, was "a noble science, which seeks to make human industry most conducive to human comfort and enjoyment!"

This "science," whatever be its true character, and whatever be its genuine "doctrines," so variously stated by the "luminaries" who have undertaken to enlighten the world by its means, has for some years past taken rank next after the physical sciences in fashion and popularity. Its effects upon the general mind, and its fruits in the sentiments and conduct of society, are such as might be expected from the Oxford Professor's account of it. As Southey said of it, what it requires of men is, "that they should harden their hearts." It is scarcely necessary to *teach* such lore as this. Selfishness is a weed which will grow fast enough without culture. The study of Political Economy makes men familiar with many subjects of the highest social importance, but I fear that it does not promote the growth of good social principles. To be selfish upon a great scale—to be formally and methodically selfish, and to regard selfishness as a kind of virtue, because it is raised to the rank of a science, seems to me to be the result of the teaching of Political Economy.

CHAPTER XIX.

RAILWAYS.

The most important event of the last quarter of a century in English history is the establishment of Railroads. The stupendous magnitude of the capital they have absorbed —the changes they have produced in the habits of society —the new aspect they have given, in some respects, to the affairs of government—the new feelings of power they have engendered—the triumphs and the disappointments of which they have been the cause—above all, the new and excessive activities to which they have given rise— must lead all who reflect upon the subject to admit that the importance of the general result of these great undertakings can scarcely be exaggerated. They have done much towards changing the old deliberative and thoughtful habits of Englishmen. People who breakfast at York and dine in London—who may be summoned from Liverpool to the metropolis in three or four minutes by the electric telegraph, and answer the summons in person within six or seven hours by the express train—acquire a habit of pressure and velocity in all they do. Even the Court of Chancery will not long be able to withstand the ideas of rapidity of motion which use and wont are turning into a second nature. But the spur which will be useful to excessive slowness may be injurious to that steadiness of pace which eventually makes the best progress. The effect of railroad habits is to make us more

American than we were, without the opportunities which
the extent of American territory, and which the nature
of her political institutions, afford, for turning her feverish
energy to good account. Thoughtfulness and prudence
are not only less valued in this country than they were,
but they are actually less valuable so far as regards the
attainment of fortune and distinction. These virtues are
too slow for the present times. Audacity and quickness
are the qualities in demand. To run risks with cleverness
—to dash through, at all hazards—to do business at all
events—to anticipate profits, and to live as if they were
realized—to rush to the point you would achieve, and
there blow off your steam with a prodigious quantity of
noise and vapour—such is now the manner of doing
business in England, and railways have done a great deal
towards establishing this fashion. Almost every one of
mature years now feels that he must either abandon the
business world altogether, or submit to a pressure and
strain which in former, and not less prosperous, times
were not imposed upon him. All persons are pushing
whatever they are engaged in to the uttermost. The
liberal man will not stop short of profusion, nor the
economist of stinginess. With less violence of manners
than formerly, there is scarcely any such thing as moderation of character and opinion. Whatever purpose a man
has in view, or whatever theory he has taken up, he is
apt, if he remains in the world, to " go a-head " with it,
and to disregard every consideration but that of gaining
his point. There is no modesty as to extent of production. If a calico-printer invents a pattern which *takes*,
he deluges the world with it. In three months he has
glutted the markets of Great Britain, and in six his
superfluous bales are crowding the warehouses of Sydney
or Hong Kong. If an author produces a book which the

public fancy, he goes on, and makes five or ten more books, all of which are but variations upon the original theme, each successive effort containing more elaboration and less truth and spirit. So it is in everything. Drive on —make hay while the sun shines—take advantage of the market, while there *is* a market—do not consider, but push on—such is the railroad temper of our times.

They who, from principle or from temperament, are averse to the new state of affairs, find that the torrent is too strong and impetuous to be resisted. Perhaps there is less individual courage among men than there used to be, especially in regard to public affairs. There are few in these days who are willing to trust to the goodness of their cause and the honesty of their purpose, and to stand their ground from a conviction that they ought to do so, whether they have followers to support them or have not. The penalty of such a course is ridicule from some, abuse from others, and unpleasant hints about imprudence, even from professing friends. This is not an age for men to stand against such discouragements. They take another course—they retire from the field of public controversy in disgust. They leave it to be trampled over by coarse and impetuously selfish men, who wring from reluctant weakness concessions which reason does not sanction,— concessions which are made, not from conviction, but from perplexity and fear. And while this is going on, the friends of a better order of things retire to their country-houses and their libraries, prophesying evil things in private, but not energetic enough to resist in public the tendencies which they deplore. The railway has made Manchester, as it were, a part of London, and infected London with the sentiments of Manchester. Even the Court catches the spirit of trade.

By a return presented to Parliament at the beginning

of the session of 1850, it appears that the progress of
railways for some years past has been as follows :—

Miles open in the United Kingdom at the end of

December, 1844	2240
June, 1845	2343
December, 1845	2536
June, 1846	2765
December, 1846	3142
June, 1847	3603
December, 1847	3945
June, 1848	4478
December, 1848	5127
June, 1849	5447

The number of passengers of all classes carried were—

Year ending June 30,

1845	33,791,253
1846	43,790,983
1847	51,352,163
1848	57,965,070
1849	60,398,159

Thus it will be seen that the increase of passengers is
by no means proportionate to the increase of miles of
railway opened. The proportion was well kept up to the
end of 1847, but since then it appears that the increase
of railway accommodation has been more rapid than the
increase of traffic. In the year ending June, 1849, the
number of first-class and of third-class passengers had
declined, when compared with the preceding year. The
following are the numbers carried of each class of passengers :—

Year ending June 30,	First Class.	Second Class.
1845	5,474,163	14,325,825
1846	6,160,354	16,931,066
1847	6,572,714	18,699,288
1848	7,190,779	21,690,509
1849	7,078,690	23,392,450

The general rate of payment for first-class passengers must have, however, been raised between 1848 and 1849, for the receipt shows a gradual increase. The money received for the above passengers was—

Year ending June 30,	First Class.	Second Class.
1845	£1,516,805	£1,598,115
1846 . . .	1,661,897	1,937,946
1847 . . .	1,675,759	2,048,080
1848 . . .	1,792,533	2,352,152
1849 . . .	1,889,645	2,502,587

We now come to the third class; the "parliamentary" class (who avail themselves of the privilege conferred by Parliament of being conveyed at the rate of a penny per mile) and a class which is called " mixed :"—

Year ending June 30.	Third-Class Passengers.	Parliamentary Class.	Mixed.
1845	13,135,820	..	855,445
1846	14,559,515	3,946,922	2,193,126
1847	15,865,311	6,985,493	3,229,357
1848	15,241,529	13,092,489	749,764
1849	14,378,377	15,432,457	116,185

It will be observed from this account, that while the number of third-class passengers has diminished, the number at the very lowest rate—the compulsory rate fixed by Parliament—has very considerably increased. The gradually increasing inability to pay, which has unfortunately marked the circumstances of the travelling classes in the last two or three years, as well as the fashion of cheapness and the eager desire to have everything at the lowest penny, are observable in the course which railway passenger-traffic has taken.

The receipts from the third-class passengers and the parliamentary-class respectively were as follow :—

Year ending June 30.	Third Class.	Parliamentary Class.	Mixed.
	£.	£.	£.
1846	738,474	293,732	93,164
1847	737,452	539,976	146,733
1848	661,038	902,851	11,807
1849	651,365	1,059,785	2,590

We now come to the general receipts, including what is earned by carrying cattle and goods of various descriptions : —

Year ending June 30.	Receipts from Passengers.	Cattle, Goods, &c.	Total Receipts.
	£.	£.	£.
1845	3,976,341	2,233,373	6,209,714
1846	4,725,215	2,840,354	7,565,569
1847	5,148,002	3,362,884	8,510,886
1848	5,720,382	4,213,170	9,933,552
1849	6,105,975	5,094,926	11,200,901

The parliamentary paper from which these abstracts are made does not bring the returns down further than the 30th June, 1849, but from the reports of the great railway companies of the kingdom for the half-year ending the 31st December, 1849, it appears that the number of first, second, and third class passengers did not increase, while the receipts from the carriage of merchandise did proceed steadily and satisfactorily.

It would take too much space to go into the statistics of all railways, but it may be worth while to enumerate the particulars of those which have their head-quarters in the metropolis. The date to which the following statements have reference is the 30th June, 1849 : —

London and North-Western Railway—miles open, 477. First-class passengers, in the *half-year* ended 30th June, 1849, 467,719 ; second-class, 1,068,576 ; third-class, 340,576 ; parliamentary class, 873,669. Receipts from passengers, 563,717*l.* ; from merchandise, &c., 563,395*l.* Total receipts for the half-year, 1,127,112*l.*

Great Western and Bristol and Exeter—miles open, 311. First-class passengers in the *half-year* ended 30th June, 1849, 199,097 ; second-class, 819,509 ; third-class, 27,538 ; parliamentary class, 270,756. Receipts from passengers, 324,163*l.* ; from merchandise, &c., 179,322*l.* Total receipts for the half-year, 503,486*l.*

Eastern Counties, including Norfolk, Northern and Eastern, and Lowestoft—miles open, 324. First-class passengers in the *half-year* ended 30th June, 1849, 213,919 ; second-class, 704,854 ; third-class, 351,436 ; parliamentary class, 202,674. Receipts from passengers, 191,329*l.* ; from cattle, merchandise, &c., 174,788*l.* Total receipts for the half-year, 366,117*l.*

London and South-Western—miles open, 216. First-class passengers in the *half-year* ended 30th June, 1849, 255,303 ; second-class, 712,142 ; third-class, 12,866 ; parliamentary class, 148,217. Receipts from passengers, 170,112*l.* ; from merchandise, &c., 84,515*l.* Total receipts for the half-year, 254,627*l.*

London, Brighton, and South Coast—miles open, 162. First-class passengers in the *half-year* ended 30th June, 1849, 232,807 ; second-class, 483,502 ; third-class, 222,425 ; parliamentary class, 194,764. Receipts from passengers, 163,757*l.* ; from merchandise, &c., 46,738*l.* Total receipts for the half-year, 210,496*l.*

South-Eastern and Dover—miles open, 144. First-class passengers in the *half-year* ended 30th June, 1849, 100,109 ; second-class, 275,315 ; third-class, 77,406. Receipts from passengers, 117,876*l.*; from merchandise, &c., 48,073*l.* Total receipts for the half-year, 165,949*l.*

When we consider the magnitude of these returns, and recollect that the railways enumerated occupied no more than 1634 miles of the 5447 which were open on the 30th of June, 1849, we may form some general notion of the extent and greatness of the railway interest. Taking into account the money lent to railway companies, as well as the amount of their share capital, and allowing also for the large premiums—more than *cent. per cent.* in a large proportion of them—which were paid for the shares, it is probable that the amount of capital sunk in these undertakings is equal to a third of the national debt. The greater part of this immense sum has been subscribed within five or six years, from the funds of the people of all classes who possessed property. The effect of this extravagant outlay, to accomplish in five years the work which had much better been distributed over thirty, has been in every way disastrous to the shareholders. The price paid for the *work* was at least double what it ought to have been. So far as regards lawyers, engineers, surveyors, and contractors for works, it was five times what it ought to have been, and what it would have been, but for the reckless haste which prevailed.* There was an all but universal madness for railway expenditure. The government of the country was unfortunately a mercan-

---

* The expenses of lawyers and of getting bills passed through Parliament were specially enormous. A writer in the Morning Chronicle of January 22, 1850, who appears to have studied the subject, estimates the law and parliamentary charges of all the railways up to that time at no less than TEN MILLIONS sterling!

tile government, which was led by the spirit of money-makers in London, Liverpool, Manchester, Glasgow, and the other great towns, and which had none of the moderation that sound moral principle would have inspired, nor of the suspicion of outrageous mercantile activity, which calm dignity of character might have suggested. The government was as mad as the people, and encouraged the excesses of wild speculation, which a wise government would have checked. The consequences of the financial folly, which the government mistook for a grand development of the spirit of trade and commerce, the country is now suffering. There never was so widely spread a financial calamity. On other occasions certain branches of trade have given way, and classes have been ruined; but the unremunerative outlay of capital upon railway undertakings has touched every class above those who live from hand to mouth. Thousands of private families, who had nothing to do with business, but who merely invested their property in these undertakings as a new species of public funds, have been reduced to the greatest difficulties by the great reduction of dividends, or their absolute cessation. What was begun in cupidity, was carried on with deception, and has ended in disaster. Projecting engineers made calculations of business and profit as flattering as they were false. Directors for a time suffered themselves to be misled, and then they misled others. When they ought to have known that a mistake had been made, and when they might have prevented the mischief from spreading, by telling the truth, they told what was not true. They paid back a part of the capital, calling it profits, and thus induced more capital to be thrown into concerns which they ought to have known were in a bad condition. Meanwhile, thousands of labourers were eating as much meat, and drinking as much beer, in each week as ought to have served them for three weeks. Barristers and solicitors, who had anything to do with railways, got absurdly rich in an incredibly short space of time. Engineers of high repute were regarded with a sort of worship, and all the goldsmiths and silversmiths of London were employed in making services of plate for them, to express the gratitude of directors and shareholders. Such was the delusion of the time—such was the eagerness with which people wasted their money, in the belief that no extravagance would outstrip the profits which railways must return! It must however be confessed that, but for this madness, which has affected almost every second person in the middle-class community with a sense of loss, if it have not obliged him to contract his expenditure, the country would not at this day have possessed the widely-extended advantages—if, upon the whole, they *are* advantages—of railway communication which it does possess.

No one can dispute that the ease and economy of journeying from the precincts of one town to the precincts of another, have been wonderfully promoted by these railways. For so far the advantage is evident. It is a great matter for those who intend to make a journey to be relieved of the obligation of taking places beforehand, and of having to depart, no matter what intervening circumstance might arise, on pain of forfeiting the fare. It is a great matter to be assured of having room in the coach; and to those whose time is of considerable value, or who fancy that it is so, it is a very great matter to be transferred so rapidly to the place where they wish to be. But it is a disadvantage that *travelling* in England is, in a general sense, at an end. You are *transferred* from place to place, but you do not *travel*. It is the same thing all the way. It is the railway, and nothing but the

railway. Sometimes you may catch the merest glimpse
of great objects, but you can get no idea of the country,
however general, from railway journeying. The roads,
the villages, the people at their ordinary business—the cos-
tume, the dialect—the bare hill sides—the hamlets—the
rural churches—the wooded dells—the streets of country
towns—the people at market—the local history and news
from the coachman, which were in former days the privilege of the outside passenger; all these points of useful
knowledge, obtained in the old mode of travelling, are
utterly lost in the new mode of transit. Young persons,
who never went from home till within the last seven years,
can have little conception of the varieties of life—of the
food for reflection—and the sundry experiences which
were imparted to the mind by a journey from country to
town, or town to country, in the old coaching days. The
inconveniences were sometimes great, and the hardships
to outside passengers in unlucky weather were not inconsiderable; but even these inconveniences and hardships were not without their value as points of experience.
Life may be too smooth and easy, and to be obliged to
feel now and then a little of that which it requires both
resolution and forbearance to endure without wincing, is
not the worst thing that can happen to a man, especially
in the season of his strength. It is true that the railways
afford great facilities for going to see noted places, and
thousands do go to such places who could not have
afforded time to go in the days of less rapid locomotion;
but it may be doubted whether this sight-seeing affords
such useful furnishing to the mind as was obtained in-
sensibly in making journeys along the old roads, in seeing
different sorts of people and different sorts of country,
and in observing at least the outside aspect of many-
coloured life.

The rapidity of railway transit necessitates, if not an equal, at least a corresponding rapidity in the transaction of business generally.   Formerly, when a man left his home, perhaps a hundred miles away, to transact business in the metropolis, it was an undertaking that seemed to warrant some repose and delay.   He allowed himself a few days after his arrival, before encountering the road again, and was not urgent to have his business despatched within an hour.   But now, when it has become possible for him to make the journey to and fro within the day, and to leave him two or three hours in which to transact his business, he presses to have it accomplished within that time.   In this, as in so many other things, we find that devices for saving time do not confer leisure, but the contrary.   One steam-engine, with the proper auxiliary machinery, will spin as much in a day as five hundred hand-spinners could do ; but there is infinitely more hurry and pressure in the spinning business than there was in former times.   A dozen power-looms make a great deal more cloth than a dozen of the old domestic looms ; but the hand-loom weaver works harder than ever he did, in his endeavour to compete with the power of machinery. The railroad certainly saves time in journeying, but there is a pressure and a hurry in getting through business since railroads came into use, which were unknown before.

The political effects of railways are in many particulars important.   As an investment and absorption of capital they are greatly influential for good or evil upon the national prosperity.   Of late years it has been a favourite abstract theory of a certain school of politicians, that legislation and government ought to abstain altogether from interference with the employment of capital, and ought to abolish all laws which aim at influencing the direction of

such employment. It is unquestionable that direct interference ought not to be attempted but with great caution,
yet to influence the employment of capital, and to endeavour to guard the public against employing it foolishly,
seems to be a very important object for a wise government;
for how can a nation be powerful if it be not prosperous,
and how can it be prosperous if the people at large have
embarked their capital in foolish undertakings, or have
foolishly embarked capital even in useful undertakings?
It appears to me that, if the legislature had wisely governed the expenditure of capital upon railways, such a
source for the gradual and profitable investment of profits
and savings would have been an immense national advantage, whereas the allowing the public to rush headlong
into undertakings which they had not the means to complete, and for which the country had no pressing occasion,
has been productive of great private distress, and has
no doubt operated most prejudicially upon the public
finances. The effect produced upon the general character
of the people is also of course an important matter of
political consideration. If the people have become generally more impatient than they were—more eager for
something to be done, and less circumspect about the
character of what is done—more urgent to get on—more
confident that safety lies in rapidity of progress rather
than in deliberation and steadiness;—if such changes as
these have taken place, they cannot but affect the course
of politics, and they demand the careful attention, if not
the control and resistance, of those to whom the guidance
of the state is confided.

But that which is most obvious, and therefore most
generally taken into consideration, with respect to the
political effect of railways, is the new physical capability
which they afford. The rapidity with which intelligence

can be communicated, and with which troops can be moved, must no doubt be regarded as highly important political facts ; but, like every other artificial aid, that of railways is more liable to disturbance than the older and slower aids to progress. In the beginning of a civil war, for instance, the railways as a mode of transporting troops would give a great advantage to the government ; but suppose plans to be determined upon and operations to be devised with reference to this mode of transmission, and an active enemy to break up a few hundred yards of the railway at intervals of twenty miles, what an advantage would then be gained *against* the government ! When an army marches after the old fashion, whoever stops the way must fight a battle. The stopping of the way decides the controversy. But if ever it become necessary to move armies by railroad in a country which is the seat of war, the road will be attacked in some place where there is no one to defend it, and the army will be stopped without the risks and losses of a battle. Upon the whole, however, and looking rather to the ordinary business of government than to the exigencies of internal or external war, it seems reasonable to conclude that railroads add considerably to the power and promptness of executive rule, or at least they might do so if the government were wielded by men of decision and vigour. They are instruments by which the power of government may be brought to bear more quickly, and the results of any stroke of policy may be more speedily known. In matters of police the advantage of them has already been experienced in some important cases. They are productive of such habits of thought and action as render government, in my opinion, more difficult, but they supply, in perhaps yet greater measure, the means of meeting that difficulty.

It is required, however, that there should be men capable of using the means.

Whatever has so widely affected the habits of living, and, as I believe, the habits of thought also, of the people, must needs have had an influence on literature; but besides this, the circumstances of railway transit demand a kind of literature of their own, and the supply to meet this demand has been very abundant. Hence a new fashion in the manufacture of literature has arisen. To produce what is cheap and yet not wholly worthless—what may be easily read and easily laid aside—what may amuse for an hour or two, and yet not be too engrossing—something that will stand between us and the tediousness of the time, without making any serious demand upon our powers of thought or of continuous attention—such is the task of those who write for railway reading, and the practice has gone much further than even railways penetrate. In these days every one admits that, without going into retirement for the special purpose, there is no time for reading books which require that men should revolve and ponder the matter as they go along. Such books are bought, and select passages from them, which appear in the reviews, are read. They are put upon the library-shelves and intended to be deliberately perused at some convenient season of leisure, but that time does not arrive. A journey, however, is to be taken by railroad, and as there is nothing to engage the attention upon the road—no variety of scene—no object of interest—the period of transit is frequently devoted to reading. Some there are who, even in a railway-carriage, can set themselves doggedly to the study of their law, or with solemn earnestness to the study of their divinity. These, however, are but few. Some feel that slight "agitation of the

spirits," as Charles Lamb used to say of the effect of
walking in the London streets, which makes reading of
any kind impossible ; but the great majority wish for a
book which they may read as it were with one eye, while
giving a sort of attention with the other to the progress
of the carriage and the names of the stations.   Hence
arrives the maxim of the publishers, that whoever wants
to command an extensive sale for his book must produce
something that the railway-traveller can read as he goes
along, and use for waste paper at the end of his journey.
It may be thought fanciful to attribute an important
practical effect upon literature to such circumstances as
these, but I believe that to railroads, and to the habits of
quick movement in everything, which have grown up in
connexion with them, may be fairly attributed much of
what is peculiar in the character of our current literature.
In particular the light and jesting method of commentary
upon public matters—the cloak of caricature with which
keen observation so frequently invests itself—arises from
the consideration that people are in such a hurry, they
must get amusement and criticism at the same time.   As
they cannot afford an hour for knowledge and an hour
for mirth, the two are wrapped together for their convenience, and thus they are, in my opinion, very often
both spoiled.   The worst symptom in all this is that we
make a boast of the practice we should be sorry for, even
while we admit that it is a kind of necessity of the time.

> " When we in our own viciousness grow hard
>   (O misery on 't!), the wise gods seal our eyes—
> .   .   .   .   .   make us
> Adore our errors ; laugh at us, while we strut
> To our confusion."

There are those who think there is nothing more to be
admired in the age we live in than the light tone of our

practical philosophy, which they regard as a judicious relief from the anxieties of ambition and the pressure of business. The fate of civilized man in a railway age is, according to their philosophy, alternately to labour and to laugh. Very different was the philosophy of that great man and greatest poet of his age, who, while I have been writing these pages, has been taken from us.* Thus *he* addressed railways and steamboats :—

> " Motions and means, on land and sea at war
> With old poetic feeling, not for this
> Shall ye, by poets even, be judged amiss !
> Nor shall your presence, howsoe'er it mar
> The loveliness of nature, prove a bar
> To the mind's gaining that prophetic sense
> Of future change, that point of wisdom, whence
> May be discover'd what in soul ye are.
> In spite of all that beauty may disown
> In your harsh features, Nature doth embrace
> Her lawful offspring in man's art ; and Time,
> Pleased with your triumphs o'er his brother Space,
> Accepts from your bold hands the proffer'd crown
> Of Hope, and smiles on you with cheer sublime."

Heaven grant that this " Hope " may not have been uttered in vain, and that the activities of our age may subside into energetic wisdom, and show our true poet to have been also a true prophet !

A paper dated the 21st of March, 1850, and prepared by Mr. J. S. Yeats, a sharebroker, shows in considerable detail the various particulars of capital, income, and expenditure, relating to thirteen of the principal railways in Great Britain. The length of line occupied by these railway companies was then 3164 miles ; the gross receipt in the last half-year from passenger and merchandise traffic 4,506,901*l.* ; the working expenses 1,632,616*l.* ;

---

* William Wordsworth, born April 7, 1770 ; died April 23, 1850.

the government duty 105,643*l.*; the local rates and taxes 135,813*l.*; the depreciation and renewal fund 157,911*l.*: making a total of 2,031,983*l.* The interest on mortgages was 634,253*l.*; the dividends on preference shares 219,770*l.*; the rents and tolls to other companies 334,096*l.* So that the gross expenditure to be deducted before any sum could be taken for dividend to the ordinary shareholders was 3,220,372*l.* in the half-year. The net traffic earnings of the half-year, applicable to dividend, were 1,286,529*l.*, with sundry other receipts amounting to 118,551*l.* The average dividend paid on the whole ordinary share-capital of 80,644,068*l.* was at the rate of 3*l.* 3*s.* 6*d.* per cent. per annum.* This capital of course does not include an aggregate mortgage debt of 31,655,097*l.*, and preference shares, &c., the dividends on which are provided for before the sum applicable to ordinary dividend is struck.

Thus, then, the average return to the holders of the stock of the greatest railways in the kingdom is not so much as 3¼ per cent. per annum, even if the holders had

---

* A paper compiled by the same hand, dated September, 1850, and bringing the account of railway affairs up to the close of the first half-year of 1850, states that

The mileage of 1850 exceeds that of 1849 by 234 miles.

Increase of receipts, 1850, from passengers	. . . £75,357
,, ,, merchandise . . .	165,705
	241,062
The gross expenditure of 1850 shows an increase of	415,056
Less decrease of rates	15,482
	399,574

The capital entitled to dividend shows an excess of . 546,062
The mortgage and loan debt an excess of . . . 2,016,531
The average dividend of the 13 companies in the first half-year of 1850 only 2*l.* 17*s.* 6*d. per cent. per annum.*

bought their stock at par; but a great deal of it is held
by persons who gave 200*l*., or more than that, for every
100*l*. stock. The unfortunate character of *their* invest-
ments may easily be calculated. The thirteen companies
to which the account in question refers are—

London and North-Western	. .	paying 5 per cent div.	
Great Western . . .	.	,, 4	,,
Lancashire and Yorkshire	. .	,, 3	,,
Midland	.	,, 2½	,,
York and North-Midland .	. .	,, 2	,,
York and Berwick . .	.	,, 2¾	,,
Eastern Counties . .	. .	,, 1½	,,
South-Western . .	. .	,, 3¼	,,
London and Brighton .	. .	,, 4¹⁶⁄₂₀	,,
South-Eastern . .	. .	,, 1¹⁶⁄₂₀	,,
Bristol and Exeter . .	.	,, 3½	,,
Edinburgh and Glasgow .	. .	,, 3	,,
North British . . .	.	,, 2	,,

These were the rates *per annum* paid for the second half-
year of 1849.

In May, 1850, the commissioners appointed in the preceding November to inquire into the state of Smithfield
Market made their Report, which contains some curious
information as to the effect of railways in supplying
London with animal food. This is observed more especially in what is called the dead-meat market. Formerly
this market (called Newgate Market) drew its chief supplies from places in Surrey, Berks, Oxford, Hants, and
Wilts, within one hundred miles of the metropolis; now
these places have to compete with the supplies brought to
Newgate Market from Suffolk, Norfolk, Lincoln, York,
Northumberland, Durham, Bristol, Liverpool, and, still
farther, from Berwick, Edinburgh, Fife, Aberdeen, &c.;
and carcase-butchers have established themselves in Hull,
Leeds, Durham, Newcastle, and Edinburgh, for the supply

of the London market. These supplies, says the Report, are partly brought by the steam-packets ; but the great proportion is now carried by railway, thus ensuring greater certainty of arrival. The Eastern Counties Company are, up to this time, the greatest carriers of meat, and they provide hampers or peds and cloths for packing the meat, for which they make a moderate charge. From Scotland some part of the meat is sent packed in boxes, but usually in hampers ; from Yorkshire generally in sacks, made to fit each carcase of mutton. From the railway termini it is conveyed and pitched in the market, on the Eastern line, by the company's own waggons, and on the other lines by Messrs. Chaplin and Horne, and Messrs. Pickford, the extensive carriers. There are no means, say the commissioners, of ascertaining with accuracy the quantity of meat sold, but they received evidence that the Eastern Counties Railway alone was carrying 600 tons of dead meat weekly, the great bulk of which was consigned to Newgate Market ; and that, in one week during the Christmas of 1849, that company pitched in the market about a thousand tons of dead meat, poultry, and game ; also that Messrs. Pickford delivered in the last four months of 1849, on an average, 18¾ tons of dead meat daily, conveyed by the North-Western Railway Company ; and from Messrs. Chaplin and Horne's letter to the commissioners, their deliveries of meat at Newgate Market may be calculated at 10 tons daily. The average deliveries of these three principal carriers may now, therefore, be taken to amount to 800 tons weekly. Calculating the price at 2s. 10d. the stone, the deliveries of meat by railway carriage from these three carriers alone will amount to 1,165,116l. in the year. It should be mentioned, however, that the supply of dead meat varies according to the season of the year, and that during the

hot months the trade in dead meat falls off to a great
extent, and a simultaneous increase takes place in the
sales of cattle and sheep at Smithfield.

The railways, however, are no less effective in bringing
live cattle to Smithfield Market, than in bringing dead
meat to Newgate Market. The great supplies of cattle
from Norfolk, Suffolk, Essex, Cambridge, and Lincoln-
shire, come, says the Report, by the Eastern Counties
Railway, the average time of the transit from Norwich
to London (110 miles) being $7\frac{1}{2}$ hours. From the mid-
land and western counties they are brought by the
North-Western and Great Western Railways. The
extent to which railway carriage is now employed in the
transport of live stock may be appreciated, say the commissioners, from the fact given in evidence to us by the
traffic-manager of the Eastern Counties Railway Company, that the stock carried on that railway in the year
1849 amounted to 57,300 oxen, 275,000 sheep, and
15,000 pigs and calves.

This traffic-manager states that the great "landing-
place" of the Eastern Counties Railway for live stock is
Tottenham, six miles below London, from whence they
are walked to the "lairs." There they rest for about
twenty-four hours, and are then taken to Smithfield at a
very early hour on Monday morning, so that they may
get into the market by two or three o'clock. The dead
meat comes to the goods station in London, from whence
it is removed to Newgate and Leadenhall Markets by
vans or waggons, and "pitched" at the various salesmen's
stalls. The delivery commences on the arrival of the first
train at one o'clock in the morning, and the servants of
the company continue to pitch the meat till six or seven
o'clock. The object is to get the meat on the standing
at five o'clock at the latest, and as much earlier as pos-

sible. In the country the company find what are called hampers, or peds, and cloths, and small butchers are induced to hire them, who make it quite a business to feed a little stock in the country, and send it up to London, paying a moderate rate for using the peds. They could not afford to find peds themselves, for, in the event of loss, it would be more than equal to any little profit that could be obtained on the sale of the meat. " The consequence has been that, by the construction of the railway through those producing districts, we have enabled men in the country to connect themselves with the London meat-markets. Formerly they were completely shut out by expensive road conveyances; they wanted cheaper communication : the establishment of railways has benefited them considerably, and it is bringing upon our railway an enormous increase of traffic. Great quantities of lean stock for the last three years have been coming out of Scotland, and going across to the grazing districts of Norfolk to be fattened. We have had that traffic now for about three years, in connexion with the London and North-Western Company, and every year we find it increasing almost twofold."

The question of the assessment of railways to the parochial rates of the kingdom has within a few years become a subject of very great interest, and was inquired into very particularly by the committee of the House of Lords on parochial assessments, which sat in May and June, 1850. In some cases the charges made appeared to be enormous, not having the slightest reference to the value of the land occupied by the railway as land, but only to the supposed value of the railway business; whereas in cotton-mills, and property of that kind, the buildings and machinery are alone considered, without any reference to actual or supposed profits. Mr. Cornewall Lewis, M.P., late Under-Sécretary of State, and now Secretary of the Treasury, gave evidence to the committee on the subject of railway assessments, and stated at some length the difficulties of the case ; the following are extracts from his evidence :—

" The assessment of railways has become practically a question of great importance, owing to the great increase in the assessable value of railways ; the assessment of railways must be now between *five and six millions a-year*. The quantity of property vested in shares in railways, the number of persons who are interested in that property, and the number of parishes through which railways pass, are now so great, that the question of rating railways has assumed a high degree of importance. When rates were first imposed upon railways, the overseers, who made the rates in each parish with the help of surveyors, applied the existing law as they best could to the rating of railways. The nearest analogy which probably could be found was that of the case of canals. The general principle is a clear one, viz. to take the net annual value of the land as improved in the hands of the railway company, without reference to their profits as carriers ; that is, to take the rent which would be paid by a tenant to whom the line should be leased. This is the principle ; but when it is attempted to apply it in practice, though when so stated it appears to be simple, very great difficulties arose. One of the greatest difficulties seems to arise from this cause : most sorts of rateable property lie exclusively within the parish which makes the rate ; for example, houses or farms, which are the ordinary subjects of rating, or a manufactory or a coal-mine, all lie within the parish in which the rate is made, and the overseer has only to consider what the probable net annual value of such occupation may be. But with regard to a railway, which

passes through a long succession of parishes, he is unable
to use any such guide ; he must consider what would be
the probable letting value of the entire line, and he must
then take such proportion of that entire value as falls
within the particular parish. There is also a further
complication arising from the presence of buildings or a
station in the parish. In some cases there is a station in
the parish, and in others there is not, and that adds to the
difficulty of making a fair rate upon the railway. Now,
the overseers of each parish make the rate without reference to the rate in any other parish. If the railway
passes through thirty or forty parishes in succession, each
parish is entitled to make its own rate, without any reference whatever to the aggregate that would be produced
by adding together the rates of the different parishes.
* * * * The overseers do not, for the most part, proceed
from any total ; they merely form a conjecture as to the
probable amount of value which belongs to that part of
the railway which is in their parish, and the process is, as
far as I am aware, *rather a rude and conjectural one.*
The railway companies further complain that they have
great difficulty in obtaining any clear statement of the
law upon the subject **of rating** ; they say that, if they
appeal upon a **particular** point of law, the court merely
decide the point that is raised, and they get no general
statement of the law of rating railways laid down, and
the result is that they are rated considerably above the
just amount. They also complain of the tribunal of
quarter sessions ; they say that they wish for some other
tribunal. Also they allege another complaint, that is,
that, unlike all other interests, they are rated upon the
profits of their trade, and they say they are rated as carriers. Now, after having read, with all the care I am
able to give to the subject, the decisions of the Court of

Queen's Bench upon the rating of railways, I am unable
to see that any such principle as that of rating railway
companies upon the profits of their trade has ever been
laid down by the court. I can likewise quote, what is
still more to the purpose than my own opinion, the opinion
of very competent anthorities on the subject, with whom
I have conversed, and who entertain a clear opinion that
the court has not laid down the principle of rating railway
companies upon the profits of their trade. All the Court
of Queen's Bench have said is this : in order to obtain the
letting value of the railway, it is necessary to consider the
profits of the carrying trade."

Mr. Cornewall Lewis says that the same difficulties
which apply to the rating of railways apply in some degree
to the rating of canals ; but the latter having been longer
in existence, the matter with them " has shaken itself
down into something like equilibrium. With railways at
present there is more friction and more disposition to liti-
gation." A noble lord was quite pleased with the *shake-
down* expression, and complimented it as " very apt."
Meanwhile the parochial assessment upon the railways is
in many cases almost intolerably high.*

P.S.—Towards the close of the parliamentary session
of 1850 another return was made to parliament respecting
railway traffic, from which it appeared that the whole
receipt of the railways in the United Kingdom, for the
year 1849, was 11,806,498*l.*, of which 6,277,892*l.* was
for passengers, and 5,528,606*l.* for cattle, goods, &c.

---

* John Hyde, Esq., of Berkhampstead parish, lately an Inspector of
Taxes, stated to the Committee of the Lords that the assessment upon
railways was stamped with injustice throughout the whole country, so
far as his knowledge extended. The most important canal and the most
important railway in the kingdom both pass through his parish. Within
the parish they are equal in length, and nearly so in breadth—the canal
is rated at 90*l.*, and the railway is rated at 4500*l.*!

Passengers in the year 1849 :—

First class	7,292,811
Second class	23,521,650
Third class	15,686,911
Parliamentary class	17,203,412
Mixed	136,755
Total passengers . . .	63,841,539

The receipts from the several classes were—

First class	£1,927,768
Second class	2,530,968
Third class	711,592
Parliamentary class	1,104,884
Mixed	2,678
Total receipts for half-year ending June 30, 1849 .	£5,455,937
,, ,, Dec. 31, 1849 .	6,350,561
Number of miles open on Dec. 31, 1849 . .	6,031

CHAPTER XX.

PUBLIC EDUCATION.

" If," says Archbishop Tillotson, " if a man, by a vast and imperious mind, and a heart large as the sand upon the sea-shore (as it is said of Solomon), could command all the knowledge of nature and art, of words and things— could attain to a mastery in all languages, and sound the depths of all arts and sciences, measure the earth and the heaven, and tell the stars, and declare their order and motions—could discourse of the interests of all states, the intrigues of all courts, the reason of all civil laws and constitutions, and give an account of the history of all ages—could speak of trees, 'from the cedar-tree that is in Lebanon even unto the hyssop that springeth out of the wall, and of beasts also, and of fowls, and of creeping things, and of fishes,'—and yet should in the mean time be destitute of the knowledge of God and Christ, and his duty : all this would be but an impertinent vanity, and a more glittering kind of ignorance, and such a man (like the philosopher who, whilst he was gazing upon the stars, fell into the ditch) would but *sapienter descendere in infernum*, be undone with all this knowledge, and with a great deal of wisdom go down to hell." This noble passage states, with an eloquence not to be surpassed, the true theory of education. However glittering and attractive intellectual accomplishments may be, and however useful in a worldly sense may be the more ordinary acquirements derived from education, yet, if religion and morality, if thoughtfulness and sound principles be not strengthened thereby, it is very questionable if any good is effected ; for knowledge will certainly not secure a man from misery in this life, and *sapienter descendere in infernum* is but small consolation in respect to the next.

As regards the amelioration of the social condition of the masses in communities which are called "civilized," more seems to be expected from education than education is ever likely to realize. But when we see the depraved habits which so greatly prevail, and when we reflect upon the danger of them, we cling to the hope that there is some one specific for the cure of that which is so appalling, and education is the remedy which is most generally agreed upon. They who know very well that education, as that term is generally understood, will do but little for the amelioration of mankind, because but few have the natural disposition to profit by it, feel it nevertheless to be but just that the advantage should be offered to as many as possible. For when we consider what the mind of a human being is, when stored with the knowledge of which it is capable of making use, and how far such a mind soars above the condition of ignorance and stupidity, we feel it but a reasonable duty to God, and to the human race, to give every mind as much opportunity as we can of rising to that lofty station to which we know some minds may, under favourable circumstances, attain. We are, moreover, aware that any portion of sound knowledge, *if rightly applied*, is a blessing, so far as it goes ; and though our experience may inform us of the thousands of instances in which it is not rightly applied, yet the conscientious man will scarcely feel himself at liberty on that account to withhold it. This is not a matter of reasoning, but of moral instinct. When we give a child food to strengthen and invigorate its body, we cannot tell but that the strength we are nourishing may be mischievously employed. We may be nurturing to manhood one who will give his body to debauchery or violence. Still, as by the blessing of Providence we cannot possibly see far enough for that, we must act as if there were no such risk. And similarly with the education of the mind. We must not omit to sow in it that seed which may produce the most glorious harvest, which may contribute largely to the welfare and happiness, not only of the individual, but of the human race, although we are aware that a contrary effect may be produced. Perplexed as we may be regarding the future result, our present duty is clear enough— it is to give to all, the best education which their circumstances and ours will permit, taking as much care as we can that the knowledge imparted shall be wholesome, and suitable to the individual to whom it is offered. To suppose that all education is alike suitable to all, is as unreasonable as to suppose that all kinds of food are alike suitable to all. Some will thrive on what is almost poison to others. Thus also it is with education ; and therefore it seems to me, that, as far as possible, there should be variety in education, so that different sorts of minds might find the occupation for which nature has best fitted them. It is obvious that to all a knowledge of religious truth should be offered, and no pains should be spared to impress such knowledge upon all to the utmost extent that they are capable of receiving it. But to suppose that all will be equally benefited in a religious sense, by a compulsory learning by rote of the Catechism, is, I think, an error. The Catechism ought, no doubt, to be taught to all, but the intelligent teacher should judge where the words have imparted ideas, and where they have not. In the latter case he should consider what other avenues

there may be to the inner mind of the pupil, and whether
it be possible to turn the soul towards God by other means
than the committing to memory that wondrous epitome
of Christian theology which the Church Catechism
contains.

In considering the advantages of education, apart from
that greatest advantage of all which Tillotson, with his
grand *copia verborum*, places in the foreground, it is usual
to dwell upon the wealth, the power, the high position in
the world, and so forth, to which education may lead.
Undoubtedly it *is* a great help to the acquisition of these
things ; but the more education is spread among the
people, the less chance there will be of *such* advantages
resulting from it.   Fifty or sixty years ago, when education was comparatively rare, whoever combined a moderate share of it with a reasonably good address, and some
favourable opportunities, was almost sure to advance himself and become prosperous.   In the present state of
society, education is so much more diffused, and the can-
didates for preferment are so much more active, and so
much more numerous, that it is idle to delude young
people with the notion that if they mind their learning
they will obtain power and prosperity.   Besides, we should
consider that these motives are not noble enough, and
that they induce young people to set up in their own
minds standards of success which they are but too prone
to erect for themselves, without any suggestion.   I therefore give my tribute of admiration to what Mrs. Austin
says in her preface to *Cousin* on Education :—" If, instead
of nurturing expectations which cannot be fulfilled," she
says, " and turning the mind on a track which must lead
to a sense of continual disappointment, and then of wrong,
we were to hold out to our humbler friends the appropriate and attainable, nay, unfailing ends of a *good*

education ; the gentle and kindly sympathies, the sense
of self-respect, and of the respect of fellow-men ; the free
exercise of the intellectual faculties ; the gratification of
a curiosity that grows by what it feeds on, and yet finds
food for ever ; the power of regulating the habits and
business of life so as to extract the greatest possible portion of comfort out of small means ; the refining and tran-
quillizing enjoyment of the beautiful in nature and art,
and the kindred perception of the beauty and utility of
virtue ; the strengthening consciousness of duty fulfilled ;
and, to crown all, the Peace which passeth all understanding ;—if we directed their aspirations this way, it is probable that we should not have to complain of being disappointed, nor they of being deceived. Who can say
that wealth can purchase better things than these ? And
who can say that they are not within the reach of any man
of sound body and mind, who by labour, not destructive
of either, can procure, for himself and his family, food,
clothing, and habitation ?" I repeat that to me these
observations seem very admirable and highly important.
The education given to young people has too often a
wrong direction, filling their minds with such objects of
ambition as they are most unlikely ever to attain to, and
such as, when they are attained to, seldom contribute to
the strengthening of virtue, or to the increase of happiness.
Most people will be ready enough to take the path to
riches and distinction when it is open to them, although
they have no special education given them in order to
point the way. But that education is indeed precious
which leads to dignity of mind independently of fortune,
and to the gratification of honourable tastes, which are
compatible even with a low estate. " Plain living and
high thinking," may undoubtedly exist together, and it
should be the object of good education to build this fact

into the structure of every young person's mind. Instead
of the possession of wealth and power, and the enjoyment
of luxurious living, being held forth as the objects to which
knowledge and mental ability should be directed, the very
contrary should be the theories of our schools. Simplicity
of life should be held up to respect, and luxury should be
continually depicted as what it is, a corrupter of manly
virtue, and an enemy of the general weal. If luxury be
necessary to happiness, then but a very small minority of
the people can ever be happy. But it is not so. A
vicious habit of wealth-worship has arisen in our country
which it ought to be the business of education to correct.
Learning, politeness, good taste, an ardent admiration of
nature, eloquence, intelligent conversation, and many
other sources of enjoyment, might be possessed without
wealth, or luxurious living. If moral dignity and intellectual accomplishments were restricted to the wealthy,
then there would be some reason in the respect we see
paid to riches ; but it is an absurdity that tries one's
patience, to see mind crouching before wealth, instead of
setting up for itself and daring to be poor. I argue upon
the assumption that there are materials for dignity and
comfort and cheerfulness in human life, irrespective of the
costliness and parade of living which so many aspire to,
and to which so few can attain. If this be not so, then
the pure pleasures of simplicity of life and self-denial are
fabulous, and the turtle-eating alderman and accomplished
scholar, rolled into one, would make your true philosopher.
But I maintain that this combination of character makes
the false philosopher, and not the true ; and every man,
whatever his mental accomplishments may be, in so far
as he is devoted to luxurious living, is a corrupter of himself. I would have it taught, and, as far as possible,
proved, in all schools, that poverty is an honourable estate,

if combined with dignity of mind, and divested of all rudeness : and I would have especial store set by all those
enjoyments and pleasing occupations which may engage
the attention independently of wealth, and concurrently
with such industrious pursuits as the absence of wealth
may render necessary. After all, and absurd as England
is in her wealth-worship, it is not so much poverty that
generally degrades a man, as the coarse and careless
habits which are so often connected with it. When
poverty lounges about in dirty clothes, or seeks enjoyment
in the brutalities of dram-shops, it is not so very unreasonable that it should be despised. But good education
would seek the correction of these evils, and, from the
very outset of the formation of young people's minds,
would endeavour to guard them against every species of
low and degrading sensualism, and would make use of
their pride to sustain them in the path of virtue and self-
restraint.

But we must ever remember that education, however
carefully conducted, cannot be relied upon for producing
a general result of either intellectual or moral excellence.
It is to be feared that a considerable majority of mankind
will ever be found incapable of much intellectual advancement. In every rank and condition of society the
greater number pursue their business as a mere routine,
and find their pleasures in other exercises than those of
the intellect. It is in vain that we dream of inducing, on
the part of the multitude, whether high or low, rich or
poor, a voluntary adoption of intellectual pursuits.
Something indeed may be effected in this direction, but
whoever expects much to be effected will experience disappointment. It therefore becomes of importance to
provide other occupation than that of the mind for the
great bulk of mankind, in order to preserve them from

falling into the vices which so rapidly grow in the rank soil of idleness and inactivity. Boys, whom no force of teaching will convert into creatures of reason and reflection—to whom books will ever be irksome, and serious discussion unintelligible and annoying—may yet be occupied in feats of strength, or exertions of manual skill. He who can never be made to comprehend the *theory* of the ordinary processes of arithmetic, may perhaps be readily taught to drive a nail straight, or even to succeed in making a dovetailed joint. It is to be wished that schools should afford opportunities for acquiring such useful knowledge.

On many occasions of public discussion, both within and without the walls of Parliament, the strongest expressions have been used to characterise the ignorance of the agricultural classes respecting the business in which they are engaged. If these complaints be true, it is manifest that not merely school education, in the ordinary sense of the word, is required, but also such education as could best be afforded, in the garden or the field, by some intelligent cultivator of the ground. On the other hand, a county member, not long since, brought a similar accusation against the manufacturers of printed calicoes, and ventured to assure the House of Commons, that, whatever ability these persons might have in making money, they were grossly ignorant both of the science and the taste which are directly connected with their business. " Is it not notorious," said Mr. Henry Drummond, " that no English manufacturer ever yet made one single useful discovery in arts or science ? We have heard a good deal of the school of Manchester. What has it ever produced that was scientific or useful ? Has it any name in chemistry to boast of ? Can it point to a Fourcroy ? Can they quote any Manchester manufacturer who has written upon any scientific subject connected with his trade ? Why, sir, it is well known that they know no more of the chemical agents required for their own print-works than the blocks they use. They had been obliged to confess that nothing but the actual cheapness of their wares obtained them a market—that there was not a person in Europe who would not prefer the more artistic taste, and the more beautiful fabrics, of the French, or indeed even of the Chinese manufacturer." * It does not appear that any member of the Manchester school attempted to repel this attack, and it will not be supposed that, when they are concerned, either apathy or diffidence can account for their silence. It may indeed be said that, as they were not accused of any ignorance of the art of making money, they did not consider that the remarks of Mr. Drummond touched them in any point to which they were concerned to reply. But it is evident that, in a business so closely connected with both science and the fine arts, as the production of the more ornamental descriptions of printed cotton manufacture, such ignorance as Mr. Drummond described, if it really exist, is disgraceful. Might not ornamental drawing be taught in the schools of the manufacturing districts, and as much of the chemistry of colours as would enable a practical man further to pursue the subject when attending to his business?

It is obvious that something is wanting in our system of education for the multitude which will in a more marked manner connect the after life of the youth or maiden emancipated from school with the lessons which in their youth they have been compelled or induced to attend to. Few things can be more mortifying to the teacher, or more melancholy to every thoughtful man, than the re-

---

* Debate, House of Commons, Feb. 19, 1850.

flection that such pains as are bestowed upon the education
of the children of the working classes seem to be in a
great measure thrown away, or at the best to be only
useful as a restraint and preventive of juvenile mischief
while the discipline of school continues.   " I do believe,"
said an eloquent preacher on an important public occasion,
" that our public men, in spite of all we say, have but a
faint notion of the moral and religious state of the mass
of the people.   Churches have been built, communicants
have increased, schools are multiplied, and so there is a
good deal of self-congratulation.   But all the while (and
it is the destructive feature of our times) there is an
immense and growing class of people untouched by us.
The increase of our Church congregations is, I suspect,
mainly from a class who in another generation were
attached to other religious communions, and truly I do
not undervalue the fact. . . . . . . Observe our National
Schools ; little as they have ever been a part of our
Church system, they are likely, I fear, to be still less so.
The present generation of artisans of the lower class in
our towns and cities—a race with whom statesmen can
never grapple—has sprung from those schools.   The
clergy view with growing anxiety the fact that vast proportions of boys, on leaving school, *leave the Church and
all religion.*   The lessons of goodness daily learned at
school are, even in childhood, daily unlearned at home,
and, when the school is finally left, the appetite for reading
is satiated throughout youth by the most demoralizing
class of periodical publications, and in manhood to peruse
even these they are generally driven from their comfortless
homes to houses of public resort.   They harden one another ; they sharpen their intellects without acquiring
knowledge ; and they grow more and more immoral, and
more and more miserable and discontented.   The Church

has no means of keeping the children she has brought up." * All this, and much more which might be advanced to the same effect, seems to indicate the want of some system of regulation and control, of which schooling shall be but the commencement—some well-organized arrangement and government, which, without unnecessarily infringing upon liberty, shall remind every one, at all seasons of life, that they belong to society, and must not neglect its interests, or outrage its rules. Or if this be deemed incompatible with the crowded state of our society and its complicated relations, then let some attempt be made to adapt the school-teaching to the probable future pursuits of the pupils. We have seen what Mr. Irons says of town-boys, the sons of artisans of the lower class. The poet Crabbe may be quoted concerning those of the country :—

> " Hark ! to that shout, that burst of empty noise,
> From a rude set of bluff obstreperous boys ;
> They who, like colts let loose, with vigour bound,
> And thoughtless spirit, o'er the beaten ground ;
> Fearless they leap, and every youngster feels
> His alma active in his hands and heels.
> These are the sons of farmers, and they come
> With partial fondness for the joys of home ;
> Their minds are coursing in their fathers' fields,
> And e'en the dream a lively pleasure yields ;
> They, much-enduring, sit th' allotted hours,
> And on a grammar waste their sprightly powers.
> They dance ; but them can measured steps delight,
> Whom horse and hounds to daring deeds excite ?
> Nor could they bear to wait from meal to meal,
> Did they not slily to the chamber steal,
> And there the produce of the basket seize—
> The mother's gift ! still studious of their ease."

As regards the irksomeness of the attempt to learn

---

* Sermon by Rev. W. J. Irons. Thanksgiving Day, Nov. 15, 1849.

grammar or anything else which requires some exercise of abstract thought, and the eagerness to throw all such pursuits aside when emancipated from the discipline of school, it belongs alike to the greater number of young persons, whether the children of artisans or aldermen—of farmers or of squires. But the restraints of school being over, to those of better condition the restraints of civilization begin. They have a position in society to support—a position which not duty alone, but vanity, and even the love of pleasure, induces them to try to maintain. To do this they must in some degree keep up what they have learned; they must also govern themselves more or less, and at least conceal the vices which perhaps they practise. Unfortunately, the mass of the lower classes are affected by such habits of society in but a very slight degree, and as yet nothing has been invented by political philosophers to stand to the lower classes in the place of the restraints of civilization. The artisan is drunk in the streets, or uses filthy and brutal language, or treats his family with savage violence; and, though he suffers from such grossness in various ways, yet he is not punished by degradation from his class. When he becomes sober, and his fierce passions have had their way, and he is calm again, he does not find that he has so disgraced himself that he may not show his face among the companions to whom he had formerly been accustomed. It is on account of this distinction between the habits of different orders of society that some kind of extended rule and discipline, beyond the term of schooling, seems needful for the lower classes of the people, so that the Church and civil society may have the means of "keeping the children they have brought up."

"The Egyptians," says our Church, "had a law that every man should weekly bring his name to the chief rulers of the province, and therewithal declare what trade of life he used, to the intent that idleness might be worthily punished, and diligent labour duly rewarded. The Athenians did chastise sluggish and slothful people no less than they did heinous and grievous offenders, considering, as the truth is, that idleness causeth much mischief. The Areopagites called every man to a strait account *how he lived;* and if they found any loiterers that did not profit the common weal by one means or other, they were driven out and banished as unprofitable members, that did only hurt and corrupt the body. And in this realm of England good and godly laws have been divers times made, that no idle vagabonds and loitering runagates should be suffered to go from town to town, from place to place, without punishment, which neither serve God nor their prince, but devour the sweet fruits of other men's labour, being common liars, drunkards, swearers, thieves, whoremasters and murderers, refusing all honest labour, and give themselves to nothing else but to invent and do mischief, whereof they are more desirous and greedy than is any lion of his prey. To remedy this inconvenience, let all parents and others which have *the care and governance of youth* so bring them up either in good learning, labour, or some honest occupation or trade, *whereby they may be able in time to come not only to sustain themselves competently, but also to relieve and supply the necessity and want of others."** And again, we are taught—" Let young men consider the precious value of their time, and waste it not in idleness, in jollity, in gaming, in banqueting, in ruffians' company. Youth is but vanity, and must be accounted for before God. How merry and glad soever thou be in thy youth, O young man, saith the preacher;

---

* Homily against Idleness.

how glad soever thy heart be in thy young days; how
fast and freely soever thou follow the ways of thine own
heart and the lust of thine own eyes; yet be thou sure
that God shall bring thee into judgment for all these
things. God of his mercy put it into the hearts and
minds of all of them that have the sword of punishment
in their hands, or have families under their governance,
to labour to redress this great enormity of all such as live
idly and unprofitably in the common weal, to the great
dishonour of God and the grievous plague of His silly
people. To leave sin unpunished, and *to neglect the good
bringing up of youth*, is nothing else but to kindle the
Lord's wrath against us, and to heap plagues upon our
own heads."

It appears, however, that the mere establishment of
schools, and the awakened attention given to the subject
of education, have not done as much as might have been
hoped for towards the "good bringing up of youth."
The Rev. W. J. E. Bennett, who has written a remarkably earnest tract on the duty of the State in respect to
education, complains in very energetic terms of the life-
less, unaffectionate, mechanical sort of instruction which
is pursued in the schools. "We require," he says, "real
masters, and *minds*, not automata, to produce real education. No doubt the failure of the National Society's
system, in grasping the minds of the poor and training
them to sound and evangelical religion, is mainly attributable to the dry, skeleton-like, monitorial classes of the
schools. The teaching is hollow, formal, and mechanical;
there is no flesh and life within it, no power or vigour, no
holding of the affections as the seat of the moral improvement of the human mind; no sympathy between the
teachers and the taught, and therefore the consequence
is, that after so many years we still find the poor, as a

class, in great commercial and manufacturing towns as well as in the metropolis, alienated from the Church. I have observed very carefully, for it has been my duty to do so, the general conduct of boys at ordinary National Schools, and I have searched among the poor for their opinions upon the subject, and, without fear of contradiction, I assert that the system, as a system, is a failure in the great work of the education of the mind and of the religious affections. Reverence for holy places, reverence for holy things, deference to superiors, good manners, purity of language, orderly conduct, solid yet humble faith in the doctrines of the Church, habitual attendance at public worship, and, above all, the reception of the Holy Communion as the seal of their lives and of their faith, is not the product among the poor of the National Society's system of education." Assuredly not; nor is so much good fruit reasonably to be expected of any system. It is not merely the children of the poor, but all classes, who are deficient in the excellent acquirements enumerated by Mr. Bennett. Even putting aside the holiness and purity which he seeks, and asking only for reverence, good manners, and orderly conduct, it may be safely asserted that members of Parliament and of the Stock Exchange, appear to have been almost as unfortunate in their schooling as the children of the poor. There is a certain careless insolence of demeanour—a parade of non-affectionateness in social intercourse—which, I think, is more glaringly offensive in the rich than in the poor, and much less excusable, because the rich ought to be considerate and courteous in proportion as they have opportunities of culture and possess weight in society. Still I cannot but think that schools in general might be much better managed than they are by a better class of teachers. Great difference of opinion exists, however, as to the proper qualifications of a teacher. To me it seems that a moderate share of knowledge, combined with an earnest character and an affectionate disposition, will better qualify a teacher for the efficient discharge of his duty than a much more considerable amount of knowledge with a character and disposition less disposed towards the humble and arduous, but most important, business, of teaching. Not sympathising in many things with the Rev. Henry Parr Hamilton, F.R.S., who writes on the subject of education, I agree with him when he says, " It may fairly be questioned whether we are not in danger of carrying a little too far the sound maxim that a schoolmaster ought to know much more than he is required to teach."* He makes, also, some important observations as to the peculiar tone which is apt to be given to the education of masters, and the probability of that education leading them to something else than their proper avocations. " While we impart to them," he says, " an accurate knowledge of the Holy Scriptures and of the doctrines and formularies of our Church, it should be our especial care to cherish in them a religious disposition, and to repress the growth of a dogmatical or a polemical spirit. In the case of master, as of scholar, we must ever make religious knowledge subservient to religious principle and religious conduct. Now I must frankly avow my fear that in some of our institutions there is danger lest we send forth students in divinity rather than pious and devoted teachers of the poor. That this fear is not wholly imaginary is, among other reasons that might be adduced, apparent from two significant statements contained in the last publication of the Committee of Council on Education. Mr. Watkins

---

* Letter to the Bishop of Ripon, 1848.

reports that he met with no less than seven masters, of whom five had been trained in diocesan training colleges, who were about to leave their schools for the purpose of admission into the holy orders of our Church. And Mr. Moseley also gives the record of a case in which the ambition of the schoolmaster to become a clergyman had obviously impaired his efficiency as a teacher. I may perhaps be permitted to remark that no one can be much surprised at these results when he reads the list of subjects in the theological department on which the student-teachers are examined." The same gentleman, after noticing Mr. Moseley's tribute to the general excellence of the system pursued at St. Mark's College, observes that " it is to be regretted he does not report favourably of the progress of the pupils in that essential branch of their studies—the art of teaching." Now, though I believe there may be an art of teaching, in the same sense as there is an art of poetry and an art of painting, yet it is in vain that we seek to impart the art of teaching as we do those other arts, in which men generally are more or less proficient, according as they are more or less instructed. That earnest sympathy which makes a man an effective teacher is a natural gift, and all the training in the world will not make an effective teacher of the man whose heart is not in his business, and who scorns the ignorance he is to enlighten.

Although it is admitted by most writers on politics from Aristotle downwards that it is the duty of the State to look to the education of the people, yet it does not appear that until of late years the State in England concerned itself with this great object. It was a work left to the Church, and to the piety and generosity of individuals. . Nor was this trust altogether in vain. It would be well for those who boast of the advancement of this

age in every good work and good feeling, beyond the
standard of our unenlightened ancestors, to ask themselves whether there would be the slightest chance in
these days of such generous endowments of colleges,
hospitals, and almshouses by the rich, as were common in
former times when great fortunes were much more uncommon?   Where is now to be found the man of wealth
who leaves it like John Lyon, of Queen Elizabeth's time,
the large-hearted yeoman who founded Harrow school,
directing his bounty to " be bestowed upon such as are most
meet for towardness, poverty, and painfulness, without
any partiality or sinister affection, as they (the governors
of Harrow) shall answer before God " ?   At that period
the Church had the power, and, if we may judge from her
statutes, had also the will, to give the people such simple
instruction as was then deemed most meet for them.
The fifty-ninth canon directs that " every parson, vicar,
or curate, upon every Sunday and holiday, before evening
prayer, shall, for half an hour or more, examine and
instruct the youth and ignorant persons in his parish in
the Ten Commandments, the Articles of the Belief, and
in the Lord's Prayer ; and shall diligently hear, instruct,
and teach them the Catechism set forth in the Book of
Common Prayer.   And all fathers, mothers, masters, and
mistresses, shall cause their children, servants, and apprentices, which have not learned the Catechism, to come
to the church at the time appointed, obediently to hear
and to be ordered by the minister, until they have learned
the same.   And if any minister neglect his duty herein,
let him be sharply reproved upon the first complaint, and
true notice thereof given to the bishop or ordinary of the
place.   If, after submitting himself, he shall willingly
offend therein again, let him be suspended ; if so the
third time, there being little hope that he will be therein

reformed, then excommunicated, and so remain until he will be reformed. And likewise, if any of the said fathers, mothers, masters, or mistresses, children, servants, or apprentices, shall neglect their duties, as the one sort in not causing them to come, and the other in refusing to learn, as aforesaid, let them be suspended by their ordinaries (if they be not children), and if they so persist by the space of a month, then let them be excommunicated." The strict rule of the Church over all education or schooling appears, moreover, in the seventy-seventh and two following canons. The first of these ordains that no man shall teach either in public school or private house, but such as shall be allowed by the bishop of the diocese, or ordinary of the place, under his hand and seal, being found meet as well for his learning and *dexterity in teaching*, as for sober and honest conversation, and also for right understanding of God's true religion. The second, that in what parish soever there is a curate who is a Master of Arts or Bachelor of Arts, and is otherwise well able to teach youth and will willingly so do, a licence to teach youth of the parish where he serveth be granted only to the said curate, except in country towns where there is a school founded already, in which case it is not meet to allow any to teach grammar but only him that is allowed for the said public school. The third relates to the duties of schoolmasters, desiring that " they all shall teach in English or Latin, as the children are able to bear, the longer or shorter Catechism heretofore by public authority set forth. And as often as any sermon shall be upon holy and festival days within the parish where they teach, they shall bring their scholars to the church where such sermon shall be made, and there see them quietly and soberly behave themselves, and shall examine them at times convenient, after their

return, what they have borne away of such sermon.
Upon other days, and at other times, they shall train
them up with such sentences of Holy Scripture as shall
be most expedient to induce them to all godliness ; and
they shall teach the grammar set forth by King Henry
VIII., and continued in the times of King Edward VI.
and Queen Elizabeth of noble memory, and *none other !*"
But what with troubles and disturbances at one time,
and afterwards from the opposite cause of too much ease
and apathy, the Church fell away from the strictness of
its attention to educational affairs. The Church, says
one of her most diligent sons, will not say that she alone
is the teacher of the people, and that even the toleration
of a Dissenter is sinful. " This she might have said
three hundred years ago. But now, when she beholds
millions of souls lost to her in this kingdom (let us confess it with humiliation) by her own negligence, she
cannot any longer say it. Three hundred years ago the
Church was one body in this country, but in the para-
lysis of her powers which since that era she has suffered,
in the loss of sanctity in her people, in the carnal lives
of her clergy, in the low Erastianism of her prelates, in
the robbery of her fair lands and endowments to feed the
eager cupidity of her aristocracy—in all these points—
known to all who have read her history in the lapse of
those three hundred years—she has no longer, alas! the
right in equity, as certainly she has no longer the ability
in power, to say that no one shall teach the people but
herself. The great bulk of dissent in this country is
Wesleyanism—not so much opposed to the Church in
doctrine, but rather in discipline. It is known that this
great body sprang out of the Church's side, and cut
itself off from her, led by one of her own priests, in consequence of the miserable state of sin and ungodly lives

of the laity, and the low, debased, worldly views of the
clergy. And all men ought to know that it is owing to
this sect principally, in conjunction with others, that
Christian education holds the place which it now does
among our people. The Dissenters led the way in education, not the Church. Let us confess this truth with
shame, by being merely recalled to the dates at which
the several societies of education took their rise; they are
as follow :—1. The first society was that called the Sunday School Society, established in London in 1785. It
was composed of Dissenters and Churchmen indiscriminately. 2. The second society was that called the
Sunday School Union, established in 1803, composed also
of Dissenters and Churchmen indiscriminately. 3. The
third society was that called the British and Foreign
School Society, established in 1808. It was composed
entirely of Dissenters, proclaiming liberty of conscience,
no creed, no catechism. 4. The fourth was that called
the National School Society, established 1811, and was
exclusively of the Church. So that the Church was as
a body twenty-six years after the first society which drew
attention to the subject of education, and three years
behind her acknowledged great rival among the Dissenters."

The following succinct and lucid history of public
education for the poor in England was given by the Bishop
of Gloucester and Bristol in his Visitation Charge of
1847 :—

" The system of mutual instruction was first promulgated, in this island, by Dr. Andrew Bell, exactly half a
century from the present time; and that invention, when
generally known, drew people's minds to the subject of
schools for the children of the poor; for it was thought
that a method by which one person could inspect the in-

struction of great numbers would reduce so materially the expense, as to render it no longer hopeless to procure some education for all the inhabitants of the country.   In the early years of the nineteenth century this became the subject of earnest discussion and controversy ; and with good reason ; for it seemed an obvious consequence, that a machinery by which large numbers could be instructed together would place in the hands of those who directed that instruction a powerful moral engine to affect the minds of the rising generation.   The sectaries were not slow in availing themselves of that engine : and as the religious differences of dissenting parents were, by some, considered a reason against their children using the Catechism of the Church, it was maintained by them that nothing should be taught in those large seminaries except such truths as all Christians, of every complexion and denomination, could agree to accept.   Many faithful ministers of the Church felt that they would not be justified before God or man in abdicating one of their most essential functions, that of watching the instruction of their young parishioners, and they recoiled from any proposal of compromising divine truths : accordingly, they were found strenuously to resist that scheme.   With the view of directing the education of the poor in the principles of the national Church, in the year 1812 was established the National Society, an institution which has ever since, by various methods, assisted our schools—by contributions towards their erection—by training teachers —by imparting advice and information— and by maintaining consistency and efficiency in an extensive and rather complicated system.   It was, I believe, about thirty years ago that this momentous subject acquired increased importance in the public eye, by the reports of an Education Committee of the House of Commons ; and it was then first suggested, that an object of such vast consequence as national education claimed the direct assistance of the State, and that nothing less than aid from the public purse could ever compass the great object of universal instruction. But it was not until the year 1833 that the least assistance was rendered by the Government or Parliament towards that work. Schools had indeed increased in number, and the public mind had become more and more favourable to the undertaking. But the countenance then first given to popular education by Parliament seems to have originated in political considerations. The population of the country had increased with surprising rapidity, and the vast numbers of poor congregated in towns, particularly in the manufacturing and mining districts, left far behind them all the efforts of private benevolence. At the same time a fearful increase was observed in the amount of crime; and an examination of the unhappy inmates of prisons proved that a great majority were destitute of every kind of instruction : on the other hand, of the educated part of the poorer classes very few were discovered in the criminal ranks. Such considerations showed the extreme danger of suffering masses of the people to grow up in ignorance of moral and religious duties, and weighed with Parliament to make a grant towards building school-rooms. The amount was, indeed, trifling compared with the demand, being only 20,000l. for England and Wales ; but the like sum was repeated for five successive years ; and, niggardly as these grants have been generally called, it would be ungrateful not to acknowledge that they did cause a great extent of good throughout the country. The money granted by the Treasury, being proportioned to the sums advanced by private subscriptions, was effectual in stimulating a large amount of individual

charity, and thus called into being a multitude of schools
that could not otherwise have had existence.   The Treasury grants being conveyed through the National Society
to Church schools, and through the British and Foreign
Society to Dissenting schools, to meet the sums respectively subscribed, the result was, that no less than five-
sixths of the whole were allotted to the former ; thereby
giving a signal proof of the greater zeal in the cause of
education which animated Churchmen.

" However, the experience of so many years too plainly
showed that the education, if such it could be called,
which was given to the poor was inadequate and unsatisfactory.   The system of mutual instruction, though to a
certain extent useful when judiciously directed, was found
not to be capable of those wonderful effects upon which
sanguine minds had calculated.   Besides, the early age
at which children were generally deprived of school instruction, through the necessities or the cupidity of their
parents, perpetually disappointed the hopes of their intellectual proficiency.   But, above all, the inadequate qualification of the masters and mistresses of National Schools
precluded all prospect of such an education as might
elevate the mind.   The smallness of their salaries, mainly
depending upon precarious subscriptions, almost excluded
persons of ability and energy from situations in which
those qualities are peculiarly required.   Frequently the
instructors of the rising generation were persons who had
been unsuccessful in their endeavours to obtain a livelihood in other lines of life, who had never turned their
attention to the subject of education, and were destitute
of the temper, discernment, and love of the profession,
which should be combined in a good teacher ; and a few
weeks' attendance in the Central School (when funds
could be found for that purpose) was seldom sufficient to

remedy previous inaptitude, or to confer appropriate
habits and address. Against these difficulties the clergy,
feeling that upon them the responsibility was cast, long
struggled with exemplary zeal and patience ; a state of
things which still continues. Many are the cases where
the whole pecuniary support of a school, beyond the
weekly pence of the children, rests with the minister ;
and whatever is of any value in the teaching proceeds
from himself, or the members of his family.

" From observation of these and other defects in our
system, and from a deep sense of the duty of a Christian
nation to bring up its people in Christian principles, the
National Society promulgated a new and comprehensive
plan, the object of which was to establish in every diocese
training schools for teachers ; to combine them with seminaries for the children of the middle classes (who had
before been unaccountably overlooked in our schemes of
national education) ; and to give permanence to these
institutions by connecting them with the cathedral establishments ; while it was hoped that all Churchmen of
influence and education might be interested in the care
and promotion of the system by the formation of Diocesan
Boards of Education. This important movement took
place in the year 1838, and, though the results, as far as
it has operated, have been beneficial to the cause of education, yet it must be confessed that the success of the
scheme has not equalled the anticipations of its benevo-
lent and enlightened projectors. The pecuniary support
which it has met with has not been hitherto sufficient to
carry into execution the contemplated objects to the
required extent : the effect, however, has, on the whole,
been considerable ; and the conviction universally produced on the public mind seems to be, that without an
appropriate education to be given to the teachers, qualify-

ing them to conduct the moral culture of the youthful mind, all efforts at useful instruction of the poor will be illusory; and that this is an object which must, at all risks and all cost, be kept in view. Nevertheless, no one can fail to see the difficulty which the circumstances of this country cast in the way of any training system: in particular, the acquirements of the pupils being of such a nature as will qualify them for many other employments better remunerated than the mastership of a charity school, it is always to be feared that the best and ablest proficients may be tempted to desert the profession for which they have been educated, to embark in one more lucrative and alluring.

" In the following year the Government made an attempt to take into their own hands the guidance of national education. This was to have been effected by various steps, by the establishment of a model school, and of a school for instructors (or *Normal School*, as it was termed), under the authority and direction of a Committee of the Privy Council, who were constituted a Board of Education, with a great latitude of discretion. The former rule of appropriating grants of public money in a just proportion to voluntary donations was to be no longer observed; but a centralized system of Government inspection of schools and of the course of instruction was announced. As these measures were proposed by statesmen who had always avowed themselves advocates and supporters of what is termed the British and Foreign system, as they opened a door to the introduction of a course of education *in which religion might have little or no share*, and as they were joyfully hailed by that party in the country which avowed hostility to the Church, there could be little doubt on the mind of anybody as to their tendency. Though the operation might have been

gradual, yet no long time would have passed before the
Church was deposed from one of its most important functions, and that upon which its ulterior usefulness among
the poorer classes mainly depends—the early instruction
of their youth. This must be regarded as the great crisis
of the education question, in which the sentiments of all
who had thought or interested themselves in the matter
found expression. The Government plan was upheld by
those who wished for schools in which instruction might
be confined, as in those of France, to secular knowledge—
as well as by those who advocated the notion of dividing
religious instruction into *general* and *special*, and wished
to communicate the former in schools, but to exclude the
latter, as bringing into collision conflicting opinions. The
prevailing judgment of the public was indicated by petitions to Parliament, of which about 3000 were against
the proposals, and about 100 in their favour. The measure was only carried in the House of Commons, with all
the weight of ministerial influence, by a majority of two,
while in the Upper House resolutions condemnatory of it
were voted by a majority of no less than one hundred and
eleven ; and an address was carried up to the Throne by
the whole House, praying Her Majesty not to enforce a
system which interfered with the province of the Established Church. It rarely happens that upon any question the preponderance of public opinion throughout all
classes has been expressed so decidedly, and at the same
time so deliberately. Its first result was of a very
remarkable character. The distinguished and eloquent
statesman, the founder of the British and Foreign School
Society, who had signalized the whole of his public life
by a zealous and energetic advocacy of the comprehensive
system of education, was so convinced of the hopelessness
of overcoming the prevalent feeling in favour of the

Church as general instructress, that he published a pamphlet, to persuade those who had co-operated with him for thirty years in that course to acquiesce in the decision which public opinion, as well as Parliament, had pronounced against them ; and urged, with his usual force of argument, that they would best show themselves the sincere, and patriotic advocates for the diffusion of knowledge, by agreeing at once to a ' Church Education Bill.' *

" It is gratifying to contemplate the moderation with which the Church used the triumph of opinion declared in her favour, and the substantial proof which she gave of the sincerity of her zeal for intellectual improvement. The deplorable ignorance in which multitudes were suffered to grow up in the populous manufacturing and mining districts, and the inadequacy of any voluntary efforts in their favour, had been used as the great argument for devolving all care of them and their instruction upon the State : accordingly, a special fund was immediately subscribed, and intrusted to the National Society, for maintaining schools in those populous districts, amounting to not less than 150,000*l.*, five times the sum voted at the time by Parliament for the whole kingdom. A disposition was likewise shown to meet, as far as possible, the views of the Government in regard to schools whose erection had been aided by parliamentary grants : t being agreed that they should be open to Government inspection, on condition that the inspectors of Church Schools were to be persons recommended by the Archbishops of the respective provinces.

" During the last seven years the system of inspection

---

* A Letter on National Education to the Duke of Bedford, K.G. From Lord Brougham. 1839.

has been in progress, and, I think, with singular benefit
to the cause of education.   The examination of a number of schools by able and intelligent observers (and such
qualifications the inspectors eminently display) has
thrown much light upon a subject in which there must
ever be some practical difficulty.   Through a comparison
of different cases, it becomes evident what methods are
most successful in practice; and it can be satisfactorily
ascertained in which instances failure is attributable to
the plan, and in which to the execution.   The Inspectors'
Reports, comprising a mine of valuable information, will
be found in the volumes of the Committee of Council,
which also communicate a variety of plans for school-
rooms and school-houses, directions useful for building
and conducting schools, improvements introduced from
time to time, and a large body of economics conducive to
the improvement of humble education.   Among all the
truths which have been established upon this interesting
subject, the most important is, that the instructor should
himself have received early training, not merely that he
may be qualified to conduct the mechanical process of a
school, but may have such acquaintance with the tempers
and characters of children, and such skill in managing
them, as experience alone can confer.   Above all, it is
necessary that he should himself be thoroughly imbued
with religious principles, without which there is little
chance of his imparting that tone of Christian discipline
which should pervade the whole of his intercourse with
the scholars.   That there may not be wanting a supply
of fit and able persons to fill these stations, it is particularly desirable that, whenever a boy is distinguished in a
National School for ability and good disposition, he should
be retained beyond the usual age, both for his own improvement and for the service of the school: and if means

can be found to constitute him a stipendiary monitor, the
real benefits of the monitorial system will be perceived,
without the objections to which it has been found liable.
Such a pupil may have further instruction after school-
hours, and, if his manners and conduct correspond with
his ability, may become an apprentice teacher: he will
then be qualified as a recipient of the higher instruction
communicated at a training establishment for schoolmasters, or, as it is the fashion to call it, a Normal
School."

The hopes which the good Bishop entertained of a continued cordiality of co-operation between the National
Society as the organ of the Church, and the Committee
of Privy Council as the Educational Department of the
Civil Government, have not been fulfilled. The parliamentary grants of public money in support of education
were indeed increased, having been, from 1839 to 1842,
30,000*l*. a-year; in 1843 and 1844, 40,000*l*. a-year; in
1845, 75,000*l*.; in 1846, 100,000*l*.; and in 1847 and
1848, 125,000*l*. a-year; but in 1846 the Committee of
Privy Council began to insist upon certain conditions of
management in the Church of England schools assisted
with public money, which led to a correspondence with
the National Society, extending over a period of three
years, and terminating in a resolution of the Society not
to recommend to promoters of schools to accept the
management clauses insisted upon by the Committee of
Privy Council. The correspondence on both sides is distinguished by considerable caution and much courtesy.
In several points the Committee of Privy Council readily
conceded what was required by the National Society, but
in the main points of imposing more restriction upon the
promoters of schools than the National Society thought
desirable, and in refusing to allow the Bishop to exercise

authority over the Church of England schools, except in what concerned directly the religious instruction of the pupils, the Committee of Privy Council continued to oppose the views of the Church. The actual and officially-recognised difference between the state of affairs as regards this subject, at the time the Bishop of Gloucester delivered his charge, and at the present time (1850), is this—that whereas the Committee of the National Society in 1846 and 1847 agreed with the Committee of Privy Council jointly to recommend certain management clauses to promoters of schools, they now have declined to recommend such clauses, and this they have done on the following grounds:—In times past the Committee of the National Society never interfered with the constitution of schools, but left them to be determined by the promoters. It was found, however, that in very numerous instances the constitution chosen by the promoters was defective. At the time mentioned the Committee of Privy Council asked the National Society to *recommend* certain clauses, to which the Society assented, with this proviso—that promoters of schools should have the same liberty of choice as had hitherto been conceded to them by the Committee of Privy Council and the National Society. The Society, however, found in the beginning of 1848 that by *recommendation* the Committee of Privy Council meant *enforcement*, and that no new school would be aided by the Committee of Privy Council in the building, which would not receive one of the four management clauses; and not only that, but the one particular clause out of the four which the Committee of Privy Council thought best for that particular school. Upon this the Committee of the National Society remonstrated against what they considered an infringement of reasonable liberty, and they also remarked upon several points in the clauses which in

their opinion would be made better by alteration.   On
most of these points the Committee of Privy Council gave
way ; but on the question of liberty that Committee would
not give way, and they still continue to enforce one of
these management clauses where public money is granted,
and that one selected by themselves.   Therefore the Committee of the National Society declined to continue to
recommend the clauses ; but they have not ceased to give
the same proportion of aid out of their funds to all cases
of school-building whether aided by the Committee of
Council or not; and therefore whether adopting one of
the management clauses or not.   The actual and formal
breach between the National Society and the Committee
of Privy Council has not gone beyond this.   In respect to
general matters the same interchange of communication
as heretofore goes on between the government department
and the National Society.   The training institutions supported by the Society are, as in times past, examined by
her Majesty's Inspectors of Schools, and certificates of
merit awarded to the pupils therein.   Payments are
also made to these institutions out of the parliamentary
grant in pursuance of such certificates, and the annual
grant of 1000*l*. towards the support of those institutions is
still paid by the Committee of Council.

While, however, the managing Committee of the National Society have gone no farther in breaking with the
government department than is implied by decisively terminating the correspondence on the subject of the management clauses, it is unquestionable that a very large body
of the clergy connected with the National Society have
been both alarmed and wounded by the course which the
Committee of Privy Council have taken—a course which
they consider to be hostile to the Church of England,
and far more restrictive as regards Church schools than

the government would venture to be in respect to the schools of Protestant Dissenters, or of Roman Catholics.

The strong feeling of the clergy against the course taken by the civil government became manifest to the public at the annual general meeting of the National Society in June, 1849, the Archbishop of Canterbury in the chair. Neither his influence, nor that of other prelates present, who were unwilling that anything wearing the appearance of very strong disapprobation of the proceedings of the Committee of Privy Council should be done by the National Society, was sufficient to prevent the Society from coming to a resolution that no terms of co-operation with the government could be satisfactory which should not allow to the clergy and laity full freedom to constitute schools upon such principles and models as are both sanctioned and commended by the order and the practice of the Church of England. It was evidently the opinion of the majority of the clergy at that important meeting, that the interference of government in the education of members of the Church of England ought to be limited to making grants of the public money in aid of the exertions of the Church. It was alleged that the real question was whether the National Society, as the educational executive of the Church, was to subordinate itself to the Committee of the Privy Council, and it was maintained that the Society ought to repudiate at once, and at whatever cost, the concurrent authority of the Committee of Council as to what should or should not be the constitution and management of a Church school. A compromise, it was said, was impossible, even on the lowest ground of the right of the Church of England to be dealt with upon the same principle as that upon which all the other religious bodies which unhappily existed in this country were dealt with by the Committee of Council on Education; not

more favourably nor less favourably, but in the same
manner and on the same principle.   It was urged that the
Committee of Privy Council said to the Roman Catholic,
" Tell us on what terms you would like us to give you
money, and you shall have it, provided only the tenure of
your school sites is legal, and you will admit the inspection of 1840." They said the same to the two divisions
of the Kirk of Scotland, to the Wesleyan, the Independent,
the Baptist, the Socinian—to any school in which any form
of religion was taught—to any school in which no form of
religion was taught; but to the Church of England they
said, " Here are other terms in your case — terms, besides, over and above the legal tenure of the site and the
inspection of 1840—terms not of your own making, or of
your own choice, or of your own approval at all, but of
our making, and our choice, and our approval, and upon
these terms we offer you money ; and whether you like
them or no, you shall not have the money upon any other
terms." Another clergyman, of European celebrity, said
that his objection to the legislative power of the Committee of Council was that in its corporate capacity that
Committee had no religion : Wesleyans, Anglicans, and
Roman Catholics were all alike in their eyes.   If they
had any partialities at all, they treated the sects as if they
were the Church, and the Church as if it were a sect.
Such sentiments as these, which were evidently in harmony
with those of a large majority of the assembled sub-
scribers to the National Society, showed that in the great
business of Christian education there was but little cordiality of sentiment or unity of purpose between the clergy
of the Church of England and the civil government of the
time.   This estrangement is much to be deplored, and it
will require the exercise of considerable judgment and
moderation on both sides to mitigate its immediate ten-

dencies, and to obviate its more remote but probable
consequences. On the one hand, there can be little doubt
that the state has exhibited a morbid jealousy of the interference of the Church which is connected with the State,
while showing a more liberal and indulgent feeling
towards Sectarians and Romanists. On the other hand,
the clergy might perhaps have taken a better method of
preserving their influence than that of directly disputing
the authority over Church of England schools which is
claimed by the State. It is no doubt—as a matter of
policy—imprudent on the part of the State to force the
Church, as it were, upon the exercise of its own sole
authority and means of influence in a matter so nearly
connected with civil affairs as education is. But if the
State, in spite of warning, persists in that imprudence, it
consists with the dignity of the Church to resort calmly
to its own inherent power—to put its own system into
action with fervent, gentle, ceaseless, self-denying earnestness, and thus to obtain influence over the pupils in spite
of management clauses springing from political liberalism,
and framed in a latitudinarian spirit. " Be ye wise as
serpents and harmless as doves." Considering the public
feeling in favour of religion and of the Church of England
which exists in this country, the clergy need not be very
solicitous to possess the aid of the State, if they will
but exert themselves in strict conformity with the system
of the Church and their own vows. In all matters which
fall within their province so much as Christian education
does, they might, by a skilful use of their means and opportunities, exert a paramount influence over the State,
instead of the State controlling them. The State is the
steward, not the owner, of the public funds. If the clergy,
denying themselves in everything else, will seek only the
triumph of their great cause, the authority they possess,

and their opportunities of persuasion, judiciously used, will bring the public over to their side; and when the public voice and the voice of religion unite in one demand, of what avail will be the Committee of Privy Council, and its secular utilitarianism? Will they not sink at once into ridiculous inferiority?

But some will say that it is absurd to occupy time and attention upon the distinctions between such education as the Privy Council prefers and such as the clergy approve, when the great question is between savage and dangerous ignorance on the one hand, and some degree of culture and information on the other. This seems plausible, but in England it is not practically true. What might be the case if our habits and the training of our youth, under the compulsion of law, were similar to the habits of continental countries, it matters not to inquire. The case is not so. The general desire of our lower classes is not so much education for their children, as employment. To earn money is the grand object. It is to be hoped it will not be always so, but it is so now. However shameful the ignorance and rudeness of large bodies of our people may be, and however dangerous to society, there seems to be no machinery for remedying the evil but that of the Church. It is probable that far too much is expected from popular education, and far more than can be realized by even the best kind of education that can be given; but as education cannot be absolutely negative in respect to religious and moral effects—as it must either promote the wisdom which is "from above," or that which is "earthly, sensual, devilish"—the question whether education shall be under safe direction is as important as the question whether there shall be education at all. There can be no doubt of the importance of bringing the purifying influence of the Church to bear upon education,

though it may be questioned whether that influence will
be any the less, because unconnected with the State, if
only the Church chooses to exert its own inherent
authority with unity, with earnestness, and with dignified
meekness.

The gratuitous education supplied in England may be
classed under four heads. First, the schools founded by
private benevolence, a custom of the olden time, but
little followed in these days. We have neither imitated
the example of our ancestors in this respect, nor even
carried out their views and applied their funds with
honesty and carefulness. Many of the trusts of old
grammar-schools or free-schools have been shamefully
neglected or abused, and, at this moment, funds are in
many cases diverted altogether from the purposes intended
by the donors, or are so applied that very little benefit is
derived in proportion to the amount of property expended.
Still these old endowments are to some extent effectual
for gratuitous education. The second class is that of
schools supported by the combined subscriptions of members of the Church, now aided to some extent by the
State.* This is by far the most important class of esta-

* Since the year 1839 Government has contributed the sum of 470,854*l.*
towards the building of school-houses, drawing out thereby voluntary
contributions to probably four times that amount. The grants have been
thus distributed :—

		Schools aided.
England	£399,368	3,255
Scotland	41,563	302
Wales	27,418	198
Islands	2,505	27

The number of children for whom accommodation was provided was
709,000. Of the whole amount granted under this head 82 per cent. was
for Church of England schools. The amount granted in aid of schools
for training teachers was 66,450*l.*, of which 35,950*l.* went to Church of
England schools.—*Edinb. Rev.*, July, 1850.

blishments for free education, and they are for the most part in connexion with the National Society. The third class consists of schools supported by the joint contributions of Protestant Dissenters or Roman Catholics, which are also assisted by the State, but the whole number of pupils in these schools is calculated as but slightly exceeding one-tenth of the number in the schools connected with the Church of England. The fourth class comprises the schools of poor-houses and prisons. In 1846 Mr. Bennett computed the number of young persons in England and Wales requiring the aid of gratuitous education to be 2,125,000, of whom 1,038,000 were unprovided with any such aid, and that number was increasing by 25,000 each year. Great exertions have been made since 1846, and are likely still to be made, for the extension of education, but it must be admitted that the prevailing spirit of the country is the spirit of trade, and that in both town and country it is not the habit of the poor to allow their children to devote their time to education, except when they cannot dispose of their time for money. Until this spirit is changed, and poor people become more willing to make sacrifices for the sake of their children's education, many will continue to be brought up in rudeness and ignorance. Again, as to the power of the State in promoting education, we must remember that, while all but a very small and very conceited minority admit religion to be the main point of education, there is no such thing as agreement upon the theory of religion which should be taught. Mr. Bennett,* after quoting Aristotle's opinion that the education of the people forms a part of the duty of the State, proceeds as follows :—

---

* On Crime and Education, p. 52.

" That a man should profess what creed he pleased was a doctrine unheard of in Aristotle's time, and so little was it heard of for centuries after, that, when some of the Greek and Roman philosophers professed the faith of Christ, they were offered the choice of sacrificing to the idols of the State religion, or the combat of the wild beasts. But it is not so with us, as all men know. Universal toleration of religious opinion is the doctrine of England, and the State itself, existing on this doctrine, and containing within itself the exemplification of this doctrine, cannot with any consistency, even had it the power or the will (but it has neither), propagate education of any one sort to the exclusion of another. The State finds itself bound round and hampered by contending interests; if it pleases one, it displeases another; and being of a democratic tendency, and owing its very existence to a democratic principle, its form of legislation must more or less tend to the satisfying of the people's pleasure, not the ruling of the people's will. In taxing the people as a people, for the benefit of all, and gathering from the people the supply of means for education, that supply must in equity be distributed among all, and consequently every man of every creed whatsoever has his equal right to a share in the distribution. Immediately, then, that the State begins her distribution the Church steps forward. The Church, being recognised by the State as one portion of the people, must have her share. On another side starts forth the Romanist. This creed is now openly tolerated, and not, as fifty years ago, persecuted with pains and penalties; nay, it is very nearly, in the State's estimation, on a parallel with the Church, for it now receives endowments from the State, as in Maynooth, which the Church does not. The Romanists are a very conspicuous body; it is doubtful whether they may not be

the prevailing body before another century has passed,
but, whether so or not, they are sufficiently conspicuous
and powerful even now to demand their share of the
people's money. Well, no sooner has their claim been
satisfied than the great body of Protestants arise in various
denominations, such as the Presbyterians, the Wesleyans,
the Anabaptists, the Independents, the Quakers, the
Plymouth Brethren, and the like, no one entirely agreeing
with another save in dissent from the Catholic Church;
and therefore no one able to join another in the education
of their children: each then must have their share.
Then, leaving Christianity and those who profess faith in
the Son of God as God, we come to the Socinians and the
Jews. They, too, cannot conscientiously suffer their
children to be taught in a faith different from their own;
and yet they, with the rest, contribute to the taxation, and
so doing, in equity, must have a corresponding share."

Such are the difficulties of the State in respect to education, arising from a want of a distinctive faith of its
own. And from such difficulties these results appear to
arise—that the crowd of smaller communities must be
left out of consideration by the State in its educational
policy, from the practical impossibility of affording separate
portions of aid to so many; and as for the larger communities, with the Church of England at their head, the duty
of the State, upon the most *liberal* view of the case, seems
to be to assist them with means in proportion to their
numbers, giving as much liberty to each, in respect to
education, as is allowed them in the public profession of
their respective tenets. To select the Church of England
for restrictions which are not so much as attempted to be
applied to other denominations of less numerical importance, appears to be a curiously inexcusable stretch of
political prejudice.

The desire of parents in the lower ranks of life to have their children earning something, rather than to have them at school, has been already adverted to. In the manufacturing districts it is notorious that at a very early age the children are sent to work in the spinning-mills, and, though the law has not been wholly silent respecting the education of children in factories,* yet it has not been effectual in practice to secure much instruction for those whose infant years are devoted to productive labour. Mr. Horner, one of the Inspectors of Factories, mentions, in his remarks prefixed to his translation of Victor Cousin's book on the Schools of Holland, that his inquiries concerning the state of education among the factory children in Manchester satisfied him that large numbers of the children were not attending schools of any kind. He officially reported to the Government, that some mill-owners held that the education clauses of the Factory Act were unnecessary, because factory children, they said, were known to be better off in that respect than other children of the working classes. Since that time, reports Mr. Horner, " I have obtained proof that, in some situations at least, the factory children form no exception to that state of destitution, as regards education, which prevails among the children of the working classes of this country, and to an extent of which few seem to be sufficiently aware." Mr. Horner made an examination of 2000 children, from 19 different factories in Manchester. Of these 1067 could not read, and 186 did not even know the alphabet. Those who " could read to any practical purpose " amounted to less than a third of the whole number. I must confess the part of Mr. Horner's statement which most surprises me is that, out of the 2000, no

---

* See 3 & 4 William IV. c. 103.

less than 611 could read *with ease* the New Testament. Of the boys, amounting to 1040, there were 441 who could sign their names. Of the girls, amounting to 960, only 100 were equally accomplished.

In the year 1843 four barristers were sent out by the Poor Law Commissioners to spy into the nakedness of the land in the rural districts, and, among other things, into the effects which the occupation of children in work had upon "their opportunities for obtaining school instruction and moral and religious education" These barristers went south, north, east, and west; that is, one took Wilts, Dorset, Devon, and Somerset; another, Kent, Surrey, and Sussex; a third, Suffolk, Norfolk, and Lincoln; and a fourth, Yorkshire and Northumberland. The Dorset and Devon gentleman reported that in the greater number of agricultural parishes there were day-schools, which were attended by a considerable number of labourers' children, both boys and girls. Children go to these schools at five, six, or seven years of age, and the boys, "if not taken away," remain till they are twelve or even older, and the girls sometimes till they are fifteen or sixteen. Reading and writing, and sometimes a little arithmetic, are taught, to which occasionally some other occupation is added: the boys not unfrequently learn some slight mechanical business, such as making nets, &c., and the girls needlework. In some parts of Dorsetshire the making of wire shirt-buttons is taught to boys and girls, the work occupying nearly all their spare time. The books that are used for teaching the children to read contain lessons of morality and religion. In a few schools singing is encouraged, particularly when the master or mistress has a taste for music. There is also, with few exceptions, a Sunday-school in every parish, at which reading is taught, and sometimes writing; but the prin-

cipal object of these schools generally is the instruction of
the children in their religious duties.   The children who
attend the day-school nearly always belong to the Sunday-
school.   Of the utility of both sorts of schools the commissioner was of opinion there could be no doubt.   Everywhere he met with evidence of the good effect produced
by them.   Among the labouring population there was an
universal feeling in their favour.   But, notwithstanding
this, it does not appear that children were kept at school
when the opportunity arrived for employing them in
labour.   The age at which boys first go out to farm-
labour varies, the commissioner says, from seven to
twelve.   Many are taken from school to go to work
before they reach the best class, and the majority of
them soon after they have reached it.   Boys taken from
school to be put out to farm-labour can generally read,
sometimes correctly; but they cannot often write with
sufficient ease for useful purposes.   But boys, though
taken from day-school to work in farm-labour, generally
attend the Sunday school, which serves to keep up, and
in many cases to improve their reading, though very
rarely to improve their writing.   There are cases, however, particularly in dairy or grazing farms, where boys
are prevented from going to the Sunday-school, by having
to attend to the cows or cattle; and what they have
learned at the day-school is in such instances, after a
time, nearly forgotten.   It also generally happens that,
when boys remain at the day-school later than the age of
seven or eight, they go out to work in the fields at particular seasons of the year, till they are finally taken away
altogether.   Their work is useful to the farmer at certain
seasons, although it may not be so all the year round.
But this occasional employment does not prevent a boy
from attending the Sunday-school.   Girls are also some-

times, but much more rarely than boys, taken from the
day school to work in the hay-harvest. Girls are also
frequently kept from school at certain times of the year,
in order to attend to their younger brothers and sisters
whilst their mothers are employed in the fields. Boys
and girls are also kept from school to help their mothers
in gleaning. The effect of these interruptions in the
attendance of children at school is frequently mischievous,
as far as their progress is concerned. A child not only
loses a certain quantity of instruction, but on its return to
school after working in the fields it appears less desirous,
and even less capable, of profiting by school instruction.
One of the witnesses examined at Whitestone, Devon,
says that " all are taken that are able to do work, and
can get it, at every season of the year." Children appren-
ticed by the parish do not attend day-school after they
are bound, although apprenticeship begins at nine years
of age. Generally, but not always, they attend a Sunday-
school. In *some* instances their reading and even writing
is attended to by their master or some member of the
family, as also their religious and moral instruction, but
such cases are rare. Upon the whole, the commissioner
is of opinion that the employment of children in agriculture deprives them of opportunities of instruction both
moral and religious, as well as of ordinary school education ; but it is rare that their attendance at Sunday-
schools is prevented by such employment, and therefore
children so employed suffer more from the loss of ordinary
school instruction than from the loss of religious instruction, the giving of which is the object of the Sunday-
schools. But it appears that the education of a farm-
labourer in his business by which he is to earn his bread
must begin early. It appears, says the commissioner, to
be the common opinion of all persons practically ac-

quainted with the agricultural labouring class, that, unless a boy begin to work in the fields when young, he never thoroughly learns his business. To make a good farm-labourer, an early familiarity with everything connected with the various kinds of work required on a farm is necessary. The age at which a boy should begin is fixed by some persons at seven, by others at eight or nine, and by others at ten or eleven, but it is generally agreed that after eleven or twelve a boy cannot learn the business of a farm-labourer so well as a boy who begins earlier.

The commissioner mentions a case at Pimperne, in Dorsetshire, where the clergyman opened an evening-school for the four winter months in the National School-room. This was attended by young persons of from eleven to twenty years of age, and was productive of very beneficial results.

In Kent, Surrey, and Sussex, we are told that the education of girls is not very seriously affected by their employment in field-labour, as in earlier years they are rarely engaged in it. Their attendance for instruction is proportionably steadier, and their stay at school longer, than that of the boys. Whether their education is, upon the whole, more successful, is questionable. The commissioner seems to regard the common in-door life of the cottage as particularly unfavourable to improvement. The domestic labour of the cottage, he says, while it more commonly checks and interrupts the general instruction of schools than agricultural employment, does not seem to furnish a practical discipline of much value for the future domestic life of the young female. To the regular and prolonged education of boys, labour in the fields is a serious obstacle, interrupting the attendance of the scholars, and early withdrawing them from school, even where the opportunities for instruction are afforded most

cheaply. That these opportunities do not exist everywhere in the same degree is the natural result of circumstances. The greater number of villages in which the
commissioner made inquiry have the benefit of schools,
endowed or supported by subscription, and generally, he
says, of recent origin. The opportunities of school instruction, where they exist in their most liberal form, are
commonly foregone for the sake of obtaining work, which
withdraws nearly all at the age of ten or eleven, and
some much earlier, and during the time of instruction,
especially the latter years of it, they are frequently absent
for the sake of earnings in the fields. When the absences
for labour occur at a very early age, as at that of seven
and eight years, they seem of themselves sufficient to
check the pupil's progress, even in the " manual exercises " learned at school. A schoolmaster in the hop
district said that in some cases the hand became so
chapped and stiffened by work, that their writing tasks
can hardly be continued, and that the sense of their own
backwardness, after repeated or long absences, so dis-
courages them, that they make slight exertions, become
unmanageable from being disheartened, and so a serious
hindrance even to others. The poverty of families, which
precludes them from obtaining the stouter kind of
clothing, and the distance of their houses from the
school in parishes which contain waste ground and are
much scattered, frequently keep the children from their
opportunities of instruction. On one day of very bad
weather forty-two, out of a total number of fifty-two,
failed to present themselves at a school so situated. The
same poverty, and its attendant indifference, acts in many
cases to prevent their seizing the opportunities for instruction at all, even during the intervals between the
periods of employment, in themselves of slight profit.

This commissioner admits that the opportunity to
attend school seems much to depend upon the pupils
themselves.   They who most dislike learning are pretty
sure to be most frequently absent on account of employment in the fields.   Great ignorance, he says, if it does
not prevail, is at least to be met with where no special
pains are taken to discover it.   It is quite common to
meet with boys engaged in farms who cannot read or
write.   The unity of God, a future state, the number of
months in the year, are matters not universally known.
These instances, not occurring in neglected districts, but
about large villages, and in the agricultural population
near towns where opportunities for instruction existed,
showed not only that there are those who do not seek
education, but that they are the persons to whom the
ordinary knowledge and convictions of society do not find
their way unless imparted by the regular method of
school teaching, and who, in consequence, if they do not
obtain such direct instruction, are not taught and human-
ized by the numerous influences which act upon others.
Where the children, however, are sent to school, the same
spirit of indifference exaggerates the effects of all real
hindrances, as it leads to any excuse for non-attendance
—the most trifling profit or inconvenience.   It is said
that it is a matter which requires much care and attention to obtain a regular attendance even at Sunday-
schools.   In this respect the lower orders are situated
very differently from those in the middle and upper
classes of society, who see clearly the benefits and necessity of an education, and oblige their children to pursue it
steadily, though, of course, they cannot enforce earnestness and real application.   This is naturally the case with
a class in society who have had an education, know from
experience what it produces, and are, besides, directed

by a steady public opinion which commands them in this
as in other matters of life.   But the poor, who have perhaps had no education themselves, have no individual
conviction of the degree and kind of benefit which it produces, and for public opinion among their own class, as,
from their isolated mode of life, it has a feebler effect,
comparatively speaking, on all points, so on this it has
scarcely an existence.   It could arise only from definite
views of life, or common hopes of social advancement and
success, such as those who live in doubt as to to-morrow's
bread hardly attain to.   As they exist from hand to mouth
in the ordinary needs of life, they are not likely to be
very prospective in their weighing and providing for its
advantages.   They are directed, therefore, mainly by the
casual influences which happen to surround them; in
some cases the influence which arises from personal
respect—the influence of their superiors ; in other cases,
that arising from personal affection—the influence of their
children.

This Commissioner goes into considerable detail in
describing the various implements, in the use of which a
good agricultural labourer must necessarily be somewhat
dexterous; and he infers, as the Dorset and Devon gentleman did, that " discipline " in the fields is necessary
as a part of his practical education from a very early
period. Following this, we find in the Commissioner's
Report a learned disquisition upon the metaphysical characteristics of arithmetic, which is ingenious enough, and
would be more so if the author had not applied to the
" science " of arithmetic observations which concern
arithmetic only as an art. The practical point is, however, that, in the counties of Kent, Surrey, and Sussex,
arithmetic learned at school is forgotten at the plough ;
and then the Commissioner proceeds to say that " the

religious instruction imparted in earlier years seems often
to meet with a fate similar to that of the arithmetic,
though not the same. What is lost in arithmetic is
purely and absolutely forgotten; but the doctrinal truths
of religion, and such few historical facts as they necessarily imply, pass away differently. The ideas themselves, as of a much more complicated nature than those
of arithmetic, remain in part, and are lost in part.
Where, therefore, the ear has forgotten the exact form of
words in which the truths were conveyed, all is error and
distortion. The impressions are sufficiently obliterated
to lose their meaning, yet remain so as to be capable of
some kind of combination which is effected by guess-work.
The ignorance of arithmetic forgotten is ignorance; the
ignorance of religious truth forgotten is confusion and
error. In both cases the salt of knowledge has lost its
savour, and indeed its form; in one, however, it has eva-
porated, in the other it has effloresced into shapes often
painfully grotesque."

The Commissioner who went into Suffolk, Norfolk,
and Lincoln does not say anything either of evaporation
or efflorescence; but his observations, though unambitious
in their manner, are much to the point. The children,
he says, usually begin to be employed in the fields at the
age of ten; but as their employment is not constant, they
commonly return to school in the intervals of work. The
effect of the new poor-law (that of 1834) and the state of
the labour-market was to throw the labouring classes
mainly on their own resources, and almost to compel the
parents to take their children from school as soon as they
could earn anything in the fields. In the counties to
which this Commissioner's inquiries extended, he found
schooling so much sacrificed to earning, that both teachers
and scholars had great difficulties to contend with, and

much time was spent in constantly going over the same
short and narrow ground. School instruction thus made
less progress than might have been expected from the
interest taken, the sums spent, and the machinery employed in it. Most children, however, learn to read, and
many to write, and there may be, says the Commissioner,
more truth than some are inclined to believe in the complaint of the farmers that education is being carried too
far. They' mean, he thinks, that educationists are apt
to value book learning at more than it is worth to the
labouring classes—that the labouring classes are educated
too much on the same plan as the leisure classes—that, as
they will have to learn most things by the rule of thumb,
that is by observation, shrewdness, and practical sagacity,
they should have their wits sharpened and their general
faculties stirred, rather than their memories stored with
knowledge, sometimes obsolete, sometimes useless for any
of the purposes of practical life.

The effect of this "jostle of notions," continues the
Commissioner, between the gentry and the clergy on the
one hand, and the employers and the poor on the other,
is to strike a sort of balance, more or less well adjusted
according to circumstances, between the education and
the earnings. *The rich rarely have a very accurate knowledge of the details of a poor man's necessities,* and therefore apply general rules where circumstances demand
exceptions. The poor have so pressing a sense of their
own immediate necessities, that they sometimes even increase those necessities by a want of foresight in choosing
the means of escaping them. For instance, they will
sometimes take a child from school to earn twopence,
when the wear and tear of the clothes will cost more than
the earnings, and the schooling will be lost into the bar-
gain. But perhaps, of the two, the poor man's reasoning

is the soundest; for as the mass of mankind are much more fitted for action without knowledge than for knowledge without action, employment is preferable to schooling where a bare livelihood is to be gained by constant labour. The Commissioner quotes a communication from the Rector of Wrentham, in Suffolk, of which the substance is, that the education of the poor in the agricultural districts has *not* advanced since the establishment of a stricter poor-law. By the change of the poor-law, this gentleman says that the moral principles of the parents have been strengthened, and their affection for their children quickened; yet, as the children must now work for their subsistence, instead of being maintained wholly or in part by the parish, as they formerly were, they have less opportunity of availing themselves of the improved means of instruction which now exist. From which fact, argues the Commissioner, this conclusion follows—that *the poor are led to estimate the prospective gain from education far below the present gain of wages for labour.* With regard to opportunities for obtaining religious education, Sunday-schools, he observes, seem to be very general, usually well attended, and to be of the greatest service in every point of view. In many cases the parents make arrangements to enable the children to attend school or church; but this varies much with the means and character of the parents, and perhaps the generality of them do *not* do so.

We now come to the shrewd and "canny" North, where the common people are certainly not wanting in general intelligence, whatever be their condition in respect of that which is commonly considered education. "What I saw of the northern peasantry," says the learned Commissioner, "impressed me very strongly in their favour. They are very intelligent, sober and courteous in their manners, and their courtesy is not cringing, but coupled with a manly independence of demeanour." As to education, however, he says that its general condition is anything but good (if book-knowledge be of the value which it is the fashion to suppose). It is very discreditable to the country, he adds, that so large a proportion of its inhabitants should be left, as they are left, in profound ignorance. The simple fact that, in a large majority of cases, what the children learn as children is not kept up afterwards, but forgotten, needs no comment. " The word education must in such cases be taken to mean really little more than a certain amount of physical deterioration incurred by wasting time in crowded and unwholesome rooms." The Commissioner, however, feels bound to say that, meagre and unsatisfactory as the instruction given commonly is, the matter is improving rather than the reverse. Infant-schools are becoming more frequent. These institutions are found to be of great value. The tempers of the children are softened, and their faculties awakened, so that they come afterwards into the day-schools with habits more or less formed of docility and self-control. Night-schools, also, where a few—a very few—of the grown-up labourers struggle gallantly with the difficulties of their position, and endeavour to maintain what they have learned, seem to be on the increase. In particular places, also, where the neighbourhood of a gentleman's house whose family interest themselves about the poor, or the labours of an energetic clergyman, have produced their natural effects, education may be in some degree more impressive in its progress, and more successful in its result; but, generally speaking, what the children of the poor learn is worth little to them, and as such is thrown aside and rapidly forgotten. The object of education, says the Commissioner, as I under-

stand it, is to fit a man for the condition of life to which
he is called, as well as circumstances admit of. Without
undervaluing it, in the proper sense of the word—without
even denying that mere discipline, no matter to what
ends, has its own advantages—a question may arise
whether reading made easy, bad writing, and worse
arithmetic, are the best preparations for a labourer's life
or not—whether the time spent at school might not be
better filled up by practical instruction upon totally different principles—whether, in short, the boys (girls *are*
taught to sew) can help thinking no more of much which
they are supposed to learn as soon as they find it irrele-
vant to their actual conditon. If education does not
quicken the faculties, it leaves its intellectual object un-
accomplished : if the method of quickening the faculties
by books be, under all circumstances, the best possible
method, let it be properly applied ; but where a people
of much natural acuteness seem to make a point of forgetting in manhood what they are taught in youth, the
action upon the faculties must be so very imperfect as to
make the instruction they receive, intellectually speaking,
no education at all. With reference to the degree in
which out door labour interferes with this education, the
question is easily answered. School, as might be supposed, is invariably sacrificed to work. If a farmer has,
even for one day, a pig or a cow to keep from straying,
away goes a boy from his books to tend the animal. In
this respect one school is just like all the rest. In winter
it is tolerably well frequented ; as the spring advances,
first one scholar drops off, and then another, till towards
harvest, when, in places where children are much employed, half the school is in the fields : it then shuts up
for six weeks altogether. After harvest it re-opens ; the
attendance at first is thin, but it keeps getting better till

about November, when it is at its height again. Still,
however, though these interruptions, in the case of intelligent children, may be vexatious to an active master,
the Commissioner is of opinion that a village boy does
not get more holidays, though he may spend them less
agreeably to himself, than as a gentleman's son he would
have found at any of the great schools. His calculation
is, that children may be taken away from school for work
about fifteen weeks in the year; but six weeks at Mid-
summer, six at Christmas, and three at Easter are the
usual holidays at schools where the sons of the gentry
are educated. " If, therefore, time were all that was
wanting to educate the children of agricultural labourers
properly, there would, I think, be time enough."

Such, then, are the opinions of the learned persons
sent forth officially to report, among other things, concerning the education of the young in the agricultural
districts. And it appears to me that it may be justly
inferred from what they say, that, generally speaking, the
means of education exist in those districts, and that, if
children are not educated, it is because the parents have
no zeal upon the point, or because the pressure of their
circumstances is such that they cannot afford to allow the
time of their children to be spent upon education. What
appears now to be wanting is, first, such an amelioration
of the general condition of the peasantry as will enable
them to spare their children from labour while obtaining
education ; and, secondly, some law which, without trench-
ing too much upon personal liberty and independence,
would operate as a strong inducement, or a mild compulsion, upon parents to take advantage of such means as
exist for affording education to their children.

At a meeting of clergy and gentry opposed to the educational proceedings of the Committee of Privy Council,

which was held in London on the 30th of May, 1850, the following resolutions were passed :—

" Whereas, by the establishment of the Normal Schools at Kneller Hall, it is proposed to provide teachers for the whole population; and whereas the published minutes of the Committee of Council on Education relating to the state of the Normal Schools propose a vague and inadequate course of religious teaching; and whereas the Church of England has no sufficient security that teachers who are to be trained in the said Normal Schools will be trained according to the doctrine and discipline of the Church, it is the opinion of this meeting that a solemn protest ought to be made against the establishment of the Normal Schools at Kneller Hall, and of any schools of the like character, and every lawful means used to press upon the legislature the duty of reconstructing it upon a basis which shall be consistent with the order and practice of the Church.

" Whereas the system of interference with the education given in Church schools, which has been engrafted on State inspection by the minutes of August and December, 1846, is a very serious encroachment upon the compact regulating the limits of State inspection established in the year 1840 ; and whereas the tendency of such system of interference is gradually to infuse a latitudinarian education into the Church schools, by means of gratuities to schoolmasters and pupil-teachers, and by the selection of school-books provided at low prices out of the annual education grant, it is the opinion of this meeting that measures ought to be taken for procuring such a settlement by the authorities of Parliament of the limits of State Inspection as shall effectually preclude the Committee of Council on Education from interfering with the education given in Church schools."

CHAPTER XXI.

THE TENTH OF APRIL, 1848.

MODERN times have afforded no such important illustration of the prevailing tone and temper of the British nation, in regard to public affairs, as was presented to the world by the circumstances of the British metropolis during the eventful 10th of April, 1848. That day was, in the British Islands, the culminating point of the revolutionary progress which, within a period of little more than two months, had shaken almost every throne of Continental Europe. In England nothing was shaken but the hopes of the disaffected. From one end of Europe to the other, the 10th of April was looked forward to by the partisans of revolution as the day which was to add London to the list of capitals submitting to the dictation of the mob. The spirit of revolt had run like wildfire from kingdom to kingdom, and capital to capital. Paris, Vienna, Naples, Berlin, Dresden, Milan, Venice, Palermo, Frankfort, and Carlsruhe, had all experienced the revolutionary shock, and none had been able completely to withstand it. Now came the turn of London, the greatest capital of all, the greatest prize that the world could afford to revolutionary adventure; the most magnificent prey to the bands of plunderers who moved about from one point of Europe to another, committing robberies under the name of revolution. London withstood the shock, and escaped without the slightest injury. Even the wild spirit of revolt, made drunk by the extraordinary success it had achieved throughout continental Europe, was frozen into fear by the calm, complete, and stern preparation which was made to encounter and to crush it. The spirit of Wellington was equal to the occasion, and seemed to pervade the might and the energy of the vast metropolis of England, while that veteran was at the head of the resisting power. The excitement was of a higher kind than that which breaks forth in passion—

> "——— and instead of rage
> Deliberate valour breathed, firm and unmoved."

The 10th of April seemed, as if by mutual consent, to be the day of trial between the rival forces of revolution and of authority, and it then plainly appeared, without any actual collision, that the revolutionists had no chance. All their points of attack had been anticipated. Everywhere there was preparation to receive them, and yet nothing was so openly done as to produce a sense of public alarm. London was armed to the teeth, and yet, in outward appearance, it was not changed. The force that had been prepared lay hushed in grim repose, and was kept out of sight. The revolutionary leaders were, however, made aware of the consequences that would ensue if they went one step beyond that which the authorities deemed to be consistent with the public safety. Foolish and frantic though they were in their political talk, they were not so mad as to rush upon certain destruction. They gave up the conflict, and from that day the spirit of revolution in England drooped and died away. The political conspirators against existing authority failed utterly, not because they were destitute of the enthusiasm meet for such an occasion, or that there were no real grievances in the condition of the people which called for redress, but because the nation had common sense enough to perceive that the ascendancy of such desperate adventurers would make matters worse instead of better. It was not that the Londoners had no taste for political improvement, but it was that they had a very decided distaste for being robbed. Not only was all the intelligence, the organization, and the resource of the country, arrayed in opposition to the mode of political action which the revolutionists of Europe had adopted, but the familiar instincts of the hundreds of thousands who had property to guard, and hearths to preserve inviolate, arrayed them in determined resistance to mob violence, whatever might be the avowed object to which that violence should be directed. There is a species of isolation in Englishmen's habits which makes them very slow to join in any political movement which is to be obtained by means of popular disturbance. They may wish a change of system, but to throw their families and fortunes into the common lot, and make all in which they are concerned the subject of general scramble, is to them intolerable. In France and Germany, whatever a man is in politics, his family are commonly the same. He keeps nothing to himself ; and when times of commotion arrive the family partake in the excitement, and they become, as it were, prepared for the changes which ambition on the one hand, or ill-fortune on the other, may occasion. Not so in England. The keenest politician at the meeting, the club, or in the houses of legislature, is, at his own fire-side, no politician at all. The sympathies he seeks there are of a totally different kind. His wife and children know nothing of the thoughts which occupy his mind relative to public affairs. While he is pondering the probabilities of a revolution, they are intent upon matters merely domestic. If then what is called " a crisis " should arrive, the family is wholly un-

prepared for sharing in its effects. They know nothing
about it.   Their concern is not with politics; or if any of
them happen to have formed opinions upon political subjects, it is as likely as not that these opinions do not
accord with those of the head of the family.   It is pretty
certain then that he has at home no encouragement to
run risks for the sake of political objects.   Himself he
may be willing enough to devote to his cause, whatever
it be, but he avoids such means of advancing his cause as
would involve his family.   With regard to them, his first
care is that they should be kept safe from all disturbance,
and, if it be proposed to redress any political grievance by
methods which are fraught with public disorder and private insecurity, he is apt to think the remedy worse than
the disease.

One circumstance which strongly affected the general
feeling in regard to the movement contemplated on the
10th of April, was the impression that foreign disturbers
were mainly concerned in it.   There can be little doubt
that this impression was well founded.   For several weeks
before the 10th of April it was obvious to all who walked
the streets that there were more foreigners than usual
among the moving groups; and from their appearance
they were not of that class who visit London for the purposes of ordinary business or amusement.   The suspicion
of the interference of such men in any public commotion
which might occur, stirred the habitual coolness of English blood into a fervour of hostility.   Desirous as we are
to show all courtesy and hospitality to foreigners who
visit us with friendly dispositions—ready as we are to
welcome foreigners even as rivals, in the peaceful pursuits
of art or of trade—there is a natural jealousy of their
interference in our political affairs.   Besides, the majority
of intelligent Englishmen had full in their recollection the

outrages which had occurred in the various continental capitals under the name of revolution, and they were at once alarmed and indignant at the chance of hands which were practised in such atrocities being allowed to mingle, and perhaps to lead, in an English disturbance. It was supposed that these foreign instigators and auxiliaries of the disaffected would, in the event of any formidable tumult, endeavour to gain possession of the public establishments. The persons employed in these establishments were all well armed for their defence on the 10th of April, and I have reason to believe that in case of any attack they were determined to settle with the foreigners in the first instance, if any had made their appearance. If an insurrection had commenced in London, and bands of foreigners, as was expected, had taken any share in it, I am persuaded that the end of the first hour would have found them all dead men, whatever might have been the fate of the English insurgents. The feeling of the government upon this subject may be inferred from the address of one of the Lords of the Admiralty, who was sent down with the Secretary, to meet the enormous establishment of Woolwich dockyard, and to address them. These officials went down on the 8th of April, and, the workmen with their officers (not less than a thousand men according to the public prints) being drawn up before them, Mr. Ward, the Secretary of the Admiralty, told them that the government, relying upon the loyalty, discipline, and efficiency of the dockyard battalion, intended on the following Monday to place the safety and guardianship of that most important and valuable national establishment in their keeping, with the full confidence that, should any enemy or evil-disposed persons make any attack upon it, or any demonstration against it, they would display loyalty to their Sovereign, attachment to the government, and determination to main-

tain peace and good order.   To this, Captain Berkeley,
one of the Lords Commissioners, added that none of them
could be ignorant of the fact that there were going about
England dangerous men, principally foreigners, who were
endeavouring to undermine the institutions of the country,
and to tamper with the loyalty of the working classes—
men who were envious of our quiet and good order, while
all around us were in a state of fearful tumult and agitation, which threatened to overthrow the whole system of
social life.   They wish, said Captain Berkeley, " to make
you like themselves.   They hate you because you have
hitherto peacefully and uninterruptedly worked on the
ground where you were born and bred, for the honest
maintenance of your wives and families.   It is a well-
known fact that hundreds of English workmen who were
employed abroad—employed on account of their superior
skill and industry—have been chased without pity from
France, without payment of their wages, without their
own clothes, and have returned to actual starvation."
These remarks were cheered by the workmen, and they
were voluntarily sworn as special constables, to preserve
the peace on the day of threatened disturbance.

As to the foreign propagandists of democratic tumult—
the *conflata improborum manus*—that had been permitted
to land upon our shores and mingle with our population,
it must be admitted that they came here not only in ignorance of the real state of affairs among us, but wholly
possessed by ideas which they soon discovered to be
absurdly erroneous.   With all the rhetorical fervour and
logical skill of the writers of foreign journals there is
generally combined a ludicrous misapprehension of matters of fact, so far as England is concerned.   The democratic writers of the Continent, while they think they are
dispensing information to Europe upon the circumstances

of Great Britain, draw pictures of the actual state of
things which are fantastically false.   They are fully persuaded that the population of these islands is palpably
divided into two classes—one, the aristocracy, proud,
harsh, insolent, and oppressive, engrossing all the advantages which the country affords; the other, the middle
and working classes, groaning under this unfeeling domi-
nation, and eager to have vengeance upon their hereditary
tyrants.   Full of these ideas, the foreign *émeute*-manu-
facturers had come hither.   It is said that many of them,
after a few days, asked " Where are these hateful aristo-
crats ? "   In our streets, full of opulence and of business,
they found one man as free to walk as another ; nor did
the omnibus, carrying its dozen passengers at sixpence
each, give way to the carriage of the nobleman or gentleman, with its liveried attendants.   If they went into those
quarters of the metropolis where every house, however
plain as to its exterior, is fitted up internally with palatial
luxury, and filled with servants of all denominations to
wait upon or anticipate the will of masters and mistresses,
they found in such localities no exclusive rank.   The rich
banker lived side by side with the rich baron ; the merchant, who had built up his fortune among bales of cotton
and bags of sugar, lived as proudly as the marquis loaded
with nominal privileges and real embarrassments.   The
judges of the courts of law, who had all toiled their way
to their high position from the middle classes, ranked with
the nobility.   The loftiest of the splendid mansions of the
aristocratic quarter, and not the least frequently opened
to the rank, the fashion, and the most costly luxury of the
metropolis, was occupied by one whose parents had stood
behind a counter and measured yards of cloth.   In short,
it was found that, as regarded the ordinary tide of life, no
particular advantage was awarded to aristocratic rank,

but the strongest swimmer almost invariably took the best position.

And, in respect to legislative authority, the foreigners who took the trouble to study the subject discovered that hereditary rank by no means predominated. The House of Peers was found to be strongly inbued with the popular sentiment. Its leading members were those who had earned their public reputation as representatives of the people in the House of Commons, or as leading members of professions in which eminence can only be obtained by a union of ability and industry with good fortune. In the House of Peers the utmost deference was found to be always paid to the decisions of the House of Commons. With respect to that part of government which the people feel most—namely, the imposition of taxes and the expenditure of the public money—it was discovered that the aristocratic branch of the legislature had no power. They might negative the plans of the House of Commons, but the constitution forbade them from even so much as proposing any scheme of their own for taxing the people, or applying the money which taxation had produced. In such matters they could only act by agreeing to what the House of Commons had previously determined.

In short, the foreign propagators of sedition found, to their no small discomfiture, that the materials of political discontent upon which they had relied did not really exist, and that all they had learned upon English politics from the democratic rhetoricians of the continental press was nothing better than ignorance or untruth. That spirit of aristocracy under which they supposed the great mass of the people to suffer with an indignant feeling, which might be easily excited into a revolt, they found to be a sentiment common to all ranks except the very lowest. Every man was straining to surpass his neighbour, and to

exhibit his superiority. The tradesman was even more
ready to take airs upon himself within his own sphere
than was the duke; and the workman who had made
money, and become a master, was far more authoritative
and exacting in respect to his servants than the nobleman who had been surrounded with attendants from his
childhood.

But while those who hoped to profit by exciting to acts
of open sedition in England found mnch to disappoint
their expectations, and to expose the ignorance or bad
faith of violently democratic journalists abroad and at
home, they also found a large amount of discontent among
the working classes of the great towns, and an eager disposition to follow the example of those street crowds who
had on the Continent obtained a momentary triumph over
conceited and neglectful governments, and had thrown
back improvement while giving success to revolution.
The "Chartists" of England, a very numerous and
very mistaken body, consisting chiefly of the working
classes, thought this a favourable opportunity for a general and decisive *demonstration*, and, growing more heated
as their organization proceeded, at last made it clear
enough that they were disposed to enforce their demands,
if the government and legislature hesitated to agree to
them. Numerous as they were, however—their boast
being that the petition to Parliament which contained
their demands was signed by more than five million persons—not one individual of public note or consideration
in the country associated himself with them. There was
one member of the House of Commons who attended
their meetings in London, and was in some sort their
medium of communication with Parliament, but he had
little weight as a legislator, and in the House of Commons his object seemed to be to represent his political

friends rather as ordinary petitioners than as the fiery and determined revolutionists which at their own meetings they seemed to wish to persuade each other that they were. For some weeks the streets of the metropolis in the neighbourhood of the public offices and the Houses of Parliament were frequented occasionally in the afternoon by crowds, who manifested a disposition towards disturbance, but were dispersed by strong bodies of police. Some windows were broken, and there were mutterings about " barricades ;" but this foreign mode of warfare went no further than a suggestion. Meanwhile, the " Chartists " of the various districts of England went so far as to appoint " delegates " to act for them in a " Convention " in London, and this convention actually met day after day, and the speeches of its members were reported in the newspapers, though the speakers were generally of the lowest condition in life, and for the most part as illiterate as they were violent. These men were not phrase-manufacturers and professional revolutionists, like those who had succeeded in producing such disastrous scenes, and in making themselves of momentary consequence, abroad. They were chiefly mistaken and violent men, who spoke honestly enough what they thought. Nor were they wrong in pointing out the great grievance of English society which was evidently the source of their complaint —namely, the uncertainty of comfortable existence for the working class in a country abounding with the means of support for all. The difficulty, and sometimes the impossibility, for even honest and careful industry to obtain employment and subsistence is a ground of complaint which, whether remediable or not, the working people may be excused for unceasingly pressing upon public attention. But the remedy proposed by the Chartists is one which neither reason, nor experience, nor any other thing which

men of common sense should rely upon, teaches to be in
the slightest degree conducive to the removal of the evil.
What they ask for is a greater amount of influence in
returning members to the House of Commons, entirely
forgetting that they have not yet learned how to choose,
and leaving entirely out of view the great fact established
by experience, that in no one instance of late years has
the popular power, when most widely exercised in returning representatives to Parliament, furnished that assembly
with a man of distinguished character and ability. Of all
the constituencies in England, those which most nearly
approach the sort of suffrage which the Chartists long to
establish universally, are the new metropolitan constituencies, called into being by the " Reform" Act of 1832.
Now, without meaning the slightest personal disrespect to
any individual, it may safely be stated that there is no
group of legislative gentlemen who could be spared from
the House of Commons with less loss to its moral dignity
and intellectual character, than these same popular members.   And yet, with the complete failure of a more
popularized legislature to afford them any relief, forming
a part of their experience, and being constantly avowed
by themselves, the Chartists could find nothing better to
ask for, and to proclaim their willingness to die for, than
a new change in the representative branch of the legislature, comprising the following particulars, which they call
the " six points" of the Charter :—

1. Universal Suffrage.
2. Annually-elected Parliaments.
3. Vote by Ballot.
4. Equal Electoral Districts.
5. Abolition of Property Qualification for Members.
6. Payment of Members for their legislative services.

In the week preceding the 10th of April, 1848, the

" convention " was actively and anxiously engaged every
day in making preparation for conveying in a sufficiently
menacing manner to the House of Commons their
" monster petition " for this change in the constitution.
They arranged to have a meeting on Kennington Common, about a mile and a half south of the Thames at
Westminster, where they were to make a display of
numbers sufficient to strike with awe the whole metropolis and its rulers.   From thence they were to march in
procession to the House of Commons, where the petition
was to be presented.   They were then to retire to the
north of the metropolis, and to return in some hours to
the House of Commons for an answer to their petition.
If it were not an answer of submission to the will of
" the people," they were then to " assume the responsibility of ulterior measures, ' and appoint a parliament of
their own.   Nothing could be more inconsistent than the
speeches delivered at the meetings of the " delegates " in
which these matters were discussed.   While some maintained that no breach of order would take place, and no
attack on property be attempted, others used the most
violent language of menace, and breathed war in every
word.   A blow they said must be struck—they were
ready to fight—if thousands were slain, other thousands
would take their place ; with many other figures of speech
of a like unpeaceful character.

The operations of the disturbers being thus indicated,
the people of the metropolis, who felt it their duty and
their interest to preserve the peace, made all possible
preparation for the coming crisis.   In every government
establishment, and in every private establishment of importance, arrangements for defence were deliberately and
actively prepared.   The Bank of England was fortified
under military advice, and less important measures of

the same character were resorted to at the government offices in Whitehall. Between the 6th of April and the morning of the 10th almost every man of the upper and middle classes in London and its vicinity, from the age of 20 to 60, was sworn as a special constable to preserve the peace : the clerks in the public offices, and in the banks of the metropolis and other large establishments, were provided with fire arms, and most of the special constables had staves. The Lord Mayor of London and other magistrates were in constant communication with the Secretary of State for the Home Department, and that department had the important assistance of the Commander-in-Chief of the army (the Duke of Wellington), who advised and carried into effect the military precautions ; while the metropolitan police, a civilian soldiery of between four and five thousand men, were carefully instructed in their proceedings for the day by their experienced commanders. Notices were sent into all the suburbs generally guarded by the police that they must be withdrawn on the 10th to act elsewhere for the defence of the metropolis. In short, the ordinary protection of property and person in London and its vicinity was committed on that day to the constables enrolled specially for the purpose, while the practised body of police acted in masses, and in military array, but armed only with their ordinary weapon, a short truncheon of wood. On the 6th of April, in the House of Commons, the Secretary of State was questioned as to the cognizance he had taken of the proceedings of the Chartist convention, and gave an answer which showed he was fully alive to the expediency of taking active measures. His announcements appeared to give much gratification to the House of Commons, though Mr. O'Connor, the Chartist member, complained that the people would be taken by surprise—that on

former occasions petitions had been presented by very
large bodies of the people—that former ministers had not
objected to it—and that until some breach of the peace
were plainly threatened no repressive measures were
called for.   Another member maintained that the Whig
Ministers, then occupying the government seats in the
House, had on former occasions rather encouraged than
repressed the expression of political opinion by great
numbers, and he thought they ought to be cautious how
they now interfered.   The remark upon what Whig
leaders had formerly done was perhaps more just than
judicious.   In moments of disturbance there does seem
to be a kind of advantage in having the Whigs in office,
especially if they have the assistance of such a man as
the Duke of Wellington.   When they are in opposition
it does not appear to accord with their principles to put
any curb upon the expression of popular opinion, whatever form that expression may take.   When they are in
the government they are protectionists of the public peace
by position, while the Tories, though out of office, are
equally so from habit and disposition.   But, in truth, all
England, of the middle and upper classes—looking to
what had so recently taken place on the Continent—was
at that time in considerable alarm for the safety of person
and property, if popular commotion were allowed to make
head even for an hour, and hence the earnestness of preparation to meet the threatened outbreak on the 10th of
April.

On the evening of the 6th a notice from the Chief
Commissioners of Police was placarded through London,
stating that " an assemblage of large numbers of people,
accompanied with circumstances tending to excite terror
and alarm in the minds of her Majesty's subjects, was
criminal and unlawful.

" That persons who take an active part in such an assemblage, and also those who by their presence wilfully countenance it, are acting contrary to law, and are liable to punishment: that by an Act of Parliament of Charles II.* it was enacted that no person or persons should repair to his Majesty or both or either of the Houses of Parliament, upon pretence of presenting or delivering any petition, complaint, remonstrance, or declaration, or other addresses, accompanied with excessive numbers of people, nor at any one time with above the number of ten persons.

" That a meeting had been called to assemble on the 10th of April at Kennington Common, and that it had been announced in the printed notices calling such meeting that it was intended to repair thence in procession to the House of Commons, accompanied with excessive numbers of the people, upon pretence of presenting a petition to the Commons House of Parliament, and that information had been received that persons had been advised to procure arms and weapons with the purpose of carrying them in such procession, and that such proposed procession was calculated to excite terror and alarm in the minds of her Majesty's subjects."

The notice then proceeded to caution and strictly enjoin all persons not to attend, or take part in, or be present at, such assemblage or procession: and all well-disposed persons were called on and required to aid in enforcing the provisions of the law, and effectually to preserve the public peace, and suppress any attempt at the disturbance thereof.

This official notice had a very great effect in determining the minds of " well-disposed persons " to prepare

---

* 13 Car. II. cap. 5.

strenuously for defence, and the result was, that never perhaps, since London was London, did such an energetic resolution to support the constituted authorities possess the minds of the middle classes as during the days which immediately preceded the 10th of April.

At length the important day came. The morning was fine, as if to usher in a holiday. Active business was evidently suspended in London. Most of the shops were wholly or partially closed. Not a soldier was to be seen anywhere, nor were the police numerous till the afternoon. But every one was well aware, that, not only were large bodies of cavalry and infantry at hand and ready for action, but that artillery, street-rockets, and everything necessary for striking a decisive blow, if any such thing had unhappily become necessary, was quite prepared. Provisions too had been thought of, and in case of any siege by the mob of the public offices, three days' provision for the armed clerks and servants had been ordered in.

From the hour of nine in the morning people were to be seen streaming towards Kennington Common. To me they looked more as if going to enjoy a holiday than to overturn a government. They were apparently working people in their Sunday suits, with rosettes of ribbon in their coats, and many of them had women in their company. From the time of the publication of the notice by the police a doubt appeared to exist whether the people would be permitted to assemble. When the day arrived, it was found that to the progress of the people to Kennington there was no objection. It was, to a military eye, a mistake, of which the military commander took advantage. The mob crossed the river by the bridges to get to the place of meeting. As soon as the multitude had passed, the bridges were taken possession of by large bodies of police. It was just what the authorities wanted.

They had got the dangerous mob out of London, and, having possession of the passes over the river, it was a comparatively easy task to keep them out.

After all, the meeting was not attended—as persons accustomed to large masses of men computed—by more than 15,000 persons. The Chartists had talked of 500,000. That number would have required ten times as much space as Kennington Common affords. While the proceedings were going on, the leaders were summoned to a conference with certain magistrates in the neighbourhood, and made acquainted with the fact that, if a procession attempted to carry the petition of the Chartists to the House of Commons, resistance would be offered. What further was said, to show how utterly and ridiculously hopeless would be the efforts of the multitude in the face of such resistance as was prepared, I cannot tell, but it may easily be imagined. The effect of the conference was that, instead of a triumphant mob marching to dictate to the House of Commons, it did not make even the slightest attempt to form a procession. The petition travelled ignobly to the House in a hack cabriolet. The overheated orators who had talked in the convention about dying in the discharge of their duty on that great day, thought it better to go home and dine ; while Messieurs the foreign amateurs of *émeutes*, having obtained, with their usual acuteness, some knowledge of the preparations made for their entertainment by the Duke of Wellington, deemed it likely that their exertions would be more available elsewhere. There was still work to be done in their line of business in Lombardy, Bohemia, and Hungary, and to these more congenial quarters they betook themselves.

The police held the bridges until the afternoon, not permitting more than two or three to pass at once.

Before dark, however, it seemed to be well understood that all the danger was over, and every avenue was as open as usual. The tremendous force of resistance which had been accumulated quietly melted away without having been seen by the public. The triumph of authority was won without a shot having been fired or a sabre drawn; and no attempt was afterwards made to revive the alarm which that triumph had dissipated.

Such was the result of deliberate, complete preparation, of calm but decisive resistance to popular menace, and of a system of government which, forbearing to be severe so long as forbearance is possible, is yet ready and able to strike, when punishment becomes the only sound policy.

END OF VOL. I.

PRINTED BY W. CLOWES AND SONS, STAMFORD STREET.